THE STRUCTURE
AND GOVERNANCE
OF LIBRARY NETWORKS

BOOKS IN LIBRARY AND INFORMATION SCIENCE

A Series of Monographs and Textbooks

EDITOR

ALLEN KENT

Director, Office of Communications Programs
University of Pittsburgh
Pittsburgh, Pennsylvania

Additional volumes in preparation

THE STRUCTURE AND GOVERNANCE OF LIBRARY NETWORKS

Proceedings of the 1978 Conference
in Pittsburgh, Pennsylvania, Co-sponsored
by National Commission on
Libraries and Information Science
and University of Pittsburgh

ALLEN KENT   THOMAS J. GALVIN

Graduate School of Library and Information Sciences
University of Pittsburgh
Pittsburgh, Pennsylvania

MARCEL DEKKER, INC.   New York and Basel

Library of Congress Cataloging in Publication Data

Main entry under title:

The Structure and governance of library networks.

    (Books in library and information science ; 27)
Includes index.
    1. Library information networks--United States--
Congresses. I. Kent, Allen. II. Galvin, Thomas J.
III. United States. National Commission on Libraries
and Information Science. IV. Pittsburgh. University.
V. Series.
Z674.8.S78   021.6'5'0973   79-12704
ISBN 0-8247-6866-3

MARCEL DEKKER, INC.

270 Madison Avenue, New York, New York 10016

Current printing (last digit):

10 9 8 7 6 5 4 3 2 1

PRINTED IN THE UNITED STATES OF AMERICA

PREFACE

"Equal opportunity of access to information" is the theme of the White House Conference on Library and Information Services scheduled for October 1979. The design and operation of library networks to facilitate the sharing of both bibliographic data and library materials, as well as human expertise, are central to the equalization of access to information for all citizens, and thus a critical element in the formulation of a national information policy.

Formation of networks and consortia at local, state, regional, and national levels is proceeding at a very rapid rate. Urgent and complex questions have emerged as a consequence of the proliferation of networks. A host of unresolved problems centering on management and organization, standardization, criteria for network membership, choices among complex technological options, interrelationships among networks, measures of network performance, and financing demand immediate attention. Among the most compelling issues are those of network design and network governance. These were the central focus of a conference convened in Pittsburgh on November 6-8, 1978 and attended by some five hundred persons from the United States and overseas.

The questions are highly complex, partly because of the rapid pace of technological development in such areas as computers, telecommunications, and in micrographics, and partly because technological and governance issues are inextricably interwoven. One thing, however, is clear—a commitment to the network concept carries with it acceptance of a high degree of mutual interdependence among individual member libraries. How much of traditional local autonomy and democratic governance structures can be retained, while at the same time preserving the rights of all members and protecting the ultimate right of the user to equality of access? How can individual and institutional values be protected, given the inevitability of an increasingly dominant network technology?

These are issues that must be addressed by the delegates to the 1979 White House Conference, as well as by the librarians, information specialists, and citizens whom they will represent.

The 1978 Pittsburgh Conference was entitled: "The Structure and Governance of Library Networks." The National Commission on Libraries and Information Science, in co-sponsoring the conference, sought to provide the opportunity for input to those who will be affected by the manner in which issues are ultimately resolved at federal, state, and local levels, as well as to encourage participation in the definition of those problems that may constitute a significant part of the agenda for the White House Conference. The state of the art in networking was reviewed, nationally known leaders reacted to the issues identified by participants, and recommendations for a national information policy were developed.

Five position papers prepared in advance were distributed to registrants prior to the conference:

1. Network Anatomy and Network Objectives (Chapter 1)

2. Network Topology: Functions of Existing Networks (Chapter 6)

3. Impact of Technology (Chapter 12)

4. The Governance of Library Networks: Purposes and Expectations (Chapter 18)

5. The Governance of Library Networks: Alternatives for the Future (Chapter 25)

The appropriate position paper was first summarized at each conference session; the principal speakers then reacted and discussion followed.

These proceedings are organized in six parts. The first five address the topics of the main sessions. The dinner speech and summaries appear in Part Six.

ACKNOWLEDGMENTS

The conference was stimulated by developments supported by the Buhl Foundation and the National Science Foundation. The Buhl Foundation has provided substantial grants to the University of Pittsburgh; first for the study of library resource sharing, and currently for the development of an experimental resource-sharing network (WEBNET) as well as for the establishment of a training center for on-line information systems. The National Science Foundation, Division of Information Science and Technology, has provided grants for a study of the use of library materials (Grant Number DSI 75-11840 A02), for the development of a campus-based information system (Grant Number G-27537), and for a study of the economics of information transfer using resource-sharing networks—network functions (Grant Number DSI 77-17635).

Mrs. Priscilla Mercier, Office of Communications Programs, University of Pittsburgh, was responsible for the administration of the conference, starting with its organization, continuing with the hosting of the event, and concluding with the post-conference activities which led to the publication of these proceedings. It is clear that her efforts were of chief importance in bringing the enterprise to fruition.

Mrs. Karen Schirra was responsible for the typing of these proceedings for publication.

Allen Kent and Thomas J. Galvin

LIST OF CONTRIBUTORS

HENRIETTE D. AVRAM, Director, Network Development Office, Library of Congress, Washington, D. C.

JOSEPH BECKER, President, Becker & Hayes, Inc., Los Angeles, California.

CHARLES BENTON, Chairman, National Commission for Libraries and Information Science, Washington, D. C.

LAWRENCE F. BUCKLAND, President, Inforonics, Inc., Littleton, Massachusetts.

JOHN W. BYSTROM, Professor of Communications, University of Hawaii at Manoa, Honolulu, Hawaii.

SUSAN H. CROOKS, Arthur D. Little, Inc., Cambridge, Massachusetts.

MELVIN S. DAY, Director, National Technical Information Service, Washington, D. C.

WILLIAM DE JOHN, Director, Pacific Northwest Bibliographic Center, University of Washington, Seattle, Washington.

C. EDWIN DOWLIN,* Ph.D. Candidate, Graduate School of Library and Information Sciences, University of Pittsburgh, Pittsburgh, Pennsylvania.

SHIRLEY ECHELMAN,** Assistant Vice President and Chief Librarian, Chemical Bank, New York, New York.

SARA FINE, Associate Professor, Department of Library Science, University of Pittsburgh, Pittsburgh, Pennsylvania.

Present Affiliations:
*Applied Management Services, Inc.   **Medical Library Association
Silver Spring, Maryland   Chicago, Illinois

ROGER FLYNN, Lecturer, Interdisciplinary Department of Information Science, University of Pittsburgh, Pittsburgh, Pennsylvania.

ERVIN J. GAINES, Director, Cleveland Public Library, Cleveland, Ohio.

THOMAS J. GALVIN, Dean, Graduate School of Library and Information Sciences, University of Pittsburgh, Pittsburgh, Pennsylvania.

VINCENT E. GIULIANO, Arthur D. Little, Inc., Cambridge, Massachusetts.

ROBERT M. HAYES, Dean, Graduate School of Library and Information Science, University of California, Los Angeles, California.

DICK W. HAYS, Associate Commissioner/Director, Office of Libraries and Learning Resources, U. S. Office of Education, Washington, D. C.

JAMES H. KENNEDY, Executive Director, AMIGOS Bibliographic Council, Dallas, Texas.

ALLEN KENT, Director, Office of Communications Programs, University of Pittsburgh, Pittsburgh, Pennsylvania.

DONALD W. KING, President, King Research, Inc., Rockville, Maryland.

BEVERLY P. LYNCH, University Librarian, University of Illinois at Chicago Circle, Chicago, Illinois.

WILLIAM D. MATHEWS, Staff Associate for Information Technology, National Commission on Libraries and Information Science, Washington, D. C.

ANTHONY W. MIELE, Director, Alabama Public Library Service, Montgomery, Alabama.

K. LEON MONTGOMERY, Associate Professor, Interdisciplinary Department of Information Science, University of Pittsburgh, Pittsburgh, Pennsylvania.

PATRICIA B. POND, Associate Dean, Graduate School of Library and Information Sciences, University of Pittsburgh, Pittsburgh, Pennsylvania.

JAMES P. RILEY, Executive Director, Federal Library Committee, Washington, D. C.

STEPHEN R. SALMON, Assistant Vice President, Library Plans and Policies, University of California Systemwide Administration, Berkeley, California.

CHARLES H. STEVENS, Executive Director, SOLINET, Atlanta, Georgia.

ROGER K. SUMMIT, Director, Lockheed Information Systems, Palo Alto, California.

RODERICK G. SWARTZ, State Librarian, Washington State Library, Olympia, Washington.

ALPHONSE F. TREZZA, Executive Director, National Commission on Libraries and Information Science, Washington, D. C.

WILLIAM J. WELSH, The Deputy Librarian of Congress, Washington, D. C.

JAMES G. WILLIAMS, Associate Professor, Interdisciplinary Department of Information Science, University of Pittsburgh, Pittsburgh, Pennsylvania.

CONTENTS

Part One
NETWORK ANATOMY AND NETWORK OBJECTIVES

Part Two
NETWORK TOPOLOGY: FUNCTIONS OF EXISTING NETWORKS

Part Three
IMPACT OF TECHNOLOGY

Part Four
THE GOVERNANCE OF LIBRARY NETWORKS:
PURPOSES AND EXPECTATIONS

Part Five
THE GOVERNANCE OF LIBRARY NETWORKS:
ALTERNATIVES FOR THE FUTURE

Part Five (continued)

Part Six
CONCLUSIONS

INTRODUCTION

Charles Benton

Chairman
National Commission for Libraries and Information Science
Washington, D. C.

It is a great pleasure for me to be here today. As the new Chairman of the
National Commission on Libraries and Information Science, it is most appropriate that my first public appearance at a library and information services
meeting be concerned with one of the major issues facing us—the structure
and governance of library networks. If we are to meet the goal of equal opportunity of access for all, regardless of the individual's location, social or
physical condition, or level of intellectual achievement, then a determination
of the structure and governance of national library and information service
networks is basic.

This structure must address the problems and concerns not only of the
research library community but of all types of libraries, both public and
private. The role of the private-for-profit sector must also be considered.
There are at least three major areas which must be considered if our overall goal is to become a reality. These are, first: the structure, management, and functioning of a national network. Second: national bibliographic
control to assure effective resource sharing. Third: literacy, to assure
access to the nation's information system for all. NCLIS expects that these
issues, among others, will be addressed at the White House Conference on
Library and Information Services, October 28 to November 1, 1979, in
Washington, D. C.

To stimulate grassroots involvement, along with professional input, the
Commission is sponsoring pre-White House conferences in the states and
territories designed to address local, state, and national issues, their interrelationships, and legislative implications. Planning for and participation
in the state conferences includes representatives of the general public as
well as professionals from all types of libraries and information centers.
Two-thirds of the participants must be lay people. We need to know what
our public, the users and the non-users, perceive as their needs for library

and information services. In addition to the state conferences, NCLIS is sponsoring three theme conferences on major national issues. The first, which has already been held and which I had the pleasure of attending in Washington, with Dr. Frederick Burkhardt presiding, was on funding. The second—the structure and governance of library networks—starts here today; and the third, scheduled for next spring, will be on literacy—not just print literacy, but media literacy and all that this implies. One of my favorite and long-term preoccupations has been trying to do something about bridging the gap between the media environment in the home dominated by television and the media environment in school, which is dominated by print. That is a real problem which we have to address.

Those of you who are participating at this conference have a major responsibility for starting, or, I should say, continuing the public dialog on the very important and controversial subject of the governance of national networks. Every group, institution, and agency has a stake in its own territorial imperatives and has its own fears of Federal interference and domination. Problems, however, must be faced and resolved with confidence and commitment —we need your thoughtful debate and constructive criticism.

Papers for this conference and the panels will offer much food for thought —controversial and new ideas, as well as traditional views. Your role is primary if the results of the conference are to help set the stage for action at the White House Conference next fall. We welcome your participation and involvement in the resolution of the problems and issues that will be aired at this conference.

Let me close by expressing the Commission's appreciation to Thomas Galvin and Allen Kent from the University of Pittsburgh for using their Annual Conference as a public forum for the discussion of the structure and governance of library networks. May I also express my thanks to Al Trezza and his staff for their role in planning this conference. I am glad to be able to participate with you, and I am certain that this will be a most stimulating and productive conference.

THE STRUCTURE
AND GOVERNANCE
OF LIBRARY NETWORKS

Part One

NETWORK ANATOMY AND NETWORK OBJECTIVES

There are several different network arrangements which can be used in providing equal opportunity of access to information. The variables to be taken into account are: type of user needs; type of member library; type of material. Current networks represent a morass of types, most with no clear interrelationship apparent. It is possible to suggest a taxonomy which can lead to integration in the long run.

The position paper distributed in advance of the conference is given in Chapter 1. Chapters 2-4 present reactions from the panelists. Chapter 5 presents the discussion at the conference.

Chapter 1

NETWORK ANATOMY AND NETWORK OBJECTIVES

Allen Kent

Director
Office of Communications Programs
University of Pittsburgh
Pittsburgh, Pennsylvania

INTRODUCTION

In 1976, the Pittsburgh conference on Resource Sharing in Libraries* addressed goals, progress, problems, economics, and performance criteria. In some sense, networking to achieve resource sharing goals was only emerging from the missionary stage. In 1978, only two years later, the pace of development has quickened, so that it is possible and necessary to become more analytic in discussing library networks. The analytic approach is made possible because the number of networks (or consortia or cooperatives) continues to increase and evidences of functions attempted and performance are beginning to surface. The analytic approach is necessary because more attention is being directed to the library functions that it makes sense to perform in a network environment.

The continuing advance in technology provides capabilities at lower unit cost, and even in capital investment. But it is becoming increasingly evident that the introduction of technology is having a profound effect on the activities of individual libraries which ally themselves to networks. The effect is seen in the ways in which specific functions are performed, with some functions relegated almost entirely to a network authority.

---

* Allen Kent and Thomas J. Galvin, editors, <u>Library Resource Sharing,</u> Marcel Dekker, Inc., New York, 1977.

The basic objective of a network is to provide better service to patrons of member libraries. "Better" can be defined in quantitative terms; for example, lower cost, access to more materials, more rapid availability of materials; "better" can also be defined in qualitative terms, such as convenience of access and hospitableness of the network environment, both for librarians and patrons. This basic objective of networks frequently entails a shift in the philosophy of member libraries from reliance on "local holdings" to reliance on "access" to materials held elsewhere. The sense of security of librarians in holding materials that patrons want must be replaced by a sense of security in the network authority being able to provide bibliographic access to what is not held locally, and also to deliver the materials to local patrons in a timely way.

Once hooked on an "access" philosophy, it is difficult for the local library to return to the "holdings" philosophy. Acquisitions policies would have changed, staffing patterns would also have been altered to react to changing functions, and reliance on technology would change local procedures—often quite dramatically.

It does not take long for the local library to realize that one trade-off in achieving the benefits of network membership is some loss of autonomy. Idiosyncratic decisions can no longer be made without "approval" by network partners, lest harm to other libraries result. This loss of autonomy has had a corollary effect—a demand for effective participation in the governance of the network. The network authority is no longer permitted authoritarian decisions, once seen by the authority as absolutely necessary to assure effective service. Frequently this was seen as despotism by network members even if considered benevolent despotism by the network authority.

And so the governance issue has become a dominant one, for the reason discussed above, as well as others: members of library networks requiring the provision of access to their holdings by other libraries must consider the legal basis for such service. For example, when the funding base for a local library comes from one city, one county, or one state and service is provided to library patrons with another funding base, the legal questions must be resolved, sometimes with new legislation; the problem is exacerbated when network membership is mixed: public and private colleges; public libraries and academic libraries; etc. It may be obvious that the resolution of such issues requires that member libraries participate formally in network governance.

Sometimes a network provides only access to central computer and/or communications services. The network authority finds it difficult to countenance a participatory governance structure, lest efficient operations be inhibited; and yet increasing dependence on such services makes such participation by member libraries necessary, lest unexpected changes in mode of service cause local disruptions.

As we view progress in networks since the 1976 Pittsburgh conference, we see a basic change in the questions being asked, shifting from "whether to join a network" to:

1. which network to join?

2. what criteria should be used in deciding?

3. how to evaluate competing networks (e.g., OCLC vs. BALLOTS, DIALOG vs. ORBIT)?

4. which functions of a network should be used?

5. what is the likelihood of system failure?

6. what quality control standards does the network enforce?

7. what is the cost?

The answers to such questions are not easy to come by; but it is necessary to obtain answers if the wheat is to be separated from the chaff, if the few performing networks are to be separated from the ones that only promise performance.

There are more than 500 U. S. networks (or consortia or cooperatives) that can be identified from the literature and recent directories. Many have foundered for a variety of reasons, such as:

(1) Emphasis on only a single library function (e.g., interlibrary loan) which is difficult to justify on a cost-effective criterion;

(2) Lack of attention to the need for a formal system design, derived from stated goals and objectives;

(3) Lack of attention to the use of appropriate technology;

(4) Lack of specificity in developing network functions;

(5) Not translating network bylaws into specific operating procedures;

(6) Unrealistic budgeting and lack of expertise in developing long-term funding.

But there are important lessons to be learned from those who have foundered, as well as from those who are surviving and becoming stronger: a first step is to examine some basics with regard to networks, starting with their anatomy.

PROLOGUE TO NETWORK ANATOMY

A library and the network to which it relates each have an "anatomy" which
in some ways can be analogized to that of the human body. For example, the
digestive system is akin to acquisitions and technical processing; the ex-
cretory system is akin to the weeding process; the cardiovascular system
is akin to the circulation system; the reproductive system may be analogized
to photocopying; the nervous system is like telecommunication; the endocrine system is akin to the governance function. Like all analogies, they
become strained and break down if carried too far, and one must move to
the core of the subject in specific terms. But before doing so, one more
analogy to human anatomy. Before modern medicine, the medical "profession" identified the "cardinal humors," which were considered responsible
for one's health and disposition: blood, phlegm, choler (yellow bile) and
melancholy (black bile). As modern medicine evolved, more penetrating
understanding was possible of the functions of the "cardinal humors," the
interactions among them, and the effect on the "health and disposition,"
permitting careful management to restore balance when the human is indis-
posed. Just so with library networks, in that many library functions were
not clearly defined, and their interactions poorly understood—if at all—
leading to malfunctioning, and inability to realize the goals and objectives of
cost-beneficial resource sharing. It is only as functions are identified ex-
haustively, as they are defined precisely, and as the mechanisms for performing them are specified, that interactions among functions can be studied,
both within and among libraries.

NETWORK ANATOMY

Three basic network anatomical structures may be distinguished: star;
hierarchical; and distributed.

The star network entails one network member holding substantially all
resources, with all other members utilizing these resources. The configuration may be diagrammed as in Figure 1.

The hierarchical network entails members sharing resources locally;
passing unsatisfied needs along to the next greater resource center. The
configuration is shown in Figure 2.

The distributed network (Figure 3) is composed of members with equal,
but different resources, with all members able to call directly on the resources of all other members.

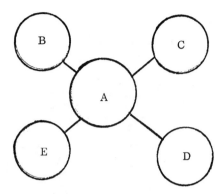

Figure 1. Star Network Structure. One network member (A)
holds all resources, with all other members (B-E)
utilizing these resources.

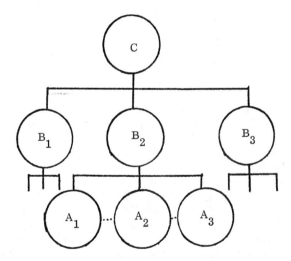

Figure 2. Hierarchical Network Structure. Network members
(A_1, A_2, A_3) share resources, with most of needs
satisfied before requesting service to the next
greater resource center (B_2); finally the few remaining unsatisfied requests are referred to the
"library of last resort" (C), which may be obliged to
check other centers (B_1, B_3) to locate required
materials.

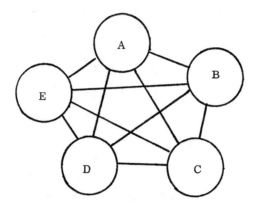

Figure 3. Distributed Network Structure. All network members
(A, B, C, D, E) hold, in theory, different resources,
which they share with one another.

Resource-sharing networks* currently in operation or in planning can be
analyzed in terms of three factors:

    (1) Type of network

    (2) Type of source material

    (3) Operations (functions) performed.

If these three factors are displayed in three dimensions (Figure 4), it is
possible to depict a structure in terms of specific operations performed by
specific network types for given types of source materials. Thus, a star
network (I) which offers bibliographic access (3) to books and monographs (B)
would be characterized symbolically as I.3.B. For example, the Research
Libraries Group (R.L.G.) would be characterized as II.3.A., since it is
working toward a distributed network (II) for four libraries (Yale, Stanford,
Columbia, New York Public-Science Technical Division) with initial emphasis
on bibliographic access (3) and on serials (A). The concept of a national
periodicals bank (III.7.A.) is being proposed as an hierarchical network (III)
for serials (A), with primary emphasis on delivery (7). The experimental
Western Pennsylvania Buhl Network (WEBNET) is developing as a distributed
network for books and monographs, but with most types of operations represented (II. 1, 2, 3, 6, 7. B.).

---

* Two terms, "network" and "resource-sharing network," are used synony-
  mously in this chapter, since the author makes the assumption that a library
  network exists for the purpose of sharing resources: bibliographic data,
  functions, materials, and human and technological resources.

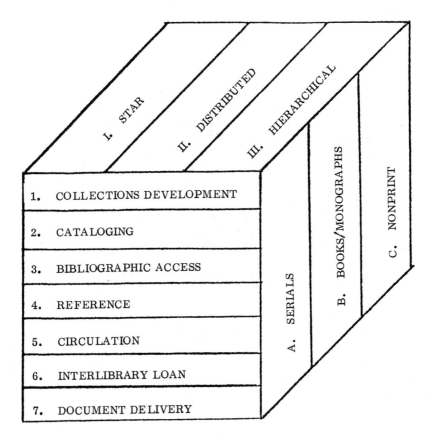

Figure 4.   Three dimensional characterization of networks in
            terms of operations (functions) and types of materials.

If one were to characterize the hundreds of resource sharing or cooperative activities in the nation, it is anticipated that one would find a morass of
types of networks, operations, and materials involved, most with no clear
interrelationships apparent, and no clear way of integrating networks which
undoubtedly will be needed for long-run cost-beneficial services.

But it is possible to untangle this morass by analytical review of the
existing networks.   This review is expected to lead to the development of
computer simulations of alternative resource sharing configurations.   The
parameters of local library environments could then be introduced into the
simulation, permitting equilibrium (break-even) points to be identified to aid
decision processes for assessing local purchasing vs. remote accessing.

If a library has the opportunity to make a choice of which network to join, the following example problem could be posed:

> Suppose that you decided—for whatever reason—that you could no longer afford to subscribe to all of your current periodicals. Further, suppose that you identified ten titles you wish to cancel (probably because of infrequent demand). But of course you would still wish to satisfy even the infrequent demand. So suppose you decided to join a resource sharing network. Let us imagine that there would be a directory of such networks to consult, and you would want to select one which would be best for your purpose. The criterion you might pose for yourself, in trying to decide, is:

> > I must have access to ten journal titles; based on past use statistics, I expect that each year I would have 20 users, asking for 50 articles from the ten journal titles, each article an average of ten pages. The users demand delivery within 24 hours of their request. Finally, the cost may not exceed 25¢ per page.

These parameters could be fed into the simulation, with an output emerging which identifies which network can meet the criterion. Or the result could be that no network can meet all the conditions, in which case the output could provide information on which conditions would need to be relaxed in order for given networks to be able to respond. (For example, 48 hours delivery instead of 24 hours, or 50¢ per page instead of 25¢.)

LIBRARY AND NETWORK FUNCTIONS

The three network anatomies (Figures 1-3) begin to achieve reality when considered in terms of services which relate to input functions (performed by librarians), output functions (performed by, or for, patrons), and administrative functions of member libraries. Generically, these functions are analogous for all types of materials, but may differ in the specific ways in which they are carried out.

Resource sharing networks may perform all or part of one or more of these functions on behalf of member libraries. The scope, cost, and efficiency of network services are influenced by the technology available (e.g., computer, communications) and the extent to which "critical mass," in terms of number of transactions, has been achieved. Also influential is the governance mechanism(s) employed.

SINGLE FUNCTION VS. MULTIPLE FUNCTION

Efficient libraries attempt to interrelate the functions performed. The stream of functions which start with collections development policies are translated into specific acquisitions decisions, leading to accessioning, accounting, and processing routines which result in materials being placed on shelves and corresponding catalog entries being filed, to be ready for patron use. Traces of these routines may be carried forward into the circulation function and further into the collection and analysis of use data. These data may then be fed back to influence the collections development policies and/or carried forward to directly influence the weeding of collections and remote storage of little-used materials. These data can also be used to assess whether cooperative, resource sharing, networking arrangements make sense for a given library.

Many networks limit their activities to a single function, interlibrary loan, frequently providing photocopies from journals rather than loaning the physical item. If all of the costs were to be considered, it is likely that the criterion established could not be met by any library or network. So it becomes useful to consider whether multiple function networks can provide services cost-effectively—since it becomes possible to amortize costs over a number of interrelated functions.

An example of a multi-function network was described at the 1976 conference, as shown in the schema in Figure 5. *   In this drawing, limited for simplicity to two libraries, each has two "terminals," one each for users and for librarians. The user (1a, 1b) is able to access a union data base (2), which provides the catalog of the holdings of libraries A and B (with locations given for each item). If the desired material is not located in the union catalog, the on-order/in-process file (3) may then be accessed. If the desired item is located in a given library, the circulation file is consulted (6a, 6b) to determine whether it is indeed available immediately. If it is available, a transaction is initiated to move the item to the point of need from the holdings of the other library (5a, 5b), with a record of the transaction maintained by the system (7).

An acquisitions librarian (8a, 8b) wishing to make a "buy/no-buy" decision would likewise consult the union data base (2) and the on-order/in-process file (3) to determine the decisions of other libraries in the system. A "buy" decision would then lead to entering the transaction in the on-order/in-process file (3), to cataloging the item when it arrives, and to entering the cata-

---

* From A. Kent and T. J. Galvin, Library Resource Sharing, Marcel Dekker, Inc., New York, 1977, pages 23-24.

loging (and location) information in the local catalog (4a, 4b) and in the union data base (2). The material itself would then become part of the local holdings (5a, 5b), ready for access.

Use statistics (7) would lead to weeding decisions (9) and consideration for remote storage (10).

In such a multi-function network, the likelihood of cost-effectiveness increases, since records of initial functions need only be updated for succeeding functions. At least as important as well is the impact of technology on the ability of functions to be interrelated cost-effectively, both within a given library as well as in a network environment.

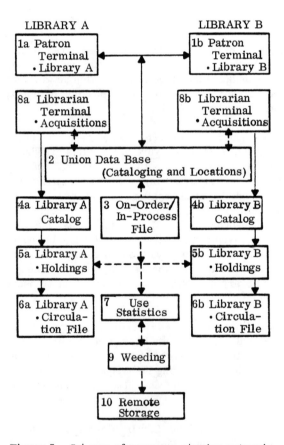

Figure 5. Schema of resource sharing network.

It is in this regard that the functions can be discussed in terms of network structure. It is unlikely that all functions of a given network can be characterized neatly as one structure. For example, the shared cataloging function of OCLC: the computer system employed can be considered as a "star" structure, since a single set of computers in one location serves all users. Even here, the developments of NELINET and WEBNET suggest movement toward hierarchical structure, with regional computer systems being developed which would serve users in the area, off-loading the OCLC system, but requiring access for some transactions. The communication system to support the shared cataloging function does not serve local libraries directly, rather through regional consortia. This suggests again a hierarchical structure, with the arrangement permitting lower costs in communication than if each library communicated directly to OCLC. The cataloging activity itself exhibits two types of structure, distributed as well as star. It is distributed when each library contributes original cataloging; it is star when the library locates the cataloging information of another library in central OCLC files.

OBJECTIVES

Resource sharing networking denotes a mode of operation whereby functions are shared in common by a number of member libraries. Objectives have not changed significantly since the 1976 conference—to provide a positive net effect: 1) on the library user in terms of access to more materials or services; and/or 2) on the library budget in terms of providing level service at less cost, increased service at level cost, or much more service at less cost than if undertaken individually. These objectives should be realized without harm to the missions of participating libraries, although their methods of operation invariably must be adjusted. Similarly, the objectives are realizable only with some changes in the habits of users.

The activities involved in realizing the objectives are (1) sharing of the burden of purchasing materials;* (2) sharing of the burden of processing the materials; (3) sharing of services; and (4) sharing of human expertise. The means for conducting these activities entails increasingly the use of technology: computers and/or telecommunications.

---

* This chapter emphasizes the sharing of library materials, although networks permit the sharing of many other types of resources. The reason for this emphasis on materials sharing is because so many networks currently have this activity as a basic, initial objective, even though the mechanisms that eventually lead to such sharing (e.g., shared cataloging) may dominate the functions actually performed currently.

Typically, resource sharing networking has been directed to disciplines
and types of libraries for which materials costs are high and/or where there
is a vocal clientele. Many areas have not been touched and yet deserve
attention. One such area is children's literature, and it is for this reason
that the author invited a colleague, Margaret Mary Kimmel, to state the
case for resource sharing in that field (see Appendix).

MIXING TYPES OF CLIENTELES, MATERIALS AND LIBRARIES

It is difficult enough to achieve library networking objectives when the member libraries are of the same type (e.g., academic). It becomes much more
difficult when a given network attempts to serve multiple types of libraries
(e.g., public, special, academic). Some libraries are obliged to be a member of several networks in order to obtain the relevant benefits from each.
Thus a library may join a regional network to achieve the benefit of geographic proximity of services to be shared; the same library may join a
national network to obtain access to a shared cataloging function; it may also
be part of a state network to satisfy cooperative objectives of the political
entity that provides funding. This frequently entails different types of materials and clienteles. But it also entails different protocols and standards that
must be rationalized, sometimes requiring new legislation to resolve anoma-
lies (e.g., regarding ownership of materials, rights of access, funding
authorities).

The challenge is to develop appropriate linkages among networks to avoid
unnecessary duplication in services.

AGREEMENTS AND GOVERNANCE

Later chapters will be dealing with the issue of network governance. However, a word is in order regarding agreements and how these may relate to
governance.

There are several basic agreements among libraries that are important
to develop if resource sharing networks are to succeed.

First, obviously, is the agreement to share currently owned materials
(that is, to permit access to the holdings among member libraries) with protocols, limitations and priorities carefully spelled out. The agreement
should provide for an independent administration of resource sharing, but
one which does not emasculate the goals and missions of the cooperating
libraries. Funding should be based on an obligation for long-term support

to permit the benefits to develop; the financial agreement should permit individual libraries to withdraw, but constrained to avoid disturbance of the network.

Second, there should be agreement on acquisitions policies, both to ensure consistent development of holdings and to avoid redundancy when this is judged jointly to be unproductive.

Third, there should be agreement on bibliographic control. Best is standardization, so that users of each cooperating library may have a consistent means of accessing the catalogs of others. If standardization is not feasible, then the second best is the provision of adequate training for users and/or access to the local reference staff to provide aid in locating materials.

Other necessary agreements include definition of loan periods and renewals, procedures for earlier return of materials if needed, payment for lost materials, and other "housekeeping" (or bookkeeping) chores.

Such agreements entail a type of governance to which individual libraries are not accustomed—a type of governance that leads to some loss of local autonomy, but which is hopefully balanced off by access to more materials, services, and human expertise than could otherwise be affordable, or afforded.

APPENDIX

A Case for Resource Sharing in Children's Literature

by Margaret Mary Kimmel

Materials for children encompass a much wider field than implied in the traditional definition of literature. Although teachers, parents and librarians often discuss children's materials in terms of books, historically children have taken as their own, stories, pictures and illustrations, toys and games, wherever they could find them. Folklore, passed from one generation to another by word of mouth, is the earliest definable material for children and relied exclusively on oral transmission until the work of the linguistic brothers Grimm brought to it a written form in the 19th century.

Scholars generally agree that folklore was an entertainment for people of all ages which children took as their own, but material for the classroom—for the "learning and edification" of the young—was developed specifically for children. The division between that material which was suitable for the educational process and that which was important outside it has grown more pronounced. Regardless of this dichotomy, however, material began to proliferate, designed and marketed for children, as early as the 1740's when John Newberry discovered a formula for success in small items he called "Pretty Little Pocket Books."

All materials collected by libraries have changed drastically, especially in the last 20 years. Materials for children are no exception. While microfiche and -form have influenced storage and retrieval processes, the visual impact of technology has radically changed the world of information for children. The production of trade books—those other than educational texts—has expanded to some 2,500 new titles each year. At the same time, there are approximately 15,000 new films aimed at children marketed yearly. Video, commercial and in-house, has reached most homes and some classrooms. The material is diverse in form and content. The client group ranges from youngsters who cannot articulate their most basic needs beyond formless babbling to scholars whose research demands are sophisticated and particularized. The issues involved can be focused on the question of access, and it is in access to these materials that networks, their design, administration, operation and financing enter the picture.

Problems in trade books typify the issue of access. There is no complete retrospective or contemporary collection of books for children in the United States. The Library of Congress may be one of the most complete, but even here some items are not kept—too flimsy (format or content), too slight, too marginal. The lack of a definitive collection might be remedied by some form of resource sharing. Even in an area so basic as interlibrary loan, however, children's books are dismissed in some ALA guidelines along with "ephemeral fiction, current 'Best Sellers,' titles announced in current alerting tools...and titles available in mass market editions." The NCLIS report has as one of its goals for action "to eventually provide every individual...with equal opportunity of access to that part of the total information resource...regardless of the individual's location, social or physical condition or level of intellectual achievement." The phrase "regardless of intellectual achievement" might lead one to believe that children and their requests are welcomed, that the ability to pursue an interest beyond the local library is encouraged. For children—or adults pursuing an interest or research in the field—access is often limited, sometimes by the reluctance of staff, but often by limitations on the system itself. In New Jersey, for instance, children's books can be sought throughout the New Jersey Library Network, but some Area Libraries accept such requests and others do not. The State Library proscribes searches for juvenile material and the Penn Union Library Catalog (ULC), with which New Jersey has a contract, has such a varied input from member libraries that it has relatively little use.

Furthermore there are serious problems of entry access to materials for children. While OCLC has a fixed field for children's books, it must accept what member libraries submit. Some libraries enter juvenile titles and some do not. Often those titles not bought by member public libraries, that exist only in schools or special collections, are excluded. Here at the University of Pittsburgh the special collection of children's books, the Elizabeth Nesbitt Collection, is entered in the Hillman Library only sporadically as items are reclassified. The Hillman catalog shows only main entry and would give no indication to a social historian interested in the lifestyle of the middle class of the 17th and 18th centuries, or to an anthropologist interested in the disposition of news by traveling vendors, that the Nesbitt Collection has more than 150 chapbooks and broadsides—very pertinent information to the research in question.

An even more basic problem of access, not for scholars but for children, exists in the relationship of the readability of subject headings and the reading level of the material. Two new publications, portfolios of illustrations by a prominent Swiss artist entitled The Changing Countryside and The Changing City, are headed "Switzerland in Art." There is no hint in the tracings of the unique format of these publications much less the suggestion that these artistic interpretations of ecological change might be of interest to a 4th or 5th grade student. In planning a system of information, an understanding of client needs, abilities and interests is essential. To enter a short story for 6 and 7 year olds called Frog and Toad Are Friends under "Reptiles and Amphibians" shows a basic lack of such a necessary understanding. The Library of Congress children's Subject Headings have only marginal impact because 1) relatively few collections of children's materials use LC; 2) even when in use, the "modifications" are superficial.

These questions are related primarily to contemporary trade books. They do not begin to identify those more complicated problems related to access of educational materials, especially to those materials that are visual. The 15,000 films per year are not even available in a comprehensive bibliographic source. There is no systematic plan for the collection of ephemeral material such as baseball cards or Star Wars regalia, yet scholars find such material a rich source of study for the mores of a society.

Institutions holding collections of materials for children, primarily schools and public libraries, have long sought to develop cooperative efforts. Little has been done to investigate the impact of service, areas of cooperation, or types of cooperative effort that are most cost effective. The suggestion by the New York State Board of Regents in 1970 that all library service to children below 6th grade should be provided by the public schools, set off an enormous amount of rhetoric, but little serious investigation. There has been one study by Ellen Altman, in a sample of public secondary schools, which indicates that interlibrary loan is feasible. The Altman study indicated that at least 48% of the collections in sampled secondary schools were unique titles and that 31.4% of the school titles were not held in the public library collection. There does not seem to be a corresponding survey of the diversity of public library collections, but if the methods of building those collections might serve as indicators, diversity should be statistically significant.

No one can deny that the technical capability exists to access any information, even children's materials. CLSI, for instance, has a touch terminal with extra large print capabilities. The problem is basically in the lack of input, of an authority file for a data base that could provide information as youngsters need it. It is a problem complicated by an attitude which regards the historical/research aspects of juvenile materials as so much "clutter" in a data base. The problem inherent in developing collections of materials for children are complex ones involving the examination and clarification of our values. The questions of including these materials in systems of information, as well as including people who understand their value in the design and management of such systems, are cumbersome and costly ones.

In the strictest sense, the goal of a collection of children's materials is to provide for a child's information needs, however they are expressed. That client group has expanded to include parent or teacher, historian, psychologist, or the social scientist whose interest in children and their environment can be related to the materials available. Traditionally the pattern of library service to children in both schools and public libraries suggests larger goals—not merely to provide information, but to stimulate and engage curiosity, to share the excitement of discovery, to develop a sense of independence in learning. Surely the question of access can accommodate and encourage, not limit, such goals.

Chapter 2

NETWORK ANATOMY AND NETWORK OBJECTIVES: RESPONSE

Melvin S. Day

Director
National Technical Information Service
Washington, D. C.

In his usual masterful and lucid manner, Professor Kent describes a number of network designs, their structure, and functions. He states very pointedly, and rightly so, that the objective of a library network is to provide better service to patrons of member libraries but, as is the case with most good things in life, there is a cost for one's participation in a network. The cost that I refer to is not in terms of dollars but rather in terms of some loss of freedom of action. Member libraries when agreeing to join a network oftentimes surrender a little of their autonomy. (I prefer the term flexibility.)

Network libraries are required to change from a "local holdings" attitude to a "shared access orientation." Understandably, as some autonomy is surrendered, network members become even more concerned that the governance of the network be by a body that is completely responsive to the stated needs and goals of the network members. And, as in all areas of cooperation between members, the terms of that cooperation need to be stated at the outset explicitly and understandably to all parties. Professor Kent concludes with a statement that many libraries have found that the loss in autonomy has been balanced by the benefits received from network participation.

Certainly the concept of networking is not new but the speed with which libraries are becoming involved with networking activities continues to accelerate and it is interesting to note the change in the pattern of questions being asked. As Professor Kent points out, for many libraries the "shall we join" question has given way to the more intricate problems of which network it shall be; of the advantages and disadvantages of each network; of the impact of participation on the individual library's budget; of the staffing and supporting services required; of the nature of the governance mechanism; and of the extent of the latitude residing with each member. Parenthetically, I might observe that although each of us is aware of the large number of network activities, to the best of my knowledge, there does not exist a comprehensive directory of available networks providing descriptive information about each. It seems to me that such a catalog would have widespread use. Perhaps the National Commission on Libraries and Information Science or the American Society for Information Science might be interested in compiling and publishing such a directory.

So much for the network participant! What about the network operator? At the National Library of Medicine there is a firm belief, to which I fully subscribe, that continuing, thoughtful network self-evaluation is critically important to the continuing success of a network activity. At the risk of over-simplification, one cannot tell what he looks like to others until he sees himself in the mirror; or although often quoted, the lines of Robert Burns retain their truth: if we could see ourselves as others see us, it would save us from many a blunder, and foolish notion. I will touch on this briefly in just a moment but before doing so let us have a quick look at a large and successful national network.

The National Library of Medicine has been the manager of and a major participant for about ten years in the National Biomedical Communications Network. Without question, a major factor contributing to the success of the library segment of the network is the relative homogeneity of the membership of the network. I wish to emphasize the term "relative." No two member libraries are identical and the nature and needs of a small community hospital library are quite different from those of a large medical school library and certainly differ from those of a medical research organization's library. Still they are inexplicably bound together by agreement on bibliographic control. They all use the same basic bibliographic tools produced by the National Library of Medicine and their local implementations are based on common practices and common standards. Fortunately, the National Library of Medicine continues to be sensitive to the growing and changing needs of the medical and hospital library communities and the willingness on the part of both the National Library and client libraries to adapt and work together is the internal force that provides the basic strength to the network.

The Biomedical Communications Network has some elements of the pyramid, or "hierarchical" (as Professor Kent calls it) structure, and some elements of the "star" configuration. For example, the document delivery process is hierarchical, beginning with 4,000 local medical and hospital libraries interconnected to 125 resource libraries, which in turn are connected to 11 regional medical libraries, and finally are in turn connected to the National Library of Medicine as the "library of last resort." In simplistic terms, most requests are filled at the local or resource library level; unfilled requests are referred up through the hierarchy to the Regional Medical Library; finally those not available within the region are referred upward to the National Library of Medicine to be filled. Within this medical library network, this year about 2.5 million interlibrary loans have been filled with almost 90% being filled within the regional environment. This type of network places most of the resources in a local setting closest to and of greatest value to the ultimate user.

On the other hand, the MEDLARS/MEDLINE computerized on-line retrieval network could be classified as a "star" network since all terminals through two national communications networks, TYMNET and TELENET, are connected directly to the central computers and data bases at the National Library of Medicine. Currently there are more than 2,000 remote terminals in about 1,000 different organizations tied directly to the NLM computers. This year it is expected that more than 1,100,000 literature searches will be completed in the network. The network performs very effectively because of the efficiency of both the high quality telecommunications system in the United States and the NLM computerized retrieval system. The reason for this "star network" is one of economics. That is, the capital investment involved is large but by amortizing the cost of operating the system over 1,000,000 searches, the unit cost of providing a search from a central facility is quite small. For an individual organization wishing to operate the current system for its own use, the cost would be prohibitively expensive.

Because of the high visibility of the National Library of Medicine and because of the large number of users, many special checks and procedures have been established to ensure a high quality of service. At every stage of the system, from the double checking of each citation as it is placed into the computer system all the way to the continuing measurement and evaluation of turnaround time for the receipt of search printouts, quality checks have been implemented to help ensure quality service. I cannot overemphasize quality as a prime requirement of every network activity.

In addition to the usual internal quality controls, it is also necessary for the network operator to know as much as possible about the network user. For example, NLM has recently entered into a contract to study the characteristics of the composite efficient searcher. Factors to be examined include:

1. whether the searcher received formal MEDLINE training from NLM;

2. whether the searcher received formal MEDLINE training from some other source;

3. whether the searcher received formal training in on-line searching from another system, such as Lockheed, SDC, or BRS;

4. other variables such as level of education, subject back-
    ground, presence or absence or other searchers on the staff
    of the same institution, type of institution served, and the
    user habits.

The results of this study together with detailed use data will help provide
NLM with information to improve the efficiency of searchers in the network,
and thus make network membership even more beneficial.

In this and other ways, a network governing body can keep an eye on the
mirror, and respond to much the same critieria used by local libraries when
deciding which network to join. Preliminary to this conference, I had on-
line searches performed against the LISA and MEDLINE data bases. LISA
is the on-line counterpart of Library and Information Science Abstracts and
produced 703 citations about library networks. Even MEDLINE, with its
highly specialized subject orientation, retrieved 256 citations. There is,
then, a meaningful volume of literature being written on this subject. It
seems to me that there is also a real need for self-evaluation by and solid,
detailed information about the networks and their activities that should also
be shared with the general library and information communities. This conference is a big step in that direction, and I salute the University of Pittsburgh,
Dean Galvin, Professor Kent, and their colleagues for making this conference
possible.

Chapter 3

NETWORK ANATOMY AND OBJECTIVES: COMMENTS

James H. Kennedy

Executive Director
AMIGOS Bibliographic Council
Dallas, Texas

While analyzing Professor Kent's paper (Chapter 1), I was trying to determine how the libraries in the Southwest would react to the fact that they should have used a computer simulation analysis to determine the cost-effectiveness for their library networks. I doubt whether many of the libraries would have required or could have justified the cost of such an analysis. Also, since most of the libraries have to share resources due to distances and limited collections, networks have been established to implement this activity of sharing. In addition to my concern as to the necessity for this type of analysis, I would also like to comment on the paper's definition of "network," role of governance, and on the objectives of networks.

DEFINITION

I believe that without a clear definition of a network, we tend to visualize the network that serves our library or region. Since this conference is examining various aspects of networks, a definition should be agreed upon. Library networks, consortia, or cooperatives for resource sharing have been in existence for many years. Due to new advances in technology, inflation coupled with decreasing support levels, and an increased demand by library and information industry users for data immediately, there has been an increased emphasis on cooperative library programs that might support various library operations. Resource sharing to most libraries means the interlibrary loan of material. In recent years, it has also meant the sharing of bibliographic data and holdings to aid the acquisitions, cataloging, collection development and reference operations of many libraries. Although these two aspects have

been the major thrust of cooperative activity, a few libraries have shared
staff and equipment.

Professor Kent apparently considers Lockheed's DIALOG, SDC's ORBIT
and perhaps a consortia of libraries that houses discarded journals or has a
courier service between the institutions as networks. However, these types
of organizations are really just offering a service and do not allow a library
to add data or material to the central facility that might be used or changed
by the other libraries. Also, most of Professor Kent's proposed network
structures are similar to communication and on-line system patterns and
would require some form of data processing in order to enhance resource
sharing and library functions.

Therefore, I believe the definition of a library network while discussing
the papers at this conference should be narrower in scope, perhaps similar
to a definition given by Brett Butler:[1]

> "An independent organization serving more than one library, using
> at least some communications technology (but not necessarily
> totally computer-based), which distributes services to user li-
> braries and, at the same time, receives information directly re-
> lated to the continuing production of the services from the user
> libraries for the purpose of sharing the resources for the librar-
> ies."

Butler amplifies his definition as follows:

> "The essential element in networking which separates it from the
> purchase of services from any outside vendor is that the use of
> the service by the library changes the service subsequently pro-
> vided to other libraries by the network."

Thus, organizations like Lockheed, BRS, University of Chicago, the Library
of Congress, and SDC would not qualify as library network organizations.

Library network organizations that are outside the scope of this proposed
definition are still important to library service. However, it is difficult
enough to compare and discuss the features, the governance, and technical
structures of organizations like OCLC, BALLOTS, WLN, SOLINET,
MINITEX, NELINET, PRLC, PALINET, AMIGOS Bibliographic Council,
and CLASS without adding organizations using no communication and data
processing technology. Hopefully, this conference's attendees will agree on
the applicable library organizations that constitute library networks.

---

[1] Brett Butler, Library Network Development and the Southern Regional
Education Board, 1976, p. 2.

ANATOMY

Now that library networks have been defined, should their "anatomy" be analyzed? Professor Kent says an analytical approach is necessary "because more attention is being directed to library functions, that it makes sense to perform them in a network environment. " He also indicates that many library functions are not clearly defined and their interactions poorly understood in library networks and that a study of network anatomy is a necessary vehicle. I submit that networks have always performed library functions and that these functions are understood by library administrators.

Networks are performing library functions and are beginning to realize the goals and objectives of cost-beneficial resource sharing. These benefits are being realized in the technical services area with the bibliographic data bases such as OCLC and BALLOTS. The options for sharing have not been exhausted but are beginning to be tapped. The group contracts that BCR, MIDLNET, and AMIGOS have established with Bibliographic Retrieval Service (BRS) and Lockheed are beginning to realize cost benefits in the reference area. There is room for more exhaustive and precise definitions of library functions, but we are not still in the dark ages as Professor Kent implies.

Professor Kent contends that there is a morass of types of networks, operations, etc. Therefore an analytical review using computer simulations of existing networks will untangle or clarify this morass. Naturally, a simulation is possible, but is it desirable or is it cost-effective? Most libraries have only a few (less than 3) networks to consider per desired function. The library in Professor Kent's example trying to determine an appropriate network to borrow material surely does not need a computer simulation to narrow its already limited choices.

Various anatomy structures of networks, namely, the star, distributed, and hierarchical, are described by Professor Kent. Normally these schemes have been used to describe different methods of communication or delivery of material between two or more organizations. Perhaps Professor Kent intends to determine which type, or combination of types, of network structures are the most cost-effective for various library functions. The results would be interesting. Such an analytical approach will require data from libraries pertaining to their operations. This data is usually lacking. William Axford[2] implies that top management does not know how to evaluate their systems and/or network systems. Thus, perhaps an analysis of network functions would be to compare each network using hypothetical library transaction and cost data.

---

[2] H. W. Axford, "The Negative Impact of Intrinsic Incrementalism, Chronic Overlayism and Pernicious OCLC-itis on the Development of Effective Resource Sharing Networks. " Library Resource Sharing, 1977, p. 153.

For most library functions the hierarchical or distributed network structure is intuitively more cost-effective in terms of resource-sharing. This of course would depend on communication or delivery costs and/or data processing costs (if applicable). Unfortunately distributed or hierarchical network structures are not as easy to construct as a star network due to political and operational constraints.

A multi-function network may be more cost-effective, but Professor Kent does not present any evidence or data to support this thesis. Surely, it costs more to create this type of system versus a single function system. There is no evidence given that the integration of networks "undoubtedly" will be needed for long-run cost-beneficial services. There is also a theory that perhaps an organization can perform one function better than several functions.

Do libraries want a multi-function network? Do they know how to use such a system? Are library administrators willing to direct their staffs toward the "access" philosophy versus the "holdings" philosophy as described by Professor Kent? How are libraries to interface their local automated systems with network systems? Should these systems be interconnected? For instance, libraries that use a shared-cataloging subsystem will not necessarily use the other functions of the network, such as interlibrary loan, acquisitions, on-line reference service, COM production, etc. There is no requirement for libraries, or at least the same group of libraries, to share resources using all the functions of a multi-function network. Hopefully, this situation will change in the near future.

Libraries within a state can usually develop cooperative programs easier than libraries within a larger region. There is no evidence to support Professor Kent's statement that "the problem (funding) is exacerbated when network membership is mixed." Multi-type library networks are necessary and each library needs the other. Those people who think otherwise, are not providing the service to their patrons. The political boundaries between libraries will disappear in the near future if enabling legislation is enacted or if users demand better service.

Naturally, to use a network efficiently, library managers and staffs are going to have to change their procedures, accept standards, and realign staff. Unfortunately, not all libraries do this. Many libraries use the network functions for their benefit only and not to further the cause for resource sharing. A national library network will have to be developed from the individual library upwards rather than from a national system downward. To do this, libraries within a region will have to decide (a) on the functions and services to be shared, (b) how to accomplish this, (c) how to interface these systems with nationwide library systems, and (d) what type of library organization is necessary to create these services.

GOVERNANCE

When such an organization is developed, governance is one of the factors to be determined. Should each user library have a vote on each policy issue or system design? Should there be a board elected by the user libraries to perform one or more of these tasks? Or should there be an independent board of selected non-members to advise the network organization's staff?

Since the network organizations' function is to serve the libraries with cost-effective service, it is definitely important that the libraries have an input into the type of services and type of products that the network generates. This is a process that is distinct from the governance of an organization. This is a different philosophy from that expounded by Professor Kent in his statement that the "loss of autonomy of a library results in a demand for effective participation in the governance of the network." I believe that if the library can approve or advise on the services produced, then the network authority can be permitted to be authoritarian.

Although other papers in the session will be dealing with the issue of network governance, a few of Professor Kent's statements should be examined. He states that "funding should be based on an obligation for a long-term support to permit the network benefits to develop. However, at the same time the agreement should permit individual libraries to withdraw." How can this be done? If individual libraries withdraw, the network organization cannot have, or plan for, long-term support.

There should be an agreement on acquisitions policies. This appears to be most difficult to achieve among libraries within a given region. It involves a high level of administrative action which is often very difficult to achieve. Many university, college, academic administrators and/or city administrators do not want to relinquish the development of their library's holdings.

Professor Kent says that the best way to have an agreement on bibliographic control is to agree upon standardization, but that standardization may not be feasible. I am not certain why standardization would not be feasible. Perhaps the bibliographic format, namely the MARC format, is too overpowering or is not necessary for future bibliographic control. Maybe there is another standard format that is more feasible for libraries to utilize. Has a research project been developed to ascertain whether or not the Library of Congress MARC format is really necessary for on-line bibliographic control? Without standardization, how do you share bibliographic data? With the increasing cost of materials, libraries must depend upon other organizations for access to some needed materials. Standardization is absolutely essential if we are to share. AACR II with its three levels of description will allow for flexibility in completeness of cataloging within a standard format.

Machine retrieval will eventually answer some of the questions Ms. Kimmel raised in her "Case for Resource Sharing in Children's Literature." With the development of a subject authority file of headings for children, the problems of retrieval could be achieved.

OBJECTIVES

The objectives of networks are well stated by Professor Kent. Most networks are trying to provide a service or product that will benefit libraries and eventually the library user in terms of more materials or better service or both. As budgets decrease or remain the same and the cost of materials and labor increase, various libraries will have to share both materials and processing of these materials.

Networks are basically extensions of libraries and their systems and services. Because of this complex environment, several areas of investigation should be considered. Henriette Avram stated these well in her paper, "How to Design a National Network in the Real World."[3]

1. The objectives of the network system must be stated in detail and agreed to by all the participants.

2. The function of the network system must be identified, in other words, determine "what" is going to be done before determining "how" it should be done.

3. The technical requirements of the system must be stated and problems identified and solved. For example, number and types of systems, protocol, standards, data base design, etc. should be decided. Unfortunately, it appears that various library funding agencies do not believe that these issues are important factors to consider before promoting networks for large libraries.

4. The "policy" issues of the system must be considered, in other words, agreement must be made to determine who will do what, when, and how.

Another aspect that many networks have not been concerned about is the delivery of materials. Telefacsimile still has major problems. Some re-

_____

[3] Avram, Henriette. "How to Design a National Network in the Real World." (Network Development Office, n.d., p. 4-5.)

search money should be given to the telefacsimile copier industry so that more efficient copying can be transmitted. In addition to this activity, services of UPS or the post office have to be given directives to assist libraries in the delivery of materials at a reasonable cost. Alternatively, various libraries can establish courier service among themselves to insure rapid delivery of required materials. Perhaps there could be an interconnection courier service throughout regions in the United States to assist in the distribution of desired materials.

In conclusion, networks are organizations that have as their goal assistance to libraries. This goal will not happen unless all the libraries in a region use the networks cooperatively in more than one activity so the network organization can develop more cost-effective services for all libraries. Libraries and their services will be changing during the next decade. There may be an increasing demand on communication and even knowledge retrieval and less on transportation and the current citation retrieval. What will be the function of library networks in this environment with computer-based technology ? Information scientists and library planners need to be developing now the functions and the technical requirements of a system that will provide information to the user when and where he needs it by interrogation of distributed data bases instead of browsing through library stacks.

Chapter 4

NETWORK ANATOMY AND NETWORK OBJECTIVES: RESPONSE

Ervin J. Gaines

Director
Cleveland Public Library
Cleveland, Ohio

Matthew Arnold, Victorian poet and critic, more than once expressed dissatisfaction with English industrial society. Among the developments that stimulated his disenchantment was what he perceived as a shift in values from ends to means, in a devotion to and reverence for methodology and machinery for their own sake. If Arnold's criticism was appropriate a century ago, it is even more trenchant today. Our society is fascinated by machinery—not only of the physical kind but of the organizational kind. In extreme instances the success of the machinery, or the protocol, or the ritual, is sufficient to evoke admiration irrespective of the purpose for which it was created. In a society like ours the form may sometimes displace the substance; the purpose of the machine may matter less than the elegance of its design. Getting to the moon was more important than being there.

Librarians are somewhat susceptible to this tendency to respect the form rather than the substance. For example, many a library has permitted itself to be injured in pursuit of the perfection of cataloging and classification, irrespective of backlogs or unmet reader needs. This is worship of machinery to the neglect of its purpose.

It is not my intention—although it would be fun—to elaborate on larger social criticism, but to apply the particular cautionary observation of Arnold to our own profession and more particularly to the major emphasis of this conference: networking.

It was inevitable, and it has come to pass, that the papers of the conference describe networks from a mechanical point of view. By doing this we may lose sight of the reason for networks—which is service.

31

The five major papers of this conference all accept without demur that a network is the sine qua non; if we concur, we are left only with the task of deciding what sort of network we are to have, when the fundamental question, perhaps, should be, do we need networks at all—or at least do we need them in profusion?

A library network, as I understand it, is a description of an activity which existed before the nomenclature was devised; but now that we have a name for the activity, we hasten to formalize it and, indeed, make networking mandatory by requiring the formation of organizations to which libraries must belong either because they will be thought unstylish if they do not, or, preferably, will be punished in their income if they do not join a network approved by the state.

When any two libraries talk to each other, we have the fundamental condition for networking, that is, exchange. Whenever one library provides a service to another we have the rudiments of network behavior. Interlibrary loan, or bibliographic exchange in any form, is the chief justification of a network. "Do you have what I don't and how can I get it" is the pre-condition for networking. If I do not perceive any deprivation in my library, then I do not need to network since I am autonomous, and autonomous libraries do not need to import service or books.

Networking is a system with a predominant flow of service from the larger to the smaller, the richer to the poorer, and a reverse flow of demand. When a librarian first asked his neighbor for a book or a citation and had his request honored, networking began.

In this traditional sense, networking is not a recent development. What is new is the formalization, the ritualization of networking—and indeed the proliferation of networking designed for different purposes. OCLC is one sort of network—a regional consortium of libraries is quite another—the difference being in the kind of service provided, the composition of the membership and the system of governance.

One now gains status by joining networks and flashing memberships like credit cards. Networking is no longer optional; it is becoming obligatory.

One of the difficulties with the promise of networks is that they entice us to improve service at remote places at the same time that the perfection of networking techniques within, say, a city public library system fails to occur. Who among us has studied the effectiveness of intra-library loan within a city library system versus inter-library loan between library systems? I suspect that we may be better prepared to find and deliver a book to Seattle than to one of our own branch libraries in Cleveland. But perhaps this perceived internal weakness is true only in Cleveland.

I am skeptical about some sorts of networks. I have repeatedly raised questions about the utility of regional consortia with additional bureaucratic apparatus superimposed upon those of local libraries. I have looked upon experiments like BARC (The Bay Area Reference Center) with, I fear, some cynicism. I have found it difficult to accept the notion that it was necessary to hire additional librarians outside the context of existing libraries to answer questions simply because they were raised in one jurisdiction and answered in another. When the BARC model was proposed for Cleveland, I refused to accede to the proposal for two reasons.

1. I thought it had not proved itself superior to direct access to a library's existing reference staff.

2. I think that mingling two staffs—each responsible to different authorities—in the context of a single library is to invite trouble.

The most useful function of most networks (in my observation) is the provision of access to bibliographic information plus access to the document itself. Other services provided by regional networks appear to me to be of marginal or dubious value. If my observation is valid, then what is the need for the formal apparatus that accompanies networks? Economic resources of the libraries, being limited, do not seem to me well used if they go to support additional bureaucracies that stand between libraries like some sort of mediators or facilitators whose efforts to speed the processes of exchange may not succeed at all.

I return to my allusion to Matthew Arnold. How many of the bureaucratic machines that have been proposed or are already in existence as a result of the stampede to develop networks, have genuinely proved their worth and have justified themselves from a cost-effective point of view?

The cost of the regional consortium in Cleveland is edging up to about $50,000 annually. I incline to the opinion that an equivalent sum of money expended on personnel attached, say, to the largest library in the area, with the sole function of responding to all comers outside the library's primary service area and of seeing that requested information or material is actually delivered, would be more effectively spent than it is through a network. When we consider all the hidden costs of networks, the need to meet, confer, pass resolutions, discuss trivia and do all those tiresome things that some librarians seem to love, meanwhile neglecting the customers—are we not like the established clergy of which John Milton complained when he said of their efforts—the hungry sheep look up and are not fed?

Professor Kent's paper on the anatomy of networks (Chapter 1) is unexceptionable. His exposition is accurate throughout. The difficulty I experi-

ence is not with what he has to say but with the unstated assumption that we
must invent more switching stations in our already cumbersome communication system that stands between the patron and the answer he seeks. We
should strive to simplify rather than complicate. We should seek speed and
accuracy in delivering service, information, and materials; and we should
concentrate less on the architecture of the system which is supposed to facilitate the process.

If there is one illness to which the library profession is susceptible, it is
the tendency to make Byzantine what is essentially Arcadian.

To illustrate how networks may become artificial, let me suggest that one
does not really need a network to make OCLC operative. I think OCLC might
function very well if it were simply a vendor. It sells one kind of library
service—Baker and Taylor or Bro Dart sell other—perhaps even competing
—systems. Does OCLC work better—and if so, is it because it is a network
of some sort—or would it be as effective or more effective if it were simply
a vendor ?

Not all systems are improved by the introduction of membership techniques
and democratic procedures. I'd hate to think of librarians telling authors
what to write as a condition of placing an order. There is something still to
be said for free markets and unaffiliated enterprise. If one library thinks of
a good way to share with other libraries, it does not follow that the sharing
must take place within the sheltering folds of a network. We may recall the
incredibly muddy definition of a network written by Sam Johnson—"Anything
reticulated as decussated with interstices between the intersections."
Johnson was a rather clear thinker. Perhaps he tripped on networks because
networks have inherent deficiencies of clarity.

Something less complex than networks may serve us better—the false is
intricate, the true is simple.

Chapter 5

OBJECTIVES: DISCUSSION

The discussion which follows has been transcribed from tape recordings, summarized and edited. Comments and questions have been attributed to speakers when their identity was provided. The editors of these proceedings take responsibility for any errors in fact or interpretation resulting from this process, since it was not feasible to provide proofs to discussants for checking.

———————————

James Kennedy (to Ervin Gaines)

You mentioned that you didn't think that network membership was necessary in order to share resources. How do you, without some form of contract, agree between institutions to do so?

Ervin Gaines

If you're talking now about sharing resources, obviously there's got to be some agreement. No library is going to let a document leave its hands unless there's some standard system or agreement. That is not what I had in mind when I made my remark. What I feared might be happening in the United States is that we will design networks simply because we don't perceive other ways of doing business, and I think there are other ways of doing business. There is still no reason why any library cannot make a contract with anybody to provide that which the library perceives that it needs for its customers. And I don't think you need a network for that. If a vendor does not supply what you want, then we hope you would stimulate another vendor to compete; and the notion of the free market is not invaluable to us. I think while it creates confusion, it also does create great opportunity. Would you have fewer publishers in the world? Wouldn't it be nice if all the books would be published by one publisher? How simple all your ordering would be. Think of the money you would save. But think of the loss. It's the loss that might be quite invisible to us when we talk about developing hard fixed efficient systems.

35

Jack Belzer - University of Pittsburgh

Regarding the remark that was made about the post office which failed. I
think it's important that we understand why it failed and perhaps learn a
lesson from it. It doesn't make sense to me for an operation like the post
office to take millions of tons of paper and move it from the east coast to the
west coast and similarly from the west coast to the east coast. With new
telecommunication methodology, I visualize going to work in the morning
after placing a cartridge into my TV set and coming home in the evening to
read my mail off the cartridge—and there will be no paper needed. I have
at the University of Pittsburgh an instant library laboratory that is capable
of holding five million pages of information on microform. You can sit at
your terminal and get access to any of it within fifteen seconds. This is just
a laboratory; it is not operational; but it may be a model of what the future
is going to hold.

I am a little concerned about pushing standards too much when the field is
at its present stage. We are moving so fast; let's not rush and freeze too
many things; let's give people opportunities.

I am also concerned about defining things that we have been doing for so
long. I sometimes like to close my eyes and dream that I'm in the next century. I think we should try to extend ourselves beyond what we're doing now
and examine whether some of the functions will still be necessary. Some of
these functions will disappear completely. What I'm trying to say is that we
are trying to replace busses with the most up to date jet planes and telling
the pilot "please follow U.S. 40." Let's not freeze it.

Maurice Freedman - School of Library Service, Columbia University

Professor Kent stated the issue has changed from "whether to join a network" to "which network one should join." It should not be at all presupposed
that the present array of networks, especially those at the national level, are
offering the full range of services or satisfying all of the basic needs of the
nation's libraries. For large segments of libraries, particularly the school
and public libraries, the divergence between base or practical services and
those truly affected and oriented to them, at least from this point of view, is
great. One example most readily comes to mind: the cataloging made available from the Library of Congress through networks such as OCLC, the
Washington Library Network, and BALLOTS, is created especially to satisfy
LC's internal needs; to the extent that it has been feasible for LC, the Library of Congress has met the needs of other communities as well. But Ms.
Kimmel indicates the inadequacies of LC's children's headings and their lack
of effectiveness for children's service (Chapter 1, Appendix). Generally,
getting the networks and our de facto national bibliographic center, LC, to
provide a cataloging service which more directly and adequately serves the

public and school libraries—and yes, the children—seems a major and yet unaddressed problem of the networks today.

It is especially gratifying that the new chairman of NCLIS is sensitive to media, as President of Films, Incorporated. The provision of access to nonprint information is an even greater problem. Libraries all over the country today, to the extent that they acquire these media, hopelessly duplicate the cataloging for these materials. Here the problem is the paucity of standardized cataloging for nonprint materials, irrespective of the cataloging orientation. So Chairman Benton's participation in a network process is welcome to the extent that someone in that position can be efficacious with respect to network services and national bibliographic services.

The three levels of cataloging of the Anglo-American Cataloging Rules, second edition, in the creation of authority files, as stated by Mr. Kennedy, doesn't in any way assure that the kinds of materials cataloged, or that the content of the cataloging, will more adequately meet the problems posed by Ms. Kimmel or the general bibliographic control needs of nonacademic libraries in the adult, young adult, and juvenile areas.

I agree that one can now choose which network to join and one indeed may cheaply and quickly obtain cataloging data from the present national networks. But the data they provide is not specifically oriented to the users of the nation's public and school libraries. Perhaps the question should be added to Professor Kent's list, "How might the present networks improve?"

Leon Montgomery (to Ervin Gaines)

If I interpret your remarks correctly, you suggest that the main flow of goods and services is primarily from big to small libraries. Did I interpret that correctly?

Ervin Gaines

I really meant: from those who have, to those who have not.

Leon Montgomery

You seem to be continuing a long held hypothesis that may be a myth; my real question is—do you have some data that tends to support your conclusions? Let me give you an example. One of the current major state university networks analyzed the data of the 180,000 books purchased last year. Seventy-five percent of the titles held at 15 campuses were unique, even though many of the campuses had similar educational missions. Do you have any data that tends to support your position?

Ervin Gaines

Nothing like the kinds of observation that you have. I suppose most of my opinion or conclusion would come from interlibrary loan behavior in areas where I'm familiar. I don't pretend to have been a student of the phenomena. If you have discovered something else, I'm sure it's very useful.

Leon Montgomery

I want to suggest that for interlibrary loan behavior, your observations are probably quite correct. But this behavior is often predicated on people not knowing where things are; library networks may in fact adjust that process to some extent.

Jack Kolb - United States Army, Pentagon

Referring to the anatomy that was suggested by Professor Kent (Chapter 1), another analogy not to be overlooked is networking in terms of switching centers that are already very well developed, that we can call upon for experience—including the utilities, the post office, communications networks, and highway networks. Most of these have some very substantial commonalities to our objectives. If we don't get adequate service from a utility because of a failure, the utility simply switches to another utility's jurisdiction to better support our needs. Thus if our networks do not serve us adequately, we should think in terms of those networks being an accessory to a further network, in a network of networks.

What has been addressed in one of the papers was economics of cost. I would like to suggest that we should be very much concerned with the economics of savings. The era of holding more, because more is better, is long gone, because additions to our holdings are doing us in, in economic terms. The sharing of holdings is what we're looking for. Within the Army we are developing a network of networks, using already developed individual nets (e.g., logistical information, medical, legal and technical).

John Linford - NELINET

I don't think that our objective is to minimize holdings. I think our objective is to allow the libraries to operate in the most effective ways they are able to operate in. We cannot say: "everybody must minimize holdings; everybody must maximize access." I think that kind of activity is going to be counterproductive.

Regarding Leon Montgomery's question, NELINET's recent interlibrary loan study suggests that large libraries borrow more from large libraries than small libraries; small libraries borrow more from small libraries than they do from large libraries. Networks must recognize that they sprang up as a result of a need, and when that need goes away, the networks ought to also. I see no reason why a network has to imbed itself in concrete just because the need happens to exist right now. As an example, interlibrary loan seems to be the kind of activity that we're dealing with on a day to day basis. But interlibrary loan now represents less than 2% of any given library's circulation activity. Why all the fuss? Well in aggregate, there's a lot of reason for it. But at some point in time, the ultimate interlibrary loan network is going to consist of circulation systems talking to one another. The clear advantage will be that you not only will know that a library has an item, you will also know that it is available, or at least you know if the system says it's available. At that stage of the game, there will be no need for massive interlibrary loan networks. The biggest problem will be, as now, document delivery.

In terms of what networks do, the ideas "do you have it?" and "can I get it?" are clearly the thrust of networks right now. But the networks have an opportunity to provide something that vendors don't provide, and that the national level networks don't provide, and that is real live hand-holding service for the members of the library network. In terms of NELINET, that translates to "automation." Our members are looking to us for help in that area, since they do not have experienced staff members with the necessary skills.

Melvin Day

I would like to add support to placing less emphasis on reducing the size of collections as the main purpose for joining a network; the main purpose should be to improve service to patrons of member libraries. If it cannot be demonstrated that membership will improve service to its patrons, I don't think I would join the network.

Carlos Cuadra - Cuadra Associates

I'd like to ask two questions. One has to do with the possible impact of minicomputers and microcomputers. At the time that people first started talking about networks, computers were very expensive and this naturally led to thinking about sharing these immense costs. Nowadays a computer that would have cost $10 million some years ago may cost $0.5 million; and the machine that could have cost $1 million five or six years ago may cost $20,000-$30,000. I'd like to ask any of the panelists whether they see any impact whatsoever of that technology on their concept of distribution of functions between centralized operations and decentralized operations at the library.

The second question I'd like to address is to Allen Kent. I enjoyed your network analogy which likens the network to systems of the body. I noticed that you used the digestive system, the cardiovascular system, the reproductive system, the endocrine system—and the brain wasn't mentioned. In most of the biological systems that I know about, the brain is what mediates all of these things, and I wondered whether there was some subtle message you were giving us about the direction and management of a national library network.

Allen Kent

I think the applause is your answer. I wish you were there when I was developing the analogy; I would have put it in.

Melvin Day

I think Carlos Cuadra raises a very good point. My own personal feeling is that we will see parallel development of networks in this country—but I think that the new technology that is being developed will also enable individual libraries sometime in the future to have available locally a much larger portion of the information that it needs to do its job. For example, one of the major reasons for the large networks today is to provide bibliographic access to the literature—primarily the journal literature. Here we have the large SDC network, Lockheed, BRS, etc., and the reason we actually tie into those networks is to enable us as an individual library to have access to data bases which are much too expensive for us to operate locally. We can't afford that kind of computer system. Carlos is absolutely correct in noting that the cost of computing is coming way down, and the ability of the small computers is increasing to do many of the jobs which previously could only be done on the large computers—that capacity is already here and will develop even further.

The National Library of Medicine has a research and development component called the Lister Hill Center for Biomedical Communications. At the present time this Center is in the process of trying to marry a video disc console to a minicomputer. Video disc works something like a long-playing record; the video disc console is being developed primarily for entertainment purposes, so you can watch programs at a later date. It will store up to 54,000 frames or a billion bytes of data on one side. The discs are produced the same way as long-playing records, they're stamped out; so the cost of producing these in batches would bring unit cost to $5 - $10. This being the case, it would be possible to have a copy of large data bases, such as MEDLINE, on one disc. This would be digital information. By the same token, you also could store pages of information. Although it is too early to talk about operational systems of this type, it is not unreasonable to expect that at some time in the future libraries will have available to them an electronic capability which will increase their capacity to provide service to their patrons above and beyond what they have at the present time. We still will have printed books and printed journals. But at some economic crossover point, for some materials, and to get access to some types of information, we will go to networks; while for other types of materials I think we will maintain local availability in electronic form. Thus it then may be cheaper to have materials available locally than to go on networks.

One advantage of the new video disc technology is that both video and digital information can be mixed, with either called out as desired.

Ervin Gaines

What Mr. Cuadra implies is certainly very valuable for us. That is, with computers and with micro-storage the opportunity to expand rather than contract holdings without much increase in the cost is a very attractive prospect indeed. Libraries may not reduce titles; they may actually increase titles because it would be so relatively low cost to obtain and retain massive bibliographies of every kind.

Melvin Day

The major problem of the future in reaching this goal is not going to be technical—it is going to be legal relating to copyright. I think we will solve the technical problems before we solve some of these other problems.

Charles Benton

The video disc isn't something that is on the drawing boards for some far distant future time; this is coming down the pike hard and will be launched by MCA Phillips in Atlanta in the middle of December 1978—operationally. The entire Encyclopedia Britannica can be put on one video disc, with 20,000 frames left over. The video disc costs less than a dollar to manufacture (its manufacturing cost—excluding binding, cover, etc.). The implications are absolutely revolutionary.

One can divide all audio visual programs for educational use into two categories: those that were available on a centralized basis (computer-assisted instruction, instructional television) and materials that were available on a decentralized basis in the school library (filmstrips, audio records). When I was President of Britannica Films, I presided over a very interesting project called Project Discovery. The concept was to remove all the logistical constraints in the use of films and filmstrips in schools by putting a library of 1,000 filmstrips and 500 films in the individual school building so that it would be accessible and available to the teacher, the children and the parents in the community. The results of that experiment were really fascinating; unfortunately, I then left the company and was unable to take it the next step, which would have been 8-mm. sound.

I hope that the technology discussion considers the implications on access vs. holdings issues and of being able to put into local libraries the kind of information through the video disc that really removes much of the pressure for access.

Stephen Salmon - University of California, Systemwide Administration

I simply want to caution Mr. Gaines and Mr. Linford against making too many hard conclusions about interlibrary loan based on present patterns of interlibrary loan. It appears that many of our existing patterns depend not only on the existence of materials in particular collections, but the existence of bibliographic information about the existence of the materials in the collections. I'm following up also on the comment by Leon Montgomery regarding overlap, or underlap, amongst collections. We've done a number of studies in California of that precise characteristic. I think the underlap is more impressive and significant, frequently, than the overlap. To give a specific example using the largest and the smallest: we found that Sonoma State College's collection was duplicated to the extent of about 75% at the University of California at Berkeley. The significant thing, however, is that 25% of that collection is not duplicated at Berkeley. It is difficult to generalize, as one might be tempted to do, and think of Berkeley as a have and think of Sonoma State as a have not; in at least some cases Sonoma State is the have and Berkeley the have not. Now there are very few faculty at the University of California/Berkeley that believe that anything good can come out of Sonoma State. This is not arrogance or at least not wholly arrogance; it is, at least in part, ignorance of the fact that there is anything at Sonoma State worth having. As we develop more effective means of making bibliographic information available and as we improve the bibliographic access mechanisms, I think we will influence our interlibrary loan patterns, and we have some evidence of that already from the performance of libraries using OCLC and other networks.

Speaker from Montgomery County, Maryland - Public Library System

I cannot think of networking in a vacuum. Tomorrow on our election ballot, we have our version of proposition 13. We will need to look at the possibility of joining networks in a very different environment. Our patrons judge us on how fast we can get best sellers from one end of the county to another, and it's very important because they're going to fund us. Public library users represent all kinds of people—employees from the National

Bureau of Standards, college and university students who come for what they can't find in their college and university library, etc. Bibliographic information is not what people want, to a great extent. They have mostly all the bibliographies they can deal with; what they want is the document. When we talk about access to information, we have to make sure that we're giving people the information in the form that they want it. It's great to have all this information on discs and on microfiche and on microfilm for storage or for use by other librarians, which may not be the form in which our users want it.

Earlier my library did convert many journals to microform, but we found that users really didn't like that material on microfiche or microfilm. They wanted those old copies of the magazines. Sometimes they wanted old magazines like the Saturday Evening Post because they wanted the ads in color for research. We had given people access to lots of stuff in a form which they couldn't use.

Networking is great, but it has got to be tailored to how your user wants this material. We've got to prove to our users that it is worthwhile for them to provide taxes to belong to regional networks. They can't see it in the way that we do. We think it is great, but we're going to have to prove to them that it really works and that they will get the service that they want. But I'm not sure that we know how much people need; for example, I don't know what anybody I can think of would do with the Encyclopedia Britannica on a video disc. Networking is a marvelous idea if we don't let our own desires dominate, and if we don't get "conned" by too many vendors into buying too much equipment and hardware that we can't maintain and the public isn't interested in.

Allen Kent

There were two points made that I'd like to comment on. (1) On the lack of desire or interest of users in Montgomery County to pay for networking because they're not convinced that it will produce results that are wanted: I wonder whether those same people are willing to pay for the building needed to store the old copies of the Saturday Evening Post that they demand in hard copy. I wonder whether the new mentality in proposition 13 will "divide the house" so to speak. Will most of the taxpayers wish to pay for those few who wish to see the ads in the Saturday Evening Post in color? (2) On the difficulty of getting a best seller from one part of the county to the other (and Ervin Gaines made a similar point): I think that is precisely the type of material that should not be put on a network. It is not the high use, the high demand material, that should be shared; I think those networks that attempt to do that by electronic and other means are missing the point. It is the little used material, the lesser used material, that is the target.

Ervin Gaines

For me this is a very important point. When I raised the question of the best seller, I didn't mean "the best seller" literally. I meant any kind of service at the neighborhood level, which is often quite weak in our library. The librarians do not themselves take advantage of the system that already exists in their neighborhoods. Have we as librarians paid close attention to perfecting systems that already exist before we go too far in developing new systems? It seems to me that there is an advantage to perfecting the systems that have been in existence for a long time or at least to analyze and understand their failures before we proliferate failure on a grander scale.

Russell Walker - Upper Arlington Public Library, Columbus, Ohio

I'd like to thank Mr. Gaines for his comments. It's refreshing to hear that point of view.

I have never seen any other industry or market make this kind of concentration on a minority aspect of the business. In other words, what we're doing is spending a tremendously disproportionate amount of time and money on a very microscopic portion of our activity; we should concentrate on marketing what we already have.

The video disc has been on the horizon now for about five or six years and even longer in the planning stages. I asked the question at ALA some years ago, "what planning is going on toward the utilization of the video disc?" We talked about its storage capability, etc., but how much planning is really going on between library people and the video disc manufacturers in utilizing this new tool?

Allen Kent

It may appear that much money is being spent in relation to what you call an "infinitesmal problem" because, specifically in the research libraries, so much of the acquisitions budget is spent on materials that is never or little used, and therefore attention is being directed to that problem.

Melvin Day

The extent of planning in the use of video disc on the part of the library community has obviously been minimal. I really don't think there will be too much planning until some actual equipment and some applications are at hand so that people can actually see and evaluate for themselves. Then I think you'll get more planning and that, hopefully, will be in the next few months.

Eileen Trauth - University of Pittsburgh

With regard to technology and its relevance to library networks, I think
it's important to keep in perspective the purpose of this conference: recommendations on policy. I think the most appropriate people to make these
recommendations are the information professionals. I don't think the issue
is whether or not this technology is here now or appropriate for now. If we
do not get involved in the use of this technology, other information professions will.

Edith Crockett - SDC Search Service

The comment that was just made is very appropriate. The technology is
here now and we have found in our user population an increasing trend for
the end user to make use of the on-line retrieval systems that are available
today. For a time, people went to libraries to retrieve materials that they
already knew about. Then there came a change with on-line retrieval systems becoming available in libraries. People went to libraries to find out
about new information that they didn't know about. The end user population
of on-line retrieval systems is growing. With the availability of electronic
document delivery services, preservation becomes a significant factor for
library networking, including the use of video discs and other types of technologies that exist now and that will be coming in the future.

Part Two

NETWORK TOPOLOGY: FUNCTIONS OF EXISTING NETWORKS

If one were to characterize the hundreds of library networks in the nation, in terms of functions performed (or services offered), one would find substantial differences. These differences may result from the type of material involved, the types of member libraries, and the technology employed. It becomes necessary to understand precisely the functions performed and to assess how these would relate to the building blocks, or modules, of a national network.

The position paper distributed in advance of the conference is given in Chapter 6. Chapters 7-10 present reactions from the panelists. Chapter 11 presents the discussion at the conference.

Chapter 6

NETWORK TOPOLOGY: FUNCTIONS OF EXISTING NETWORKS

James G. Williams   Roger Flynn

Associate Professor   and   Lecturer
Interdisciplinary Department   Interdisciplinary Department
of Information Science   of Information Science

University of Pittsburgh
Pittsburgh, Pennsylvania

"We're not perfect, but we have connections."
(Cooperating Libraries in Consortium—brochure)

INTRODUCTION

The primary purpose of this chapter is to discuss network functions. However, these functions are dependent on various other factors, such as the
network topology, the resources shared, the geographical area covered, the
type of member libraries and the technology utilized to implement the functions. Hence, this discussion intertwines some descriptive aspects of the
functions as well as some prescriptive aspects.

The need to study network functions is critical to the design of library
networks of the future. This is most important for any national network or
for existing networks that are changing in terms of size, functions or technology. The functions to be performed by a network determine its physical
structure as well as its logical organization. The interaction among functions
needs to be understood in order to design cost-effective networks and to be
able to make valid judgments regarding their performance. We believe that
designing networks to fit a specific set of functions is preferable to designing
functions to fit a specific network. A network designed to perform a specific
function such as cataloging is not necessarily well suited to perform the circulation function and vice versa. If the relationship between these functions
is not known and utilized in the design of a network to perform both functions,

it is unlikely that the network will be cost-effective in its operations. Therefore, it seems appropriate that the network functions be understood in terms of their individual requirements and their impact on other functions. The impact of a function performed by a network upon other functions performed within the member libraries, or by another network utilized by the member libraries, is also important to the design and evaluation of library networks.

The basis for much of what follows has been derived from a survey of networks in the United States and Canada conducted by the Office of Communications Programs at the University of Pittsburgh. * The wealth of data supplied by more than 150 networks have provided us with the opportunity to arrive at some judgments and assess some of the problems related to network functions.

AN OVERVIEW

A network can be viewed as a physical network and as a logical network. The physical network is the concern of those who must operate it so that it will support the logical network. The physical network is concerned with physical channels of communications, equipment, physical interconnection of network nodes (levels), speed of processing data, file structures, etc. The logical network is the concern of those who must use the network in attempting to meet the objectives established by each network member. The logical network is function-oriented in that those who use the network think of performing a function and the logical relationships among network nodes, data files, data elements, etc. The logical structure of a network may or may not have any resemblance to its physical structure.

> For example, when a library requests an interlibrary loan via a network, the requesting library views the transaction from the logical point of view as a direct connection between the requesting library and the lending library. In fact, the logical view of the entire interlibrary loan function may be that of a completely decentralized network. The actual physical network may be a completely centralized one that appears to the user as decentralized. The desired logical structure of the network to satisfy the user functions imposes constraints upon the physical components of the network and upon how they operate.

Networks currently perform an array of functions involving numerous activities, a variety of technological methods, a diversity of human expertise, and a plethora of problems.

---

* Study funded in part by NSF grant DSI 77-17635.

Network functions fall into three primary classes:

1) those that serve the patron directly,

2) those that serve the member libraries directly and the patron indirectly, and

3) those that support the network structure.

The first two general function types might be termed goal-oriented. They attempt to fulfill the primary goal of the network (service to the patron) and its necessary condition (the survival of the library). As indicated in the survey, these goals correspond to the general network objectives of:

1. Sharing resources, and

2. Reducing and/or controlling the rate of rising costs.

The third general type, functions that support network activities, is "means-oriented." It consists of activities that contribute to the accomplishment of the other two primary goals.

For example, the functions that serve the patron directly would include:

1. Interlibrary loan, with its reliance on the photocopying and delivery of materials;

2. Inter-system reference, with its reliance on a communications subsystem;

3. Inter-system referral, with its reliance on a file of resources and the communications system; and

4. Continuing education, whether for professionals within the network, or for patrons in general.

Those that serve the library interests directly and the patron indirectly would include:

1. Cooperative acquisitions programs,

2. The technical processing involved in acquisitions,

3. Cataloging and other means of resource identification and location, and

4. Circulation control systems.

And functions that support the network activities might involve:

1. The creation and operation of systems that implement the functions mentioned above (systems support);

2. Evaluation activities, such as the collection of statistics, analysis of performance, and user evaluation studies;

3. Staff and user training activities;

4. The determination of costs and setting of fees;

5. Communications activities such as publication, the holding of meetings, etc.

The impetus for establishing a network is to provide improved library service more economically by pooling resources. Since the primary goal of a library is to provide users with access to information at the lowest possible costs, and since all library activities such as acquisitions, cataloging, processing, reference, circulation, etc., are performed with this in mind, it is difficult to imagine that a unified acquisitions function within a network cannot perform more cost-effectively than by having each library attempt to perform this function separately. But like all ideals there are other considerations such as:

1. Cooperative acquisitions cannot be effectively implemented without an effective interlibrary loan system because the fear of not being able to borrow what is not bought will destroy its intent.

2. Cooperative acquisitions will fail if an adequate delivery system does not exist.

3. The policies governing unified acquisitions are difficult to establish, difficult to implement and difficult to evaluate.

Keeping in mind that library functions do not exist in isolation but are related to each other, it is important for any attempt at networking to consider not only the individual function the libraries decide to perform, but also the relationships among each of the other functions libraries perform. It may be that the benefits derived by performing one function via the network may result in a higher cost for performing another function through the individual libraries, thus completely offsetting the networking benefit. For example, a network policy of resource sharing and cooperative acquisitions will result in increased interlibrary loan activity. If this activity is not also network-supported at an efficient level, the individual library may find that the costs incurred in filling interlibrary loan requests more than offset the benefits derived from cooperative acquisitions. This would lead one to infer that a network must look at the cost benefits across all functions rather than a single function in order to make reasonable network design and utilization decisions.

DESCRIPTION OF NETWORKS

Definition of a Network

A general definition of a network might be: an interconnected or interrelated chain, group or system attempting to achieve some specified common and mutually beneficial objectives. This definition does not necessarily include certain of the characteristics of a library network as defined by Brett Butler in his paper, "State of the Art in Networking."[1] But is is a useful definition in examining the notion of networks as defined by activities in the library and information field. Butler's definition of a library network includes the following components:

1. A dependent system which operates multilaterally "in concert" in response to the common desires of a group of member libraries, as opposed to various shared or cooperative services which are offered unilaterally to libraries of all types by vendors or other libraries.

2. A duplex element which enables two-way communication, which separates a network from a publication, or an information service which is one-way.

3. Digital which excludes various multi-library functions that fulfill other characteristics but do not involve some use of computers, telecommunications or digital manipulation.

4. The distribution of information which may take the forms of catalog cards, print-outs, CRT displays, micro-images, etc.

5. An independent organization separate from administrative, political and fiscal bounds of its members.

Butler uses the concept of digital transmission, storage and manipulation whereas many library and information activities labeled "networks" have no explicit digital aspects. Therefore, as a starting point we accept the general definition above in discussing the network topologies and functions as found in the field with the notion that some of these are resource sharing systems but not networks as per the Butler definition.

The important aspects to be discussed in this chapter are the topologies and functions that are, could, and should be included in a true network. It is our contention that those resource sharing systems that are not true networks could be converted into networks via the application of computers and telecommunications technology. The topologies of and functions performed by many resource sharing systems are similar to those that would be performed in a networking environment.

The term "topology" as discussed here relates to the structural and geographic relationships among elements in a network as well as relationships among networks. The term "functions" relates to the services offered by the network.

Network Topology

Networks vary widely in terms of their explicit structures and geographic distribution, but have some common implicit structures and geographic distributions when considered in terms of network-to-network relationships. An interesting relationship that we have noticed is that the more formal the governance structure of a network, the more clearly defined are the network topology and the functions performed by the network.

In discussing network structure, we commonly think of (1) totally centralized (star), (2) totally decentralized, (3) distributed centralized or (4) hierarchical (Figure 1).

There are examples of each type of network in existence as found in the data collected in our survey of networks. OCLC would be classified as a totally centralized network, RLG (Research Libraries Group) as a decentralized network, Bell Labs or the Suburban Library System in Illinois (outside Chicago) as a distributed centralized network, and the National Library of Medicine (NLM) as a hierarchical network. But upon closer examination, few if any networks are of pure type. OCLC is centralized in the physical sense but not in terms of how it is utilized by libraries. Some libraries utilize OCLC as part of a distributed centralized network. That is, an OCLC node is also a central node for another network. Figure 2 depicts such a topology.

In such a structure the central node in the library network queries and captures data from OCLC that it, in turn, makes available to its nodes for circulation, bibliographic access, etc. This illustrates the importance of viewing networks in network-to-network relationships as opposed to a network as an isolated entity.

Many resource sharing systems that do not necessarily meet the Butler criteria for a "true" network are structured in an hierarchical manner. Although the network shown in Figure 3 is hierarchical when viewed in isolation, it is not strictly hierarchical in terms of its relationship with other networks and its operational characteristics in relation to the functions it performs. This network is interconnected with OCLC, New York Times, and Lockheed. Thus, its operational structure, as seen in Figure 4, is a combination of a distributed centralized and an hierarchical structure. The operational network structure is much more complicated than the structure when viewed in isolation.

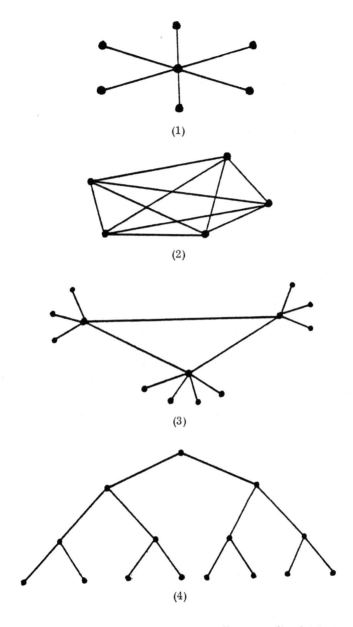

Figure 1. Network structures: (1) totally centralized (star) network; (2) totally decentralized network; (3) distributed centralized network; (4) hierarchical network.

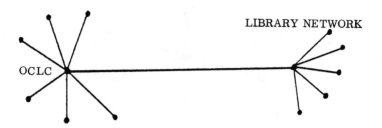

Figure 2.   OCLC as a distributed centralized network.

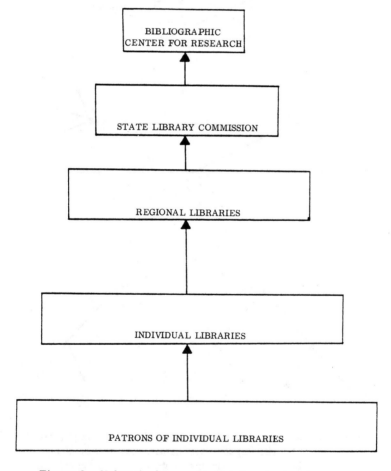

Figure 3.   Nebraska hierarchical network structure.

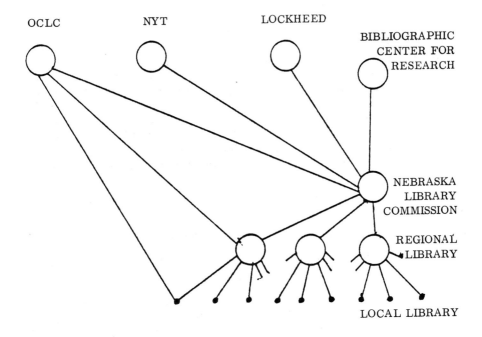

Figure 4. Nebraska as an operational network to network structure.

Usually, the structure presented by an individual network does not present itself in terms of other networks but in terms of functions that can be performed in relation to its network members. Thus, OCLC is viewed as a resource for cataloging, search and verification, etc., but not as another network structure which interfaces with and impacts on the individual network. If all networks are viewed in terms of a network-to-network structure, most are interconnected.

Yet, although networks are related in the sense that they are connected to nodes in other networks, there is often no two-way communication between them. For example, nodes in two networks may be connected to Lockheed but Lockheed does not permit them to communicate with each other. If nodes in two networks are connected to OCLC, they may communicate with each other in an indirect manner by leaving a message in terms of a catalog record or creating a message in the "save" file that another node may display. But, the ability to be connected in a direct and interactive manner does not usually exist among networks. Technically, this two-way communication is possible, but the economic, political, administrative and legal aspects have not been determined.

In examining the distribution of geographic network types, certain patterns begin to emerge. For example, as might be expected, the national networks are often based in the area surrounding Washington, D. C., although notable exceptions exist (OCLC, BALLOTS, CRL). Networks covering several states are found more frequently in the West, where the geographical area is large in comparison to population density; while networks covering only a portion of a state (urban, several counties) are more common in the heavily populated areas, such as the East, the Midwest and California. It may be advisable, in planning a national network, to de-emphasize political boundaries for the more realistic parameters of geographic distance and user population. The factors that seem most influential in determining the geographic area of a network are:

1. The number of libraries per square mile which is usually related to population density;

2. The types of functions the network performs;

3. The funding patterns of library service; and

4. The types of libraries involved.

Thus, networks in the less densely populated regions tend to span large areas. Networks providing "processing" functions, such as cataloging (OCLC) tend to be centralized and often span larger geographic areas. Networks that provide access to bibliographic data bases tend to be centralized (commercial vendors) or hierarchical (access to NLM's MEDLINE), and span large geographic areas. A network designed for interlibrary loan tends to be a completely decentralized structure that covers a small geographic area, typically, a single state or some portion of a state. Networks supported by a particular funding agency, such as the state library, often follow the geographic pattern of distribution of that funding agency.

The technology employed also seems to be related to the structure of the network. Decentralized networks use low level communications technology such as TWX, hierarchical structured networks use the telephone systems with people interacting at each level; while centralized systems tend to use high levels of technology such as large computers.

FUNCTION DEFINITIONS

The Pitt survey of networks revealed that networks perform many functions that might not be obvious at first glance. The functions range from the very common interlibrary loan to the less common function of serving as a clearinghouse for materials. In the initial list of functions performed, the following were the most frequently mentioned:

1. interlibrary loan	12. cataloging
2. reference	13. processing
3. delivery	14. storage
4. acquisitions	15. literature searching
5. union lists	16. collections development
6. continuing education	17. abstracting/indexing
7. bibliographic access	18. referral
8. photocopying	19. consulting
9. circulation	20. accounting and management
10. communications	21. microfilming
11. publications	

The list is long and multi-faceted and some functions are not listed as they actually appeared in the survey responses. The authors have thus introduced a mapping of all functions described by the survey respondents into 17 general headings. The headings (and brief definitions) given below have been made general enough to include the many variations in input, processing and output that seem to accomplish the same general objectives.

A. Management Function. This function is limited to those activities necessary to control and evaluate the network operations, including financial accounting.

B. Administrative Function. This includes those activities necessary to support all other network functions (such as coordination, resource allocation, planning, policy making, and funding). These activities shape the network's structure and insure its continued operation.

C. Acquisitions Function. The procurement of packages of information in whatever media necessary to meet the needs and limitations of the network's objectives.

D. Cataloging and Catalog Production Function. The cataloging function has two parts: descriptive cataloging and subject cataloging. Descriptive cataloging attempts to provide identification data for a package of information in terms of form of entry while subject cataloging attempts to provide locational and subject access data for an information package. Catalog production may be in card, book, electronic or micro-image form. It may be in individual or union catalog.

E. Processing/Preparation Function. The production of spine labels and book cards, stamping and inserting other items in packages of information, as well as shelving and filing would be included in this function.

F. Information Retrieval Function. This function attempts to locate packages of information or answer factual questions by utilizing available access points to a data base such as author, title, subject headings, classification numbers, etc.

G. Circulation Function. This is an inventory control activity that maintains a record of who has what packages of information. Many statistics generated by this function are useful in making decisions concerning other functions, such as acquisitions.

H. Serials Control Function. This is an order entry/inventory control activity that attempts to perform such tasks as serials check-in, subscription renewal, claiming and tracking the status and location of serials.

I. Interlibrary Loan Function. The primary tasks incorporated in this function are acting as an agent for patrons who desire to borrow a package of information outside their own library and lending packages of information to other institutions or individuals as well as maintaining a record of each such transaction.

J. Delivery Function. This function involves the transmission or transportation of a package of information from one location to another with maximum efficiency and effectiveness.

K. Storage Function. This is the storage of packages of information at a remote location for on-demand delivery. The information selected for such storage might meet some predetermined criteria and is usually stored remotely to make room for current or frequently used information.

L. Referral Function. Requests for information that cannot be satisfied by the receiving institution/library are referred to another institution/library. This may involve referring either the requestor or the request itself to another library.

M. Communications Function. This involves establishing and maintaining channels of communications among members of the network. This may take many forms such as TWX, privately operated interlibrary delivery service, area telephone service, telecommunications network or postal delivery service.

N. Education Function. Training users (library staff and patrons) how to use network capabilities and equipment as well as providing opportunities for continuing education on broader topics would be included under this function. Preparation of training materials such as user manuals, workshop syllabi, newsletters, computer-aided learning packages, etc. would also be involved.

O. Standardization Function. This includes establishing minimum standards for each network function so as to create a minimum level of compatibility within a specific network as well as among networks.

P. Marketing Function. Network functions and the tasks they accomplish must be known to both members as well as potential members. In addition, evaluation of present services and of the demand for new services must be an on-going process. These, as well as fair and cost recovery pricing, are the responsibility of marketing. The publication of brochures and other useful documents is also within the marketing area.

Q. Systems Development and Support. The implementation of the various activities of the network require the development of many systems. Once these systems become operational, they require both day-to-day maintenance and periodic development. This includes such activities as documentation, programming, testing, equipment operation and maintenance, supervision, consultation, trouble shooting, production, error correction, and the various activities of system analysis, design and implementation.

The survey of information networks revealed a wide variation in emphasis on such activities. However, each activity was mentioned by one or more of the networks reporting.

NETWORK PROBLEMS, PROMISES AND POSSIBILITIES

This section deals with the various inferences we have made about the functions in a networking environment. These opinions are based on the descriptive information about network functions, as gleaned from the survey data we have collected to date.

A. MANAGEMENT FUNCTION

It seems apparent that network management varies widely in its ability to control the network operations. Many networks have survived in spite of themselves via available funds and strong member library support. In our opinion, this function is not well conceptualized and there do not seem to be enough adequately trained personnel to perform the network management function. This problem should be addressed by educational institutions and professional associations.

Current educational approaches in library science are notably weak in the areas of business management, operations research, data collection methods, statistical analysis, and the various tools necessary to the running of a net-

work. While it is feasible to bring non-librarian managers into the area of
library networking, it also seems feasible to redirect educational procedures
(both degree and continuing education programs) toward these areas of expertise that are currently lacking.

B. ADMINISTRATIVE FUNCTIONS

We believe this function also suffers from a lack of adequately trained, experienced personnel. This is particularly evident in the policy-formulation
and fee-setting areas. The formulation of policies in a networking environment is analogous to policy-making in a large commercial firm with a con-
glomerate of separate companies which have a primary objective in common
(e.g., making a profit) but with separate sets of problems, procedures, etc.
As important as policies are to the successful operation of a network, its
ultimate survival depends on financial stability.

Funding. It is our opinion that only those networks based on a fee structure that can be maintained without grant money will be viable in the long run.
This fee structure may be determined by taking into account a combination
of budgeted funds and member fees. The strongest networks are those that
offer services in such a cost-effective manner that membership is desirable
because it is profitable to the individual member, and when all services provided by the network are paid for by membership fees. This opinion has
been strengthened by the reaction of librarians in California upon passage of
proposition 13 (see Advanced Technology Libraries, Vol. 7, No. 6).

The setting of fee structures involves philosophical problems over and
above the accounting problems involved in assessing true costs. The matter
of membership fees (when they exist) is usually handled in one of two ways:

1. Fixed Fee
2. Scaled Fee

The scaled approach is based on two premises:

1. Those that have more can afford to pay more (similar to the
   graduated income tax);

2. Larger libraries will serve more users and create more
   transactions, thus placing a greater burden on the network.

However, it does not take into account two other factors:

1. A library joining with a larger amount of resources is penal-
   ized precisely for the great wealth of resources it brings
   into the network.

2. The large library with a large collection may tend not to use
    the network services in relation to what they pay for belong-
    ing to the network, while small libraries may utilize net-
    work services a great deal, in relation to what they pay;
    thereby the per use cost by large libraries may be much
    higher than for small libraries. This conflicts with the phi-
    losophy of equal access with equal cost to all.

If the concept of a network is taken in its complete form, there is one
logical collection and one logical body of users. It would seem then that the
fees assessed would be equitably distributed among all users in direct relationship to the costs incurred by the network. At first glance, this philosophy would seem to dictate a fixed fee structure. However, this assumption
is fallacious if applied to a fee assessed per member library. The fixed fee
of the small library is spread over a wider number of users than the fixed
fee of the small library, thus resulting in a smaller per capita price for network services in the large library. This again mitigates against the concept
of equal access to all.

Possibly, then, a scaled fee based on population is the answer. The one
difficulty involved in setting the fee according to population served is the
determination of the population. Should the determination be made on the
basis of number of potential users? Should those who have a borrower's
card be the factor? Or those who actually do access materials and/or information, as indicated by the circulation and reference records?

Since, in actuality, not all potential users access the resources, and not
all actual users access them equally often, should the fee be based on total
transactions? The concept of a fee based on number of transactions is already familiar in such services as cataloging (OCLC, BALLOTS) and in
bibliographic access to data bases (Lockheed, SDC). It may be the only viable measure for a truly cost-effective network to adopt. And, besides
being cost-effective, it is operationally implementable in a much easier
fashion than a fee structure based on the population served.

Policy. The lack of formal agreements in developing a network's structure undermines both the approach of funding and planning. One reason
given for the demise of networks besides lack of funding is lack of interest:

> As a network system...disbanded in 1975. Each agency
> within the network began to work independently of the
> others.
> -- Network reply to survey

The network must be assured of the continued participation of the members,
and each member must have the assurance of continued support from the

network. This "double reassurance" cannot be achieved without formal agreements between the parties involved.

Planning. The development of a viable network demands planning not only among network members, but between the members and the clients they serve. For example, in an academic library, the collection should be developed in order to service the needs of the educational programs being offered. As indicated in previous discussions of networking,[2] this is not a one-time process. Institutional plans change, and, over time, it is possible for one institution to have the educational program, another institution to have the resources. However, if the concept of the network as a single logical collection is taken seriously, it may prove feasible to move the collection. Whether such drastic deviation from current practice will be acceptable to users and librarians is a question that must be addressed.

Certainly, it seems reasonable that users who do not need the resources should not miss them; and it seems reasonable that a single large "interlibrary loan" of an entire collection (or portion of a collection) is preferable to unending individual requests. It will be part of the job of marketing and training to indicate the reasonableness of such an approach to users and librarians alike.

C. ACQUISITIONS

We believe the function of cooperative acquisitions is critical to any successful library network. We use the term "cooperative acquisitions" to cover all types of acquisition programs whether joint ownership, centralized purchasing, specialized areas of acquisition, etc. The network functions of communication; interlibrary loan, including delivery; and interlibrary reference will place an additional cost into the already overburdened budget. This cost must be alleviated in other ways, and one of the more impactive methods of alleviation is to reduce the costs of acquisitions (without reducing the total resources) by introducing a cooperative acquisitions program.

The value of cooperative acquisitions can be seen in the following simplified illustration. Suppose that the network is a hierarchical structure of three levels, with the nodes at each lower level being served by a single node at the immediately higher level:

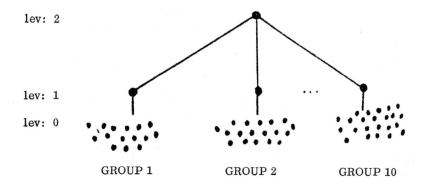

lev: 2

lev: 1

lev: 0

GROUP 1   GROUP 2   GROUP 10

Suppose further that the network is created to acquire books, and that the average cost of a book (buying and processing) is $50. Books acquired at level zero incur the entire cost of $50 per book per library, so that a library acquiring 5,000 books locally would spend $250,000. However, books acquired at level 1 would be available to all libraries, but the cost per library would be only $5 per book, since the cost would be distributed among ten lower node libraries. Thus, a "regional center" at level 1 could acquire 10,000 books at a cost per library at level zero of $50,000 or $5 per book. At level 2, the cost per book acquired would be spread over 100 libraries, so that the effective cost per library at level zero would be $0.50; at this price, the regional node at level 2 could acquire 20,000 books at a cost of $10,000 per library. Thus we have the following situation:

Level	Books acquired	Cost incurred at level 0
0	5,000	$250,000
1	10,000	50,000
2	20,000	10,000
	35,000	$310,000

The books acquired locally consume about 80% of the library's materials budget for about 15% of the books acquired; while books acquired at level 2 consume 3% of the budget for over 55% of the books acquired. By contrast, the cost for acquiring all 35,000 books locally would be about $1.75 million.

As in all simplified models, there are flaws in the representation. The savings in acquisition costs may be offset by costs incurred in servicing interlibrary loans. Furthermore, the impact of such buying policies on the publishing industry would no doubt affect the cost of books acquired at the higher levels of the network. For example, in the extreme, a network of 10,000 libraries could be constructed in five levels of "groups of 10," with the cost of a book acquired at the highest level being 1/2¢ per library at level zero; however, the purchase of one book to service 10,000 libraries would not likely result in a publisher setting the price at the level of $15-$20. Yet, with all its difficulties, the concept is plain: it's cheaper to buy books cooperatively than it is to buy them locally.

The next question to be addressed is: given that the concept of cooperative acquisitions is adopted, what will the policy be for the selection of materials. Currently, this problem is addressed in one of the following ways:

1. An existing subject area strength is recognized, and the member library with that strength is encouraged to collect in this area.

2. Areas are assigned to the member libraries, with the expectation that subject strength will result.

3. The probability that a book will be demanded locally is examined, with the high probability items being acquired locally.

Actually, the first and second options represent the same basic philosophy. A library with a subject specialty most likely services users in that area, so that those books have a higher probability of circulating locally than they would have of circulating at another library. However, the third option makes the determination of the probability of use more explicit, and seems to be a viable decision rule.

According to the study of the book and monograph usage at the Hillman Library, carried out at the University of Pittsburgh,[3] a threshold of six local circulations in a six-year period would have resulted in about 70% of the material not being acquired. One major fear in such wholesale "nonacquisition" is that material that would have been useful will not have been acquired; that is, the items we chose not to get will turn out to be precisely the items we later need. It is in order to combat this fear that the "back-up" acquisition is provided by nodes at higher levels of the network, with the ultimate network node being faced with the "last-copy decision."

A second fear is that the item will not be easily accessible if it is not held locally. Traditionally, this fear has been substantiated by tedious and slow-moving interlibrary loan procedures. However, in the network structure, interlibrary loan becomes a central concern, and a relatively fast response is imperative. Because of the change in priority given interlibrary loan, networks are reporting deliveries ranging from "same day" to a few days for most book requests, with projections in the vicinity of two weeks for "worst-case" national requests. These response times would seem adequate for most interlibrary requests, although the longer waits implied in requests at the national level might be alleviated in a national network structure, so that 90-95% of the requests might be filled within a week's time, with a lower percentage being filled in one or two days.

The parameters of local acquisitions versus length of wait for interlibrary loan do interact inversely, so that a working solution will be found by "co-considering" several factors:

1. Volume of requests,

2. Volume of local requests at given selection threshold (probability of use),

3. Volume of interlibrary requests at given selection threshold,

4. Cost of local acquisitions,

5. Cost of interlibrary communications and delivery, and

6. Desirable response time for a given category of acquisition.

Because of the variety of possible combinations, the interaction of these parameters will probably be best studied with the use of simulation. Furthermore, the parameters take on different values with the study of different media being acquired: for example, the cost of acquiring a book will be different than the cost of acquiring a journal or a film. The response time required in requesting a journal article will be different from that required in requesting a piece of equipment. Hence, these parameters should be entered into a model with appropriate probability distributions, for each medium to be acquired by the network.

D. CATALOGING/CATALOGS

The cataloging function is not an isolated activity that can be treated apart from other functions in a library system if the total benefits of shared cataloging in a networking environment are to be realized. Those networks that were designed to perform a single function such as cataloging must have the flexibility to provide members with the capability to integrate other functions into systems operated by individual members. This will require some policy changes on the part of those who now offer a single service such as cataloging and face network-to-network relationships as well as more freedom for the end-user in terms of how he or she manipulates the data. The true cost-effectiveness of the shared cataloging function will not be realized until it can be fully integrated into other library functions on an automated basis without restriction and based on established standards known to all and usable by all.

Performance Objectives. Much has been written about the merits of shared cataloging and therefore it will not be discussed here. The issue is what capabilities should a network-based, shared-cataloging function provide and at what cost? OCLC, BALLOTS, Washington Library Network, and others provide a network-based cataloging function. Each has provided certain capabilities that are essential to performing this function. Some provide authority lists to ensure quality control while others do not. Some provide for subject access and Boolean logic searches. Some provide keyword access and truncation capabilities so that the user does not need to know the exact form of entry or the exact wording in a bibliographic data item. All have similar objectives but each has made certain assumptions in designing its system to meet those objectives.

The minimal objectives of a network-based cataloging function might be stated as:

A. To provide on-line access to a shared cataloging system that will guarantee a 90% hit rate on items to be cataloged.

B. To provide search capabilities for the on-line catalog that permit a 90% chance of finding the desired item when only 10% of the correct information is known about the item.

C. To provide authority list quality control to ensure with a 95% probability that the entry being made is the correct one.

D. To provide the cataloging function in a manner that permits its integration with other functions that may be automated in a member library or via the network itself.

E. To provide a catalog that can be utilized as the on-line catalog for the patrons at each member institution.

F. To provide network members with the capability of producing specialized products from the catalog data base.

G. Provide the cataloging function at no less than 2/3 of the cost to perform the same function using any other method.

H. To provide for inter-network access and to transfer, if necessary, the cataloging data stored in other networks at any location in the world.

Form of Catalog. The production of a catalog which results from the cataloging function may take many forms. The most common form is the catalog card. This form is probably the most expensive to maintain and certainly the most expensive for the patron to utilize, since he/she must travel to the card catalog. In addition, it is difficult to perform complex searches, since the access points are limited and the search logic must be carried out by the patron.

The COM catalog removes some of the problems of accessibility since many copies can be produced and storied at multiple locations. The major disadvantages of a COM catalog are the updating problems and the need for special equipment to manipulate it. The book catalog also suffers from the updating problem, as well as the expense of producing multiple copies.

The electronic catalog stored on-line offers the greatest accessibility, availability and flexibility. Its advantages are immediate access via a large number of access points to a large number of locations, and offers powerful searching capabilities. In addition, an on-line catalog is the easiest to integrate into other library functions and offers a low per-transaction cost. With the coming changes in the Anglo American Cataloging Rules, a computerized system for performing the cataloging function would soften the negative ramifications of the proposed changes. In fact, an adequately designed cataloging system should be affected very little by such changes.

The disadvantages of the on-line catalog are: (1) a large initial investment in computer equipment, (2) the need for special terminal devices for access, and (3) the requirement for specialized personnel to operate the computer system. It is just these disadvantages that can be better absorbed by a broad-based network system than by an individual institution. In considering a national network, it may be more feasible to have several centers, in a distributed fashion, to avoid an overload on a single processing center.

E. PROCESSING/PREPARATION

The concept of coordinated acquisitions and facilitated interlibrary loan implies a heavier use of telecommunications facilities. This will no doubt result in an unwelcome increase in network costs, and is one of the major reasons that costs must be reduced in other areas, e.g., in lessening the rate of rising costs in acquisitions and in achieving network economies of scale in many of the technical processing functions, such as cataloging. The area of processing activities is one of the most attractive in which to reduce costs by removing duplication of effort and achieving economies of scale.

It is evident from the network survey data that the processing/preparation function operates best in a centralized manner. However, it is possible that a distributed organization of several processing centers may be necessary, due to problems such as volume of transactions and distance between nodes.

F. INFORMATION RETRIEVAL FUNCTION

This is an area that can benefit greatly from cooperative efforts. The resources used in the information retrieval (reference) function are among the most costly to acquire. Cooperative acquisitions programs in obtaining these reference works, as practiced in the New York Metro System, can help to reduce these costs. Furthermore, if access to informational data bases such as those provided by Lockheed, SDC, BRS or the NYT, is considered to be analogous to the problem of "collections development," a similar savings can be obtained. The access point(s) may be centrally or hierarchically located, as in the Nebraska Library Network, in which case member libraries obtain access by phoning or using a teletype to place requests. Or member libraries may obtain local access at cheaper rates through a network contract which assures the vendor of a greater volume of use, as in the MIDLNET operation.

Finally, if the information retrieval function is to be carried out efficiently, the technology to implement a reasonably fast response, and minimize human handling of requests, is necessary. This technology, especially if computer-based, can usually be purchased more economically by a network than by the individual member libraries. Furthermore, the software and hardware to support these communications activities can be more readily maintained through the network than through the member libraries.

Information retrieval seems to be one area that will always demand inter-system dialog. It would usually not be feasible for local networks. The immense effort involved in creating a data base, indexing, abstracting, updating, forwarding of materials from the data base seems to require the specialized efforts of "information brokers." Thus, the mechanized data base is viewed as a resource in the same vein as the printed reference work; and the data base supplier is analogous to the publisher/supplier of monographs, periodicals or more traditional non-print materials.

G. CIRCULATION FUNCTION

Topology. It appears that the circulation function requires a great deal of local control, and therefore should be restricted to a relatively small geographic region. In addition, the circulation function generates a great many transactions and requires updating of rather large files of data. This type of activity can only respond in the required time frame if queues are small and files can be updated in a relatively short time frame. If a large public library generates 7,300,000 circulation transactions over a 365 day year, 10 hour day, then there are 2,000 transactions generated each hour, or 3.3 per minute. If we assume a network of 20 members with a mix of small, medium and large libraries, and an average of two transactions per minute per library, we might have 40 circulation transactions per minute, or one transaction every 1.5 seconds. One can imagine the impact of having 200 such libraries in a network, where a transaction would occur every 1/3 of a second. Actually, the problem is worse than it may appear, since circulation occurs at peak periods. Thus, 60 percent of all circulations may occur over a four-hour period each day. This could result in one transaction every 1/18 of a second during these peak periods. Also, the transactions required to add and modify records in the patron and title file would generate a considerable number of transactions as well. Placing these potential system loads in perspective, relative to present technology, it would appear that size and volume become limiting factors for a totally centralized system covering a wide geographic area incorporating a great many libraries.

An approach that has been discussed is that of a large regional or national on-line network that would provide the circulation function. OCLC has been associated with the concept of a national on-line circulation control system. This appears to be a logical conclusion since OCLC has a union catalog of holdings. But when one considers the missing elements necessary for such a national system, the conclusion becomes somewhat absurd. A patron file would have to be maintained, multiple copies would require unique identifications and multiple locations within a given library system would also require unique identification. In addition to file conversion and maintenance problems, the telecommunications traffic and the file-updating activities generated by such a circulation system would cause intolerable queues using present technology and techniques.

It might be mentioned that automated circulation systems have been incorporated in bookmobiles via radio transmission or data collection devices. This is an important feature of many library systems and would be a factor in considering the implementation of a network-based circulation function.

Statistics on Use. The statistics generated by a circulation control function could be essential in making acquisition decisions and marketing library/ network services. Most networks are already gathering such data, and, in an automated network, the statistics can be gleaned as a by-product of other operations. Utilizing the data so gathered, the manager can judge whether or not certain policies are proving effective.

An example of how a single statistic from the circulation system might be used is the number of reserves placed against a given title. A decision rule commonly used by libraries is when the number of reserves for a specific title reaches 10, another copy will be acquired. Another example might be the analysis of queue lengths to decide that setting a threshold of "90% probability of being used" before an item is acquired locally is too high, causing an overload in the communications, interlibrary loan and the delivery units. These simply serve as examples of how an automated network might automatically use its statistics to aid the decision-making requirements of librarians.

Circulation statistics may also provide a realistic picture of the costs of operating a library network. Since actual use and actual users can be accounted for, these statistics can also provide use patterns such as peak circulation times, as well as marketing information relating to who does and who does not utilize library service. Use statistics by subject area, as well as patron profile, may lead to different marketing strategies and acquisition patterns.

H. SERIALS CONTROL FUNCTION

The serials control function is related to the information retrieval function, the interlibrary loan function, the storage function and the delivery function. The retrieval function is utilized to locate and verify the serials for patrons and librarians; the interlibrary loan function is used to request a serial title or parts thereof in some form; the storage function must deal with the problem of preserving serials over a long period of time; and the delivery function must assure that serials or parts of serials or copies thereof are transmitted from the storage location to the requestor. Each of these functions impacts on the serials control function and vice versa.

The economic factors and legal factors involved with serials control and the related functions are complex and difficult to control but are central to making current information available to patrons of network libraries. Use data for serials is not well researched, and is difficult to collect, since serials do not typically circulate, but some indications of use can be obtained via the interlibrary loan function, as well as "in-house" use studies.

It seems logical to maintain several levels of serials control in a networking environment. The lowest level is the local library system. At this level the serials acquired within the system are controlled by the local library. The control system must be designed so that the serials data can be made available to other libraries in the same network as well as other networks. This provides for several alternatives for storing and processing the serials data. The data may reside at a central location within the nation such as OCLC or the Library of Congress, with access by the local library, and the central site performing the data storage and data processing functions. The problems associated with large centralized systems may make this approach unfeasible.

A second approach would favor a decentralized network wherein regional centers would provide the storage and data processing capabilities, and the regional centers would be interconnected. This would provide the same capabilities as a centralized network but without the problems associated with volume in totally centralized systems. Of course, the problems of interfacing networks become a major barrier. These include technical, legal, economic and social problems. Another alternative would be to maintain all storage of data and processing at the local level, with interconnections among all library systems. This alternative is fraught with high costs and compounded with interface problems.

We believe that a system of interconnected regional centers provides the better alternative to providing the serials control function in a cost-effective and reliable manner. The authors also believe that a national center should be a node in this network for controlling serials that are not elsewhere in the network, the node of "last resort. "

I. INTERLIBRARY LOAN

Transparency. This function is handled mechanically by networks, but lags behind current conceptual capabilities by 10 years or more. With the continuing development of networking, resource sharing, cooperative acquisitions, and library automation, interlibrary loan will be viewed conceptually in terms of all the collections in individual libraries as being one collection available to all patrons in a transparent mode. "Transparency" has already been accomplished in networks such as Bell Labs and the Ohio State University Libraries, which allow the user to transmit a request by telephone or computer terminal, often from his or her office, have that request filled from any node in the network (if the item is held by the network), and have the needed item delivered at his or her location. It is this mode of "use-facilitation" that will transform interlibrary loan from a "second class task" to one of the key network functions.

File Structures. Aspects of the interlibrary loan procedure involve the creation and maintenance of fairly large file structures:

1. Identification and location of materials,

2. Identification and location of patrons, and

3. Transaction data (circulation).

The files involved in circulation have already been discussed, so that attention is restricted here to the materials file and the patron file.

All the data necessary for the creation of the materials file are available as by-products of the acquisitions and cataloging functions. For example, in the acquisition of books, the author and title of the material acquired (and frequently subject headings), as well as the library that orders the item and hence is holding it, are a matter of record.

The primary decisions revolve around the means of accessing the materials: author? title? author-title? subject? If access is by author or author-title, the data are static and of limited size; the processing is clerical in nature, and the file may be created and maintained automatically. If access by subject is allowed, the file structure tends to become more complex, the processing more difficult, and the size of the file increases.

The types of access desirable are a function of the type of material acquired and also a function of the person searching the file. For example, a
file of audio-visual materials might be accessed by title and/or subject,
while a journal article might also require access by author. A search performed by the user might require a subject approach, while access made by
a cataloger might be handled by author and/or title. It may be desirable to
create separate file structures for the different types of access.

It may also be desirable to place limits on the use of certain modes of
access: for example, a user who is browsing may be requested to select a
subfile to browse through, e.g., psychology, and be limited to a "representative sample" of the file. This would tend to control the use of time-consum-
ing, expensive searches of huge files. Flexibility could also be offered by
allowing more extensive searching, but with subsidization of the costs. Thus,
a "normal" search would be provided at either a nominal fee or no fee to the
user, but "extra" facilities would be offered only upon request and on a cost-
recovery basis.

The problem of identification and location of the user is parallel to the
identification and location of materials. In fact, it is simpler to identify and
locate the user by name or user-number or both, with address providing the
location. The source of these data should be the initial contact of the user
with the library system. If possible, the data could be captured in machine-
readable form, so that further entry is unnecessary.

Means would also have to be provided for the updating of identification/
location data (e.g., change of address or cancellation of a subscription).
These are well-defined problems in the area of data processing. However,
they do require human cooperation. In terms of the materials file, the task
devolves on member libraries to notify the "file keeper" of any materials
that are lost, disposed of, or relocated. This is already a practice in networks wherein other members are notified of "deacquisition decisions," so
that another library might have the chance to claim the material not wanted
locally.

The notification of change of user address is a problem in current library
activities. This is due to the fact that it is beneficial to the user to be "non-
locatable" in case of overdue or lost materials. However, in a network
employing delivery to the user, it would be beneficial to the user to keep the
network posted on address changes, just as it is beneficial to notify a magazine publisher of an address change when one subscribes to that magazine.
Thus, the changes in technology would potentially present at least one beneficial change in the behavioral area.

Besides identifying the materials and users, and giving their location, it
is necessary to keep "status" information: in the case of materials, this

would be "charged-discharged"; in the case of users, "good standing or not good standing." These are also well-defined problems in the area of data processing, and they do not present behavioral difficulties.

Placing Requests On-line. Once the holdings of the network are identified by the user, the next step is to place a request for any desired items. In the ideal case, the request would be placed in machine-readable form in real time, so that its processing could begin immediately. The actual entry of the request may be made by the user or by an intermediary. Once the request is entered, the system would search the holdings file for the item requested. Assuming that the item were held in the network, the status would be checked, and if the item were available, an estimated time of delivery could be computed, the user notified immediately, the request confirmed, and the delivery process begun. If the item were charged out, or it were not held in the network, the user could be notified. In the case of a charged item, the expected date of availability could be given and a "hold" placed, if requested. In the case of an item not held by the network, other networks could be contacted at the request of the user, if such a service agreement with other networks existed. In any case, the status of the request would be established in "real-time." As indicated above, the examination of "holds" and/or requests to other networks can serve as a barometer indicating that acquisition by the local library or by the network is desirable. The work of Morse[4] and Chen[5] indicate how these decisions might be made with the aid of use data, cost data, and the tools of operations research.

J. DELIVERY FUNCTION

The choice of technology to implement delivery is a function of several factors: distance traversed, response time necessary, size of object and cost of service being primary. Some networks, such as the University of California Libraries, employ more than one technology. It would seem that a national network would also have to employ various types of delivery. Whether the services are provided by the network itself or contracted out to other organizations depends on the scope of the service. Many networks employ a system-operated vehicular service in a limited geographic area, while making use of the U.S. mail for more distant delivery. The primary emphasis in the delivery function should be a shift toward direct delivery to the user.

A concommitant concern of the delivery function is the question of "OS&D" (over, short and damaged). The question of who keeps track of the item once it has entered the interlibrary loan network circulation is a question of both policy and technical processing. Should each lending library be saddled with the problem of receiving overdue books, fines for lost materials, etc., or should this be a function of the network as a whole? It would seem that in

the concept of the network as a single logical collection, the chore would be
a networking problem. However, the actual contact with the user, searches
of libraries, and so on, must be carried out locally, thus involving the
receiving library, rather than the lending library in the retrieval process.

K. STORAGE FUNCTION

The implementation of a national network will no doubt require several modes
of handling the problem of storage allocation. For certain materials, such
as books, it would seem that a national network would have to depend on a
hierarchical storage organization. For other materials, such as data bases,
a more centralized location might be possible, although it is doubtful whether
a purely centralized access to resources would be implemented, due to the
geographical distances involved, problems of "back-up files" and volume.
Items requiring a fast response from request to delivery, or items that can
be accessed by the user directly, would more than likely demand a more
distributed storage structure.

The problem of deallocation of resources is a function of demand for an
item. For example, one rule used by the Center for Research Libraries is
that items to be forwarded there for storage should have been "unused for ten
years." No one rule will suffice for all forms of resources and all nodes
(levels) of a network. However, the processes involved in making the decision are the same processes executed in making selection decisions: probability of future demand versus probability of non-use, and cost of local
storage versus costs of non-local storage or no storage at all.

It is likely that the concept of media cycling can be applicable to the problem of storage. For example, in the early life of a book, when it is more
likely to be used, the original might be stored locally; as the book ages and
probability of use declines, the item might be stored at a node that is not
local, e.g., a regional library in a hierarchical structure. As space becomes
tight at the node of "last storage," media cycling, e.g., to a microfiche copy,
might be effected. An excellent study of the costs of journal storage via (1)
new construction, with binding of original journal article, (2) with fiche copy
produced locally, and (3) with fiche copy purchased with the journal itself,
has been carried out by the University of California Libraries.[6] Similar cost-
effectiveness studies must be carried out for each medium to be stored.

L. REFERRAL FUNCTION

The network referral function goes beyond the concept of sharing data and
material resources to the concept of sharing human knowledge. It is not a
priority function in most of today's libraries or library networks. However,
it is a concept that can make the library a true information center rather

than a materials warehouse. Through the utilization of other human resources, whether individuals or organizations, the library can serve as an
access point to diagnosis of needs, planning analysis, application, evaluation
and other activities concommitant to information storage and retrieval.

The implementation of this function requires little more than the creation,
maintenance and searching of automated "identification and location" files,
similar to those utilized in circulation and interlibrary loan. As mentioned
in the descriptive portion of the paper, data might be collected on the performance, cooperativeness, etc. of the referenced agency or person.

One difficulty in both creating the file structure and maintaining its "cur-
rentness" will be the elicitation of cooperating "referees. " This will no
doubt be a task entrusted to the marketing function of the network.

M. COMMUNICATIONS FUNCTION

The concept of coordinated acquisitions, cataloging, circulation control,
serials control, facilitated interlibrary loan, interlibrary references and
retrieval implies a number of on-line files, to be accessed in real time, and
this implies a heavier use of telecommunications facilities.

The communications technology utilized will no doubt be composed of more
than one type. An ideal example of coordinated communications is the Ohio
State University Libraries, which combine the telephone with computer-based
telecommunications facilities to provide a telephone-answering service that
allows access to the collection by a user from the user's home or office.
This technology is then tied into the delivery system, so that requests for
materials are dispatched to the user, most often on the day of request. It is
just such a system of bringing materials to the user, regardless of physical
location, that is seen as the core concept of a national network.

One other form of communications that has been mentioned is the publication of union lists. This function has been treated under cataloging/catalogs,
but it is one of the most popular methods of communicating holdings from
library to library to user. The publication of these lists is very often done
manually, in a labor-intensive manner; however, given a strongly automated
system, with machine-readable data bases of holdings, this function could be
made an on-line routine of the daily network activities.

N. EDUCATION FUNCTION

Continuing Education. This is one of the "avant-garde" functions implemented by the networks. It is similar to the referral function in that an
attempt is made to share human expertise. However, the approach differs

in that the expertise is brought to the user in continuing education, in a fashion analogous to the ideal delivery system. In the light of continuing education requirements for maintaining certification in many professions, this function can make the network attractive in a very real sense. While many programs are instituted for professional librarians, the special-purpose consortia have developed this function for specialists other than librarians.

Training. Besides the training in technological matters, the initial period of networking will no doubt require "training in attitude." The concept of a collection that is not "local," the forced cooperation and sometimes inconvenient lack of autonomy that will accompany the networking structure will no doubt meet with resistance. In fact, the participants in the 1977 Library Resource Sharing conference in Pittsburgh saw this problem as one of the major obstacles to networking.[7] This obstacle is seen as being offset only by the gains that can be achieved through networking: increased access to resources and a more cost-effective solution to the provision of this access. The Southwest Missouri Library Network has made this concern one of their primary objectives. The treatment of the attitudinal problem should be a one-time task, with the next generation of users and librarians taking for granted the concept of a local collection, delivery of materials to the user, cooperative acquisitions and processing, etc.

The implementation of technical training is usually accomplished through a combination of printed brochures and training sessions. The implementation of attitudinal training is accomplished through personal communication, meetings and brochures. Attitudinal training is, of course, a marketing function, while the technical training falls into the area of systems support.

O. STANDARDIZATION FUNCTION

The difficulty in arranging standardization for a library network is that the problem is being addressed in midstream. Each member library has a long history of unique ways of doing things, with large files already created. To convert all these items to a standard format would be prohibitive in terms of time and cost. It would seem more likely that a double approach be taken:

1. Devise packages to translate the protocols of individual libraries into the protocols of the network, at least in regard to format in which data is stored;

2. Resort to a common format for all records created after a given date.

This approach has already been taken by some of the networks responding. Again, in the words of the RLG (Research Libraries Group):

The Research Libraries Group should not embark on an independent project to convert retrospective catalog data to machine-readable form. The four libraries should be aware of, and develop the capability for taking advantage of nationwide efforts in the areas of retrospective conversion;

The RLG should move toward the establishment of a common bibliographic system and data base covering (at least) future accessions. Basic requirements in this area are (1) agreement on and implementation of standard cataloging practices which will allow the merging of records and (2) a machine-based system designed to input, transmit, store, and process bibliographic data with the capability of producing desired outputs.

Research Libraries Group,
Proposals for Cooperation

One of the items to be standardized is the record format of data. Another is the query language used to access the data. Practice has resulted in a proliferation of methods of both storage and access, with separate training required for learning to access another network. This problem can only be alleviated if the equivalent of the ANSI standards for Fortran, Cobol and Data Base Systems is attempted in the area of library activities. For many networks, not yet automated, the use of a standard protocol is not a problem. For those that already do have a protocol, the substitution of a standard protocol with suitable training should not be a monumental problem.

Besides differences in procedures for creating and accessing files, there are currently a wide range of prices offered by different services. That these prices are not always based on costs is evident by the decrease of charges for services when competitors enter the market place. It may be desirable to regulate pricing structures through a network commission, setting standard tariffs for the functions common to library networks. This is already achieved for certain services, such as telephone and U.S. mail, and would result in a more accurate estimation of costs.

While standardization is a difficult problem, it is really a "one-time problem," with much cooperation, debate, research and experimentation in the beginning, followed by a decision and relative stability, subject only to periodic review and modification. Hence, it is a problem area for the beginning of a network, but a routine function thereafter.

P. MARKETING/PUBLICATION FUNCTION

Marketing. While libraries and library networks attempt to deal with the intellectual and mechanical aspects of providing access to information, they

cannot ignore the marketing function. On-line catalogs, automated data
bases, and delivery to your doorstep are valueless unless the patron can be
made aware of their existence and enticed to use them. While non-profit
organizations, such as the library, have traditionally been remiss in this
area, concerted efforts to publicize network activities have been implemented
by many of the networks reporting in our survey. New York Metro, Environment Canada, and the Illinois Research Council are three that perform such
activities.

The literature received from network members in our survey illustrates
that the marketing and publication function is performed in a hierarchical
manner. A local library markets its services by utilizing regional network
marketing information and regional networks utilize national network marketing data in their marketing and publication efforts. This same trend is
true in a downward mode as well. That is, national networks use regional
marketing and publication data and regional networks use local network information.

The problem lies in the lack of an adequate investment in such efforts
except in a relatively few cases. This is evident in the scope and quality of
marketing and publication activities. A notable exception is the Environment
Canada Library Network. The brochures distributed by Environment Canada
are comparable in quality to any produced by commercial firms. In the light
of contention for limited budgeted funds, it would seem that these marketing
procedures will play a greater role than ever in network activities.

Publication. This function has already been treated in several of the other
network operations. For example, in the pursuit of bibliographic access,
union lists are often published. In establishing training programs, brochures
may be printed, as they are in marketing the network's services. Communication activities involve the production of newsletters, and evaluation activities involve the production of annual reports as well as periodic reports.

While supported by the network, the actual publication of materials may
be contracted out to another organization, although some networks may support the function entirely self-sufficiently. One aspect of the publication
function that can benefit from network activities in reducing cost and time to
execute is the publication of union lists. In the automated network, these
publications can be a by-product of the files maintained for network processes. In fact, the flexibility of automated sorting will often allow greater
flexibility and reliability in format of these lists than manual printing has
allowed.

The production of reports will also be facilitated by the continual recordkeeping of the automated network, with statistical studies becoming routine

rather than the subject of commissioned studies. The savings involved in producing union lists and statistical reports as by-products of automated networking will serve to absorb some of the costs involved in implementing the automated system.

Union Lists. Use of printed and/or microfilm union lists of holdings will continue even in an on-line network, since they allow for more leisurely perusal than a terminal device. More importantly, they allow the user to obtain an idea of what is contained in a particular file before searching that file on the terminal. Users accessing a mechanized data base without a printed thesaurus have often voiced the complaint that they do not "have a feel" for what is contained in the data base. The use of published lists can alleviate this problem.

By sorting or otherwise processing the file in different manners, the lists can be provided for each type of access to the files (author, title, subject), and might be produced for "subject subsets" of the file, so that a separate listing is available for different disciplinary areas. While this might decrease total recall for subjects spanning more than one area, the use of automated means to produce the lists will allow for items to be listed more than once when deemed desirable.

Q. SYSTEMS DEVELOPMENT AND SUPPORT

As has been evident throughout this report, the design and implementation of sophisticated technical systems will be an integral part of network operations. Individual libraries will not usually have the personnel to support such activities, which will therefore devolve upon the network itself or the outside support. On a national plane, it would seem that the distributed approach to system support might be implemented. This would involve regional centers that would service given areas. These centers would be interconnected for both communications and delivery in order to facilitate the sharing of expertise and equipment. The design of systems might be handled centrally, with the product systems developed at one location. These products would then be distributed to the regional system support centers, as well as to local networks and/or individual libraries.

THE RELATIVE IMPORTANCE OF FUNCTIONS AND PROBLEMS

In the preceding discussion, all functions and related problems were treated with approximately equal emphasis. The reason we did not make any attempt to judge the magnitude of a problem or function is because we believe they are situation dependent. That is, what may be a serious problem to one network may be considered a minor or non-existent problem for another network.

But since it seems appropriate to make such judgments in light of those we have already made, the following is a brief discussion of those items we believe to be most critical in the operation and survival of a library network.

The number one area of importance is that of network management and administration. The setting of operational and planning policies as well as fee structures and evaluation measures is not only of major importance but an area in which expertise seems to be lacking. The second major problem as we see it is in the area of standardization. Without some minimal standards, a national network becomes virtually impossible from a cost-effective point of view. The third area of importance is the implementation of cooperative acquisitions. This area consumes tremendous resources, results in duplication of effort, has the highest amount of uncertainty and entails the greatest amount of risk. On the other hand, it provides for high return if it can be implemented successfully. Fourth on our list of importance is the document delivery function. This is fraught with problems that at present data computer and telecommunications technology cannot deal with on a cost-effective basis. The final item on our list of most important problems is the communication function which involves marketing, publication, continuing education and training. This cuts across all other functions and is the glue which holds a network together and builds the demand for services as well as ensures continued and effective use of network services.

Although each of the functions has a relative importance in a particular context, the above functions seem to pervade all networks. Another area of concern to us was not of a particular function but the integration of functions into an overall network. It appears that networks are designed with one or two functions as their goals but not with the flexibility to incorporate other functions within the network or to incorporate the individual member functions with network functions.

REFERENCES

1. Butler, Brett. "State of the Art in Networking." Journal of Library Automation, Volume 8, Number 3, September, 1975, pp. 200-220.

2. Dunlap, Connie. Quotation from "Resource Sharing Goals: Discussion," p. 57, in Kent, Allen and Galvin, Thomas J., editors, Library Resource Sharing: Proceedings of the 1976 Conference on Resource Sharing in Libraries, New York: Marcel Dekker, 1977.

3. Kent, Allen, principal investigator. "A Cost-Benefit Model of Some Critical Library Operations in Terms of Use of Materials," Final Report, April 1978. Research supported in part by the National Science Foundation under grant no. DSI 75-11840A03.

4. Morse, Philip M. _Library Effectiveness: A Systems Approach,_ Cambridge, MIT Press, 1968.

5. Chen, Ching-Chih. _Applications of Operations Research Mode as to Libraries: A Case Study on the Use of Monographs in the Frances A. Countway Library of Medicine, Harvard University,_ Cambridge, MIT Press, 1976.

6. The University of California Libraries, A Plan for Development—1978-1988, Office of the Executive Director of Universitywide Planning, July, 1977.

7. Kent, Allen and Galvin, Thomas J. _Library Resource Sharing: Proceedings of the 1976 Conference on Resource Sharing in Libraries,_ New York, Marcel Dekker, 1977.

Chapter 7

NETWORK FUNCTIONS: REACTIONS

Joseph Becker

President
Becker & Hayes, Inc.
Los Angeles, California

My purpose is to comment on the network topology paper by Jim Williams and Roger Flynn dealing with the functions of existing library networks (Chapter 6). It is, I believe, a useful paper. Not only does it set forth a comprehensive list of library network functions, but it also uses these functions to explain how networks operate. "Topology" is the study of a particular place or region, and I think Williams and Flynn have done the conference a service by giving us their view of the domain of library networks in functional terms.

There are two parts of the paper on which I wish to comment. The first is the authors' definition of the word "network"; and the second is the authors' list of library network functions.

The paper defines the word network as "an interconnected or interrelated chain, group, or system attempting to achieve some specified common and mutually beneficial objectives." This definition is broad enough in scope and meaning to accommodate almost any association of activities: from airlines, multinational organizations, and grocery chains to library consortia, library systems, and library networks.

Eight years ago, Ray Swank, at the Airlie Conference on Library Networks, also tried to define a library network, but to this day we do not have a definition which the profession as a whole embraces with enthusiasm. While the definition offered in Williams and Flynn's paper is a clear, general statement, it neither provides a sharp demarcation of the limits of meaning of a library network nor does it convey its distinguishing features.

The job, however, is a formidable one. A large part of the problem is that we are dealing with a concept rather than a word. Concepts are explained; words are defined. The authors do refer to the "notion" of a network, as they call it, but I believe they fell into the same trap I, Brett Butler, Samuel Johnson and others have, in trying to define the word.

The confusion which exists in the library field over the word network has led some library groups to call themselves a network for no other reason than because they aspired to become one. I think the important thing in talking or writing about networks is to be specific about the type of network under discussion. Unless the descriptive adjective is carried along with the noun, it is virtually impossible to understand the context in which the word network is being used. Similarly, the adoption by the authors of abstract modifiers such as "true network" and "pure network" hinders rather than enhances understanding.

Reading the papers of this conference, one finds a bewildering array of networks and many ways of classifying them. Networks are perceived from many points of view such as:

- By the signals they carry:
    digital network
    video network
    analog network
    communications network

- By their logical structure:
    star or centralized network
    decentralized network
    distributive network
    hierarchical network

- By their institutional focus:
    public library network
    academic library network
    special library network
    and even, intertype network

- By the functions they perform:
    cataloging network
    bibliographic network
    interlibrary loan network
    reference information network

- By the subjects they treat:
    medical information network
    agricultural information network
    energy information network

- By the equipment they employ:
    teletype network
    telephone network
    radio network
    television network
    computer network

- By the geographic area they encompass:
    statewide network
    regional network
    multi-state network
    national network
    international network

Is it any wonder the word defies defintion? Although we can explain the concept and even describe the characteristics of different types of networks, the likelihood that we will ever be able to define the word "network" with precision in a library context seems remote.

One way I have found to explain the organizational concept of a library network to library students is by describing its prerequisites. For example, a library network exists when <u>two or more</u> libraries...

- A library network will, of course, involve libraries and it will most certainly involve more than one library -

...when two or more libraries <u>engage formally</u>...

- The word "engage" implies a commitment by members to be part of a cooperative venture. While the word "formally" implies the existence of an agreement, contract, or other legal instrument which delineates and assigns explicit roles and responsibilities to members and to their governing body -

...when two or more libraries engage formally in a <u>common pattern of information exchange</u>...

- "Common pattern" suggests that uniform standards, procedures, and protocols are in force and the phrase "information exchange" implies a two-way, interactive relationship between and among members in the sharing of information resources -

The explanatory statement now reads: when two or more libraries engage formally in a common pattern of information exchange, <u>through communications</u>:

- The use of the phrase "through communications" indicates that the members are interconnected by the same communications system. For example, advanced library networks may use a

computer-based communications system to achieve this
interconnection -

And finally, for some functionally interdependent purpose:

  - "Purpose" means that the network has a group reason for
  being and "functionally interdependent" means that the members of the group are prepared to share the workload and
  rely on one another -

In summary, when two or more libraries engage formally in a common
pattern of information exchange, through communications, for some functionally interdependent purpose, we have a library network.

The purpose of any network in the most general sense—no matter what
the objectives—is to facilitate the widest possible interchange of information
among the members and thereby improve access by users. Thus, if we
begin to think of the word "network" conceptually rather than semantically
and, if we always use the word with its related descriptive adjective, the
combination could lead to improved understanding in the field and maybe even
help to speed-up the library network development process nationally.

In the second half of their paper, the authors present a distilled list of
functions performed by operating library networks. These were derived
from a survey of 150 networks covering every kind of cooperative endeavor.
But, the criteria used to select the institutions in the first place is not explained in the paper. The National Center for Educational Statistics in the
U.S. Office of Education is in the midst of surveying a thousand or more
library networks and cooperative library organizations. This is part of a
project designed to collect information about library networks annually and
systematically so that an historical, statistical data base can be built for
use in studying nationwide library network developments and trends. Part V
of OE's survey instrument contains a list of cooperative services and activities, and when I compared this list with the Williams and Flynn list, I found
them to be almost identical. I am confident, therefore, that they have given
us a list of cooperative library functions and services that are both comprehensive and complete. It is important to point out, however, that most of
the functions on the list are traditional library functions cast in a cooperative
context. In only a few cases does the fact of the network's own existence
imply some new function or service.

Since this is a national network conference, I mapped the seventeen or so
functions against the national network concept spelled out in the NCLIS program document in order to see how well they fit and if others might emerge.

Before giving you the results, let me take a moment to describe the components of a national network as seen from the Commission's perspective.

The idea of a nationwide library network is contained in the national program document which the Commission published in 1975. It is based on the belief that information in the United States is a national resource and that all citizens, therefore, have an equal right to access this resource from any location in the country.

A nationwide network of libraries and information centers means an integrated system encompassing statewide networks, multistate networks, and specialized networks in the public and private sectors. It would be a network of networks. The Commission sees this network of networks as a flexible, evolving, voluntary confederation of the nation's vast independent information resources. No library or information service would be forced to join the national network, but the federal government would provide technical inducements and funding incentives to state governments and the private sector to strengthen their ability to affiliate. The federal government would also be responsible for funding the planning and operation of the interstate aspects of the network, such as facilitating interconnection between states, establishing technical standards, sustaining and supporting national collections, designating or creating national services, and so forth. As envisioned by the Commission, the national network would have five components: a bibliographic component; a collections component; an information services component; a communications component; and a support component.

The bibliographic component of the national network would consist of designated institutions such as OCLC, BALLOTS, WLN, or others that are dedicated to the computer processing of machine-readable bibliographic information into by-products required by libraries and information centers. These organizations would essentially serve as national utilities and the federal government would encourage, protect, and support them as necessary to ensure their continued operation.

The national network would also make unique and major resource collections available nationwide. The federal government would achieve this by offering to compensate the institutions that owned the collections for the added services they performed in behalf of the national network. Although the federal government would designate the collections as national collections, the institutions would of course have the option of accepting or rejecting a national responsibility for developing and sustaining their particular collections. The Commission recognizes that there are many institutions in our country whose collections include one-of-a-kind resources of widespread interest and potential benefit to the entire population. It would identify these collections and provide incremental funding to enable them to serve more people than their primary clientele.

Another responsibility of the federal government would be to sponsor and support information services in the public and private sectors when it can be reasonably demonstrated that such central services would benefit a majority of libraries and information centers throughout the country and/or achieve economies of scale. Examples of such services might include a national periodicals center, a national audio/visual repository, and other national back-up services such as those which the Library of Congress and other federal agencies could provide.

The fourth component would be the telecommunications component. Since the main purpose of a nationwide network is to place the user in contact with his or her materials, finding ways of speeding up the delivery of information on an interstate basis constitutes one of the more important aspects of the national network concept. A nationwide network must incorporate appropriate means of communicating rapidly and effectively with the facility at which the desired materials are located. It therefore implies a system of inter-library communications—an electronic mailbox if you will—which stores and forwards messages, keeps track of charges and copyright fees, and does the financial accounting.

A future telecommunications system for a nationwide network will eventually need to integrate audio, video, and digital signals into a single system. The Commission foresees the possibility of using the expanding Federal Telecommunications Service as the interstate grid, but other approaches are also practical. The Commission believes that rapid and inexpensive telecommunications among the members of a national network could turn out to be the greatest boon ever to the national distribution of knowledge for education and learning.

Finally, the national network would have a support component. The support component would be a planning and development activity. It would seek solutions to common library network research problems, it would support continuing education for librarians and information managers engaged in network operations, it would develop standards and protocols for interstate use, it would promote the services of the nationwide network to citizens, and it would serve as a coordinating arm for interfacing our United States network with similar networks in other countries.

If we think of the federal role as that of forming a network of networks, it then becomes clear, at the philosophic level, that the major goal of the federal government is to support, enhance, and otherwise facilitate the growth of networks at the state and local level. This leaves to the local institution the responsibility of deciding which functions to emphasize and who to link up with.

At the technical level, however, there are additional functions—not mentioned in the list given by Williams and Flynn—which must be planned for at the national level. These would include, for example,

- A directory and switching function for the network so that users would know—just as they use yellow pages—where the most relevant source of information was to meet a specific information demand and what were the conditions of use.

- A mediative function wherein service would be sustained in a closed loop as long as the user wished to interact.

- A teleconferencing function that enabled the user to socialize, in an information sense, with people expert in his area of interest.

- An evaluation function wherein the network would monitor its own performance and be capable of self improvement.

From an organizational perspective, a national network has three major objectives:

- To help local and state networks grow from the bottom up;

- To help put in place services and collections needed to back up local and statewide networks; and,

- To help introduce standards.

Chapter 8

REMARKS ON "NETWORK TOPOLOGY:
FUNCTIONS OF EXISTING NETWORKS"

Stephen R. Salmon

Assistant Vice President
Library Plans and Policies
University of California Systemwide Administration
Berkeley, California

I must confess that my initial difficulty with this paper (Chapter 6) was getting through the first two words. "Network" can mean so many things, and "topology"—well, topology refers to the properties of a configuration that are unaltered by elastic deformations. In other words, what doesn't change even when something is pushed out of shape. Now I could talk at some length about what happens when a network or the people in it get pushed out of shape, but I doubt that this was what was intended. An old textbook on topology I had at home defined it more precisely as "the study of continuity." Continuity is perhaps characteristic of some networks but not, unfortunately, of others, so that didn't help much either. I finally decided to read the paper, and it appears that what we are talking about, so far as networks are concerned, is groups—a group by definition having some unifying relationship—and for topology, I read structure and functions. I'm not sure Messrs. Williams and Flynn will accept this, but in the remarks that follow, I'll be commenting on the structure and functions of various groups, libraries being understood as members of those groups.

Once I got beyond the first two words, I found much to agree with, and I think the paper is genuinely useful as a starting point. I also found several instances in which I disagree with the paper, however, and other places where major considerations have been omitted.

Let me start by itemizing some minor points. One network function of which there is no mention, and which I think should be added, is the conservation and preservation of library materials. Libraries and their users are increasingly concerned about the deterioration of library materials, but few individual libraries have the resources to do anything effective about the problem alone. As a consequence, several networks are beginning to develop cooperative programs in this area, and I think this trend will grow.

The suggested "minimal objectives" for shared cataloging seem to me completely unrealistic. The "hit rate" for an individual library will depend on the nature of the materials acquired by that library, as well as on the nature of the data base in the shared cataloging system, so a guaranteed hit rate of 90 percent could not easily apply to large or specialized libraries— or if it did, the system would be inappropriate for general libraries. And requiring that there be a 90 percent chance of finding the desired item when only 10 percent of the correct information is known appears impossible without further explanation. Suppose the 10 percent correctly known were the size of the book? Or that the author entry correctly began with "United States Congress"?

The description of the University of California study of storage options is misleading in several respects. First of all, this study included most forms of library materials, not just journals. Second, the analysis of various microform options assumed microfilm, not microfiche. Third, the question of binding was raised in connection with microform as a substitute, not in connection with new construction. And lastly, the study considered options other than new construction and microfilming, including weeding and compact shelving. I should also report that the analysis of various options for housing of library collections was carried out using a fairly comprehensive computerized model, which is available to other institutions for use.

Regarding standardization, which is described as the second most important problem for networks, it seems to me that it will always be necessary to allow some flexibility for libraries (and library users) with specialized requirements. The problem, more precisely, is differentiating these legitimate variations from the whimsical and unconscionably fussy ones made by many cataloging departments and idiosyncratic librarians.

Now let me discuss three major areas of disagreement with the paper. First of all, I continue to be disturbed at the failure of researchers to distinguish carefully between "use" and "circulation." I will agree that all circulation may be considered use—the exceptions would amount to a quibble— but I cannot agree that use should or can be equated with circulation, as the authors appear to do.

We must also keep in mind the distinction between what is used and what is useful. There are a number of reasons for the fact that materials are not used, only one of which is that they are not useful. Other possible reasons for non-use are that the material is improperly cataloged, or improperly labelled, or improperly shelved; it may be properly cataloged, but the cataloging rules don't put it where potential users look for it; or it is at the bindery precisely when it is needed.

The last point gives me an opportunity to voice a pet peeve which I share with many users: the librarian's predilection for whipping materials off to the bindery when a volume is complete, right at a time when the material may be approaching its peak in usefulness, there to remain inaccessible for weeks or months on end, and possibly until it has ceased being useful.

In addition to problems with the paper's concept of use, there are difficulties relating to some implicit assumptions regarding the sharing of resources and cooperation among libraries. The paper quite rightly points out that effective sharing of resources will require changes in attitudes on the part of librarians and library users, but I think the authors underestimate the problem. An instance is the suggestion that collections be moved from libraries where they are not used to libraries where they might be. So long as membership in prestigious organizations such as the Association of Research Libraries is determined in part by the size of a library's holdings, the larger libraries will continue to be heavily oriented toward what the paper calls the "holdings" approach. And so long as faculty members continue to view the adequacy of their libraries in terms of the holdings count rather than the services provided, this predisposition will be reinforced.

Whether or not resources can be shared effectively depends critically on two factors which the paper does not take into account adequately. The first is what I have called elsewhere the immediacy of need. If a book must be obtained within an hour or a day in order for the need to be satisfied, sharing that book in a system that can only make it available in two days is unsatisfactory. It therefore becomes important to devise a means of determining the likelihood of particular materials being needed by particular users within various time periods. Those which are likely to be needed immediately must be owned (or at least housed) locally; those which are likely to be needed within, say, two days, may be housed in a region; and for those which are likely to be needed only within a month or so, we may safely rely on more remote locations. Please note two further considerations: the immediacy of need may be completely independent of the frequency of need and circulation is therefore of limited use in measuring immediacy of need. Second, the characteristics which determine immediacy of need may be characteristics of the user rather than characteristics of the materials.

The second factor which determines whether resources can be shared effectively, but which the paper ignores, is whether the identity of the items needed is known or not. All of the assertions about sharing of resources implicitly assume that the user knows which items are wanted, or that the user can determine their identity through the use of a catalog or other means.

In research institutions, however (and I suspect in many other libraries as well), users may need to consult a body of material in order to determine the relevance of particular items to their needs. I have learned the hard way not to call this "browsing," so I suggest we call it "at-the-shelf consultation." Under whatever term, however, it is a factor which limits resource sharing, and the limitation is proportional to the remoteness of the materials shared. This limitation must be taken into account in any attempt to design networks and to predict and evaluate their performance.

A third major respect in which I disagree with the paper relates to assumptions regarding costs. I agree with the statement that the goal of a library is to provide users with access to information—in fact, I wrote an identical statement in another publication. But I deliberately did not add the phrase appended here, "at the lowest possible costs." This may be a goal of a particular library, but it is not an inherent or necessary part of the definition.

The whole subject of costs, in fact, deserves more attention and analysis than is present in the paper. For example, there is frequently a confusion, or at least no distinction, between total costs and unit costs. This is important, because failure to make the distinction can result in false conclusions. An example is where the authors say that sharing of resources may result in increased interlibrary loan activity, and a library may then find "that the costs incurred in filling interlibrary loan requests more than offset the benefits derived from cooperative acquisitions." If the word "costs" means total costs, then they may indeed be greater; if, however, it means the unit costs of loans or filling individual needs, they may be lower, and presumably would be.

This leads to a much larger question ignored by the authors: what happens if libraries do share resources effectively, and make more materials available to their users, and as a consequence of the improved service the use of the libraries in question goes up? Is this good or bad? I have heard it argued, on more than one occasion and by eminent librarians, that it is bad, because it creates an additional workload that the library will find difficulty in handling.

The logical extensions of such an attitude are obvious, and, at least to me, professionally unacceptable. Yet the practical problems of such an increase in workload are real enough; what are the alternative approaches? I believe librarians must think increasingly in terms of market creation, and realize that improved services, if they are truly improved and desired by people, inevitably create an increased market, which translates into resources. We must avoid the trap of assuming that the market for library services is necessarily limited to its present dimensions. Let me give an obvious example: if one had assessed the office copying market in the carbon paper era, it would have been easy to come to false conclusions about what people wanted in the way of office copying, and what they were willing to pay for. But if new mechanisms are introduced that make the activity more effective and convenient—such as a Xerox machine—then the level of activity and the market become vastly different. We must not, therefore, avoid creating a larger market; in fact, we should be enlarging it enthusiastically, and the resources will follow. Our energies should also be directed toward solving the transitional problems during the inevitable time lag between increased demand and the availability of increased resources to meet it.

Discussions of costs inevitably bring up the question of fees for service. Russell Shank, in his inaugural address as President of the American Library Association, spoke eloquently of the dangers of creating a "greenback curtain" separating those who can afford to pay for information from those who cannot, and this has rightly become one of the most important professional issues of our day. However, the paper in question is not always clear in its discussion of this matter whether we are talking about fees to libraries as members of a network, or fees to library patrons. In most cases, whether a patron pays or not depends on whether the community wants to offer the service without fee and is willing to pay for it collectively.

A further confusion appears in the discussion of the effect of fees on large and small libraries. If small libraries have a small number of users and large ones have a large number, the unit costs may be the same, whether paid by users individually, or paid collectively through taxes. We will not be able to deal effectively with this important matter unless we keep such distinctions in mind.

Let me summarize, then, what I think needs to be said about the functions and services of networks in addition to what has been discussed in the paper. First, we must be more precise and analytical in defining such functions and services, particularly in discussing the concepts of use. Second, the extent to which resources can be shared effectively in a network will continue to be limited by such factors as the deeply-ingrained attitudes of many librarians and users, and by the nature and immediacy of need for such resources. Third, the success with which services are offered through a network, or indeed through an individual library, will depend on unit costs as much as total costs; on our ability to create and enlarge an adequate market for those services; and on the willingness of people to pay for enhanced services, whether individually or collectively. I am convinced that the need and desire for library service is there, and marketable, if we can do a better job of supplying that market, and I am also convinced that networks offer one promising way of doing so.

Chapter 9

NETWORK TOPOLOGY AND THE FEDERAL LIBRARY COMMITTEE

James P. Riley

Executive Director
Federal Library Committee
Washington, D. C.

The Federal Library Committee (FLC) was established, in 1965, for the purpose of serving to promote optimum exchange of experience and skills and sharing of resources among Federal libraries, and to promote more effective service to the nation-at-large. Thus, the FLC conducts surveys, studies, projects, contracts and services, in order to achieve better use of Federal library resources and facilities and to provide more effective planning, development and operation of Federal library and information services.

FLC during its first ten years dealt with library functions within Federal libraries, surveying and studying such functions, giving especial attention to common procedures and practices in order to determine what could be done in consort to assist one another and with an eye toward making policy changes or setting policy to which its members would adhere. The work was usually extensive and exhaustive, resulting in good studies but little if any action toward change or establishing policy. These were good times, however, for FLC members. It was a good beginning, a satisfying experience for many. FLC activities provided for a coming together, opportunity for free discussions and shared experiences which were conducted and gained through various task forces, working groups, panels, and subcommittee participation. The subjects of study and discussion were interesting and time for completion was not imminent. The pace was quite relaxed and the demand for the completion of work was not now or yesterday.

Nineteen hundred seventy-three/seventy-four saw the beginning of a real change for FLC—and there is no turning back. In June 1973, FLC negotiated a contract with the Ohio College Library Center to conduct a Federal library experiment in cooperative cataloging (FLECC), using the OCLC data base, and to develop and implement on-line, dial-up access to OCLC. Most of the Federal libraries are field libraries, having small collections and located outside of Washington, D. C., and frequently not located near a large city. These libraries are usually operated by a single person who does have the use of a dial-up terminal. Thus, the agreement to provide dial-up terminal access was required. In January 1974, eight Federal libraries in the Washington, D. C. area began using the OCLC system for cooperative cataloging, using the OCLC Beehive 100 CRT terminal. And in July 1974 the dial-up terminal access was operational. The experiment was conducted for two years. During the second year, an outside consulting firm was hired to evaluate the experiment. The results showed that cooperative cataloging was effective and beneficial for Federal libraries. The participating agency library members met and decided to continue the activity. Since it was now no longer experimental, the members decided to call the activity the Federal library and information network, FEDLINK. The members think of FEDLINK as being the Federal library link in the emerging national library and information network. On September 30, 1978, there were 157 Federal libraries or information centers, representing 36 states and serving users in the 50 states, using the OCLC system. Today, the FLC Executive Director's Office serves as an operating network service center, similar to other network centers, as AMIGOS, NELINET, SOLINET and others, providing many of the services described in the paper, Network Topology (Chapter 6).

I shall now discuss some of the things mentioned in Mr. Williams' paper that relate in a certain way to FLC/FEDLINK activity; and, also, a few things that we are engaged in that are not mentioned and that are somewhat unique to our operation.

The FLC/FEDLINK is a Federal library and information network but not all Federal libraries and information centers are FEDLINK members. Only when a library or information center makes use of one of the FEDLINK services do they become a member and have a representative on the membership committee. Within FLC, the FEDLINK operation provides all activities and services relating to networking. At the same time, the FLC executive office conducts various other activities and services that are not a part of FEDLINK —not a part of networking.

The FEDLINK staff serves library and information centers' interests directly and patrons indirectly; and, also, they fully support the network. They serve the interests and patrons through cooperative programs and services, and support the network through planning, system design, development, implementation, training, review, analysis, evaluation, cost comparisons, budgeting, communication, and publications. Also, the staff must conduct successful public relations and show dedication and stability.

Networking requires a commitment on the part of all participants. Commitment may be difficult to obtain and more difficult to sustain. Members frequently have good intentions regarding commitment; however, demands on one's cooperation, which sometimes for the larger and more resourceful library cooperation seems to be only one way, causing stress and strain conditions. The "haves" began to lose their concern for the needs of the "have nots." Also, a change in library management, or department or agency management, may cease to support networking activity.

Mr. Williams' statement of looking at all cost across all functions for network planning appears reasonable; however, in reality it may not happen that way because all functions do not start up at the same time and some experience long delays.

Regarding the question of training librarians for management and administrative positions in networking versus hiring non-librarians who are trained and educated professionaly to work in these areas—we may have somewhat of a dilemma today. Since librarian positions have become tighter and our work is changing—in many cases, retraining for librarians is not only practical but commendable. On the other hand, networking requires that such expertise be not only on board immediately but that the best trained person in management and administration be in the position, which usually means the non-librarian. Not all network offices can be as fortunate as ours: the FEDLINK Network Coordinator has a degree in library science, as well as an MBA.

The funding of networks varies. The FEDLINK members determine by vote the charges to an institution to cover the cost for service and the office staffing. In the beginning, the members decided on an initiation fee only, then later they added a fixed fee and a sliding scale fee (or proportional fee) relating to volume of use of services. Today, the fee is a 10 to 12 percent surcharge on all services plus a reduced initiation fee for new members.

Cooperative acquisition, "critical to any successful network," seems to be very important to the authors of the position paper. We agree it is important; however, it is not presently a function within FEDLINK.

Two functions which are definitely required in networks are communication and standardization. The network service center has the very important responsibility of communication—keeping the membership informed. It seems that no matter how hard one tries to keep all informed, one never really ever succeeds. It is a most difficult task which demands daily attention. One always has to seek ways for improvement. In our FEDLINK office we are also responsible for telecommunication which I will discuss later.

Standardization must be the concern of all participants, since it is required in order to conduct activities and services in an orderly and efficient manner. In FEDLINK, the membership has technical working groups which address standards and quality control.

The continuing education function is not solely a network function, hence it is conducted by FLC and may include education programs relating to networking activities. FLC plans and schedules management and informational workshops which are held in major cities. These workshops are for Federal librarians and information specialists and limited to 50 participants. They are open to the public when the limit is not reached. In addition, FLC is developing, through contract, self-instructional home-study courses, supported by related regional workshops, to extend and upgrade the knowledge and expertise of Federal librarians. These courses should be of special use to our field librarians.

Contracting and membership associations are functions not mentioned that are a major activity of FLC/FEDLINK. I assume that other network offices negotiate and monitor contracts for the network. Association membership can be an important function depending on the emphasis given by the membership or the network office. Also, an association membership does tell you something useful about the network. For example, FLC/FEDLINK is a member of the Council for Computerized Library Networks and, also, is represented at the OCLC, Inc. Network Directors' meetings.

Now—how is FLC/FEDLINK unique? How is it different from other network service centers? All Federal libraries are potential members of FEDLINK—all 2,500 of them. We expect to have in the near future Federal libraries as members from each of the 50 states, as well as overseas. FEDLINK is the only nationwide network where the member institutions have the same funding source.

FLC/FEDLINK is responsible for its own telecommunications. In addition to OCLC telecommunication engineers, we work with AT&T and the General Services Administration, Automated Data & Telecommunications Division personnel, ordering GSA TELPAK, discounted rate, telecommunications, direct-line access to OCLC for Federal libraries in any part of the country. Since many of the Federal libraries joining FEDLINK today are not located in the Washington, D. C. area, we began contracting with regional and state network service centers to provide implementation and training to FEDLINK members who applied for access to the OCLC services that are located within the boundary of the respective network. Having such contractual agreements and sharing bibliographic resources useful and available to the Federal government has enabled the FLC office to experiment with the sharing of our telecommunications with a contractual network center. The reality of the FEDLINK nationwide network, and the sharing of its telecommunications with others, leads one to believe that FEDLINK will serve as a major component of the emerging national library and information network. It may be beneficial to all of us if experimentation and modeling for a national network be conducted with FEDLINK.

The Federal libraries have another interesting and important characteristic, almost all types of libraries are found within the Federal sector: national, archival, academic, recreational, educational and training, military, hospital, special, research, and mission-oriented departments, agencies, institutions, and organizations.

In concluding, the conference is essentially concerned with the structure and governance of library networks. The persons involved in the planning and implementation of network governance and the relationship to a national library and information network must give more serious consideration in their deliberations to the role of FEDLINK and the availability and use of Federal library and information resources.

Chapter 10

NETWORK FUNCTIONS: RESPONSE

Roderick G. Swartz

State Librarian
Washington State Library
Olympia, Washington

As final panelist of this session, I would like to remind us that as a result of this paper (Chapter 6), this discussion and this conference, we are identifying issues to be addressed at an important national conference in the fall of 1979.

In the case of the current session, we are addressing issues of service, possibly the most important of our topics. I would like to comment on those issues the authors start toward—or do not start toward—addressing. But first, I would like to make two comments on the context in which these issues are being identified.

First, it always amazes me that when librarians get together to discuss networking or any other national issue, we tend to talk just "libraries" rather than "libraries within the entire spectrum of informational and cultural services. " And many times we tend to look back into time rather than forward into the future.

Many contemporary library speeches and articles open with reference to the truths of American librarianship discovered during the last quarter of the nineteenth century. It seems amazing how valid these century old pronouncements still sound. They still ring true because many times libraries have really not changed the way in which they do business over these ten decades. Our basic service process, with minor changes, has been founded on library service patterns which developed in nineteenth century New England. Some librarians today are running operations similar to those of our professional ancestors of over three generations ago.

Networking is an opportunity to step back and look at ourselves as being in the future information and cultural business. Yet networking many times appears in our conversation as the "in" solution, just as the community must have addressed an "in" solution fifty or one hundred years ago.

Today's "in" solution many times appears not as an alternative future, but a band-aid on the present situation. "I will take this...this and this from the present variety of networks in order to sustain my current operation." This appears to me as a 1960's mentality applied to an 1980's problem. It is only when we see networking as an alternative and new service approach, and not something in addition, will we see us moving in a positive direction.

Second, even as we develop this full service network into a national network, we have to realize that we do so against an ever changing backdrop. Three examples should illustrate.

Recently I participated in a conference at the Aspen Institute at Aspen, Colorado. Participants included communicators, educators and librarians. Educational trends discussed included: 1) the general growth and demand for education; 2) education spread out over a person's lifetime and therefore interrupted; and 3) re-education for new job opportunities.

Such social change certainly implies a closer working relationship among libraries, since an individual will use an ever increasing variety of libraries during a lifetime. Technological changes are proceeding at a pace ever faster as we slowly develop our networks. Every magazine from the data processing field speaks of distributed systems, yet the library approach remains still largely centralized.

Finally, there is the growth of the bureaucracy and the current rebellion against it. A Washington state paper recently interviewed several former state administrators who have returned to private industry. Their comments on governmental management included the following:

1) Certainly state government is less efficient than private industry, since it must be responsive to all demands.

2) Certainly the budget process at the state level works against good management, since it is sinful to return money to the budget office, even if saved due to good fiscal management.

3) Certainly there are gaps in the growth and education of middle management, which one does not see in private industry.

4) Certainly decision-making is more open to the audit of public criticism.

Yet most libraries have to exist in this governmental structure, while others in information-cultural services are not hampered by living in this structure.

We have to recognize that: 1) we are changing the way we do business, and 2) we are effecting that change in an ever changing environment.

In looking at the services provided in a networking environment, the authors (Chapter 6) have given us a nice shopping list of choices but have left us hanging with regard to:

1) Any future configuration of these services;

2) Any strong sense of major issues to be addressed at a national level.

With regard to the first issue, I suspect they are supporters of full-service networks as indicated from two statements in their paper:

... "We believe that designing networks to fit a specific set of functions is preferable to designing functions to fit a specific network."

... "Another area of concern. . . (was) the integration of functions into an overall network. It appears that networks are designed with one or two functions as their goals, but not with the flexibility to incorporate other functions within the network. . ."

Both statements imply a full-service network, a new approach, rather than a salvaging operation. But they do not address what services should be provided at what level—i. e., local, state, regional or national. This is an issue which needs to be addressed on a nationwide basis.

With regard to the second concern, the authors do spotlight, at the end of their paper, several major issues, but fail to put them in the context of national interests or issues. I would like to agree with a couple of these, expand on a couple of others, and add a couple of issues on my own.

The authors emphasize the need for strong network management and administration, which is really a major issue to be addressed. We are looking for individuals who have good management and marketing techniques, know business and accounting procedures, have the appropriate technical skills, and are able to interact with people, especially groups, on a day-to-day basis. It is difficult to find an individual with just a few of these skills, let alone a person who encompasses all of these needed backgrounds.

Certainly the argument that standards are a necessity is a valid one. This means technical standards, but it also implies an effort to maintain a quality of service, which reaches to various publics within this country.

The authors push for the implementation of a cooperative acquisitions program, seeing the network as a single logical collection, which needs to be developed as a single entity. Certainly this concept deserves support, yet there is a lack of attention in the paper to the economics of such a concept. Librarians have not really come face to face with the true impact of such approaches on the private sector, and what this will ultimately mean for resource sharing. This needs to be given much more attention in the future.

While the authors touch on the lack of development in the document delivery function, they do not move on into a discussion of alternative routes for information transfer. Obviously networks are not looking toward newer and innovative ways to deliver information.

The report cited continuing education as an "avant garde" feature of networking. This is discouraging, since continuing education should be a major focal point for networks. If we see networking as a change to the way we do business, then an educational process has to take place at the local level to insure such changes proceed. Continuing education cannot be considered a frill, but it has to be at the heart of the matter.

The issue of tying resources together with the American public is an important one, which cannot be forgotten. In the opening remarks it was made clear that unless we make an effort to meet this challenge, networking will not meet its full potential.

Finally, the issue of costs. Little concern seemed to be expressed in the article's findings on the question of costs of services and the relative merits of different services in terms of costs.

Each of us from our own experience favors a particular network anatomy, technology or governance structure. In the case of the network I represent —the Washington Library Network—we have opted for a state-based network with regional potential, a sophisticated computer and telecommunications technology, and a participatory governance structure. Regardless of such approaches, it is the service pattern, the quantity and quality of services at various junctions in the future national library network, which will determine its success and the success of its state and regional components.

Chapter 11

TOPOLOGY: DISCUSSION

The discussion which follows has been transcribed from tape recordings, summarized and edited. Comments and questions have been attributed to speakers when their identity was provided. The editors of these proceedings take responsibility for any errors in fact or interpretation resulting from this process, since it was not feasible to provide proofs to discussants for checking.

Allen Kent (to Roderick Swartz)

Why be so concerned when we make a decision independently to buy or not buy a book? When they make the decision to buy or not buy, or perhaps not buy, the publishers—the profit-seeking publishers—take care of their problems in many ways. Won't the profit sector find a way to cope without us worrying about it so much?

Roderick Swartz

Many of us do not understand the economics of the library, information, and book industry, and the interaction between librarianship and that industry. I've seen very few articles on the general economics of what resource sharing will do to the private sector and the eventual impact.

Allen Kent

The commercial and the noncommercial sector took a good step forward to protect their interest. The Copyright Clearinghouse Center is a new way of doing business and attempts to adjust to the problems created by the marketplace.

James Williams (to Joseph Becker)

In dealing with the 40-50 functions given in our survey, we tried to cluster related functions under general headings. Thus, we clustered preservation and conservation with storage.

George Kobulnicky - West Virginia Northern Community College

Considering funding implications of proposition 13 and other limitations on tax-supported libraries, are we, Professor Kent, going to be able to afford the cost for paying for the network?

Allen Kent

In a free enterprise system, the choices are yours to make. In coping with the proposition 13 situation, the choices are yours to make. Are you going to fight against it in your community? Are you going to attempt to find other ways of getting revenue? If you are able to get that revenue, then how would you spend it—network? storage? The choice is really up to you. The options are developing to place whatever money you have, whatever revenue you can develop in whatever way you decide—so make up your mind.

Eric de Grolier - Paris, UNESCO, and Montreal

There are four dimensions or aspects of networks which in my opinion have been neglected or set aside in the paper, which are very remarkable in other aspects. These are:

(1) International - As one coming from another, bordering country, I'm very much interested in the international aspects of networks in general and especially in the regional international networks—networks across national borders, as in the Canadian or the Mexican borders. I suspect that there are many relations between Canadian (and especially Quebec) networks and the southern neighbors like Vermont, Massachusetts, Ohio.

(2) Global Information Networks - Here is a conference on library networks, but in Canada and in Quebec especially we are very much interested in global information networks; I mean networks extending across various information organizations other than libraries, like archives, museums, research institutions, invisible colleges, booksellers, publishers, and so on.

(3) Linguistic - It is now impossible to reason only in English terms. In Quebec, we are reasoning in Anglo-French networks.

(4) Organization of Knowledge - My thesis is that the networking idea is changing the whole organization of knowledge in
libraries and other information institutions and that in the
future information retrieval systems, for instance, will
be profoundly changed by the networking aspect.

Allen Kent

As Professor de Grolier talked about the international or **regional** international aspects, I thought of the issues that have come up in the United
States with regard to crossing state boundaries. Sometimes we think these
are different countries with regard to constraints. What has been found, for
example, with WLN? Have you crossed state boundaries? What are the
inhibitions, if any?

Roderick Swartz

We are crossing state boundaries and the major issue we find is immediate desire to be involved in the governance of whatever it is that they have
bought into. We've also had some experience across the border. We've had
discussions with our Canadian neighbors in the Pacific northwest, and we
find that all the problems of crossing state borders are there; but also there
are a number of other issues: certain diplomacies that have to be met; certain issues of national pride with two countries working with each other.

Stephen Salmon - University of California, Systemwide Administration

There is a temptation to overlook the gains that can be made by including
the international dimension; I agree with Professor de Grolier. A specific
example is the University of Toronto Library Automation System. That
organization is a thriving one, with dozens of members in the network. They
have submitted a very strong bid to the University of California for supplying
of technical processing services, and yet they are curiously absent from all
of the discussion about a national network. The national network concept is
being delineated in such a way that we tend to exclude, too often, the obvious
international implications; or we include them only in a casual way.

Russell Walker - Upper Arlington Public Library, Columbus, Ohio

Many of my questions relate to Mr. Becker's statements. We spent quite
a bit of time in the early part of this session defining words such as networking, and then we added some truly ambiguous terms like equal access. What
is "equal access"? I submit to you that this is an impossibility, perhaps
"better access" but not "equal access." We also mentioned "rebate" for
providing information. I wonder if anybody has ever considered not rebating
the major libraries providing information but perhaps restructuring them.

The statement was made about networks monitoring their own performance.
I think this is another impossibility. I think they ought to be monitored by an
independent body. Mr. Swartz made the statement about tying resources of
various libraries together. My question is regarding the definition of "resources": don't some other things have to take place first, like consolidation
of administration, because obviously resources would mean much more to
me than simply materials?

Roderick Swartz

I think that the goal of equal access is probably an unreachable goal; in
the recent publications of NCLIS they have turned that toward "equal access
opportunity." I don't think that because a goal is completely unobtainable
doesn't mean one still shouldn't work toward it.

When I talk about "resources" I'm not talking just about library materials
but about total resources, including human resources. It is necessary to
have some type of a governance structure, not necessarily a merging of
administrations—in our case an Executive Council and a representative
assembly—so that there is some involvement in the decision-making process.
We have interstate compacts that we can use to tie these things together
legally; we have structures both at the state and the regional level; forums
for decision-making and policy-setting that allow us to move these programs
ahead without a totally centralized operation.

James Williams

If Mr. Becker was referring to some of the technical aspects of modern
networks, it is feasible insofar as traffic flows, switching, switching lines,
and circuits—taking care of loan leveling for interlibrary loan. Given some
decision rules, it is possible.

Allen Kent

Comment on the first point: equal access to information. For the past
two years I've been serving as chair of an ad hoc ALA committee on equal
access to information. An end point (convergence) came unexpectedly from
a very diverse committee, with a report submitted to the Executive Board
of ALA. This report takes the form of specifications for a "request for proposal" which would assess: (1) the status of providing services free or for
a fee; (2) the alternatives considered before choosing to offer services free
or for a fee; and (3) the impact of the policy on the user.

Shirley Echelman

If NCLIS has such a clear plan for what the national library and information service network shall be, and Becker's remarks indicate that the plan

remains essentially unchanged from that which was published in 1975, why
are we all working ourselves to the bone and spending so much money on
Governors' Conferences and the White House Conference? Does NCLIS expect anything at all from these conferences that will give them information
on what the national library resource should be like except for rubber stamp
approval of their plan? And if NCLIS got anything more, what effect would
that have on what seems to me to be a very well-established and impactive
plan?

Carlos Cuadra

I don't know whether Joseph Becker used the word "plan" or not; if he
did, I suspect he didn't mean to use it. I think it has been agreed for several
years that what is described in the Commission document is not a plan. I
think that to the systems designer a plan says what you are trying to do to
help you to get from here to there, what you are going to use to do it with,
and what is the schedule and timetable in which you're going to do it. The
document doesn't do any of these things. It states some general objectives
and indicates the degree of concurrence with those objectives that have been
found with the library and information community as a whole. It is a far cry
from the kind of programming statement that is called a plan. And I'm sure
that the various states will be contributing a great deal of information both in
terms of their needs, ideas, mechanisms for implementing the ideas, and
resources that will be taken into account both by NCLIS and the library community. There is nothing I know of that is cut and dry, foreordained.

William Welsh

I've been serving, on behalf of Daniel Boorstin, on the Commission for
three years. And I must confess I was quite surprised at the references that
Joseph Becker made to this plan this morning. Because I had not heard that
before. Maybe it was because I was not listening very carefully. But I agree
completely with Carlos Cuadra: I don't believe it was what Joseph Becker
intended. And I think if you will be patient and wait until Wednesday when
we discuss governance and at least hear some of the remarks I make about
the role of the Commission, you'll see that the Commission is not capable,
by mandate, of doing whatever Joe described as the plan. So this gathering
is absolutely intended to provide a whole series of answers and some questions that are facing the profession.

Joseph Anderson - State Librarian of Nevada

We're preparing in Nevada for our Governor's Conference at the end of
this month. I think that our general public is not so much different from the
general public of other states. We're finding that the general public agrees
with and understands most of the basic functions we're talking about here in

a network context; they are acutely concerned about governance. From state legislators to distinguished members of the general public to people who are entepreneurs in the private sector as well as administrators in other areas of public life, a major concern is the spector of federal control. These are very hot issues in the West—not only in libraries but also in areas of public policy with regard to public lands, energy, water resources and their management and development. It is my feeling that the library community has failed to obtain a public policy review on whether or not the information transfer process itself is worthy of public policy formation. We have not made clear what we're hoping to accomplish with a White House Conference. We are tired in Nevada of defending again the idea of holding a White House Conference on this issue because it is seen by many people as just another exercise coming from a special interest group; this is difficult to beat down at the general public level.

According to last week's Kiplinger letter, forty-six states will be dealing with some aspect of the tax initiative environment, and we'll all have to deal with that in our own jurisdictions. But I am not familiar with any attempt of the library community at large or any segment thereof (except one small effort made in COSLA back in 1973) at seeking policy review by such groups as the National Governors' Association or the regional groupings of them, the conference of state legislators, or the council of state government.

Should federal funding policies change by fiscal 1982 as to what we should do at the state level, both for library development within our states as well as working at the multistate level?

William DeJohn - Pacific Northwest Bibliographic Center

The Pacific Northwest Bibliographic Center in Seattle has been sharing resources with the Canadian province of British Columbia for over 38 years. And this year we have opened up agreements with the provinces of Saskatchewan and Alberta. It works, it's reciprocal: they loan to us, we loan to them; no problems other than the border problems of mail delivery, etc. They are quite a source for old British fiction which is extremely difficult to find, and they're very cooperative. A representative from British Columbia, the University of British Columbia, sits on my Board of Directors as a non-voting member; we'll be discussing our by-laws this year to see how Alberta and Saskatchewan are going to involve themselves in our governance since they are full funding provinces for PNBC Services.

Now I have a question for James Williams. I didn't notice in your paper any reference to what I call interlibrary reference and referral, or interlibrary information services—and by that I mean the total concept of the reference interview. Did you subsume it under another topic?

James Williams

There was a large section on this topic in the very long first draft of the paper.

William DeJohn

I think it is one of the important aspects of a nationwide network. We must train library staff members (professional and nonprofessional) to understand what the nationwide network is and how to access it at its various levels.

Stephen Salmon

Before we leave the referral aspect, there was an interesting study done in the San Diego metropolitan area by a person named John Haak. A set of questions was addressed to a number of public agencies and two disturbing results emerged. In very few cases did other public agencies refer the questioners to a library even though many of the questions deliberately involved subjects on which the libraries had extensive resources (for example, questions about Indians). Also, the questions addressed to the libraries, and to some extent other public agencies, tended to be rephrased for the questioner in ways that that agency could then answer—and what was answered was not the original question.

Unidentified Speaker

Perhaps I should have followed the gentleman from Nevada, since my comments are closely related to the issues he raised. The grassroots from the Commonwealth of Virginia will be very glad to know that we are not alone in our concern. We have been assured that NCLIS does not have the power to take the kinds of action that have been referred to. On the other hand, advance materials we received in preparation for a Governor's Conference indicated clearly to me that NCLIS is intending to ask for an extension of power—new enabling legislation to extend its programs. I'm not saying that that is bad, but there is a lot to be reviewed before we get that far. And the fact that so many of these ideas have been conveyed to us as already decided is a matter for great concern, because it tends to indicate a set of mind that is telling and not asking, and yet we are going through the maneuvers of asking. I'm hoping very much that this conference itself can turn that around; to turn it around if the fact is true—to turn it around in our understanding of the process if it is not true.

Alphonse Trezza

I frankly was trying to avoid speaking until Wednesday afternoon, but I do want to try to clarify a very serious misunderstanding. Everything that has been written and mailed from NCLIS I have read and approved, so I know that there isn't a single piece of material that went out which in any way indicated that the results of either the state or the national White House conferences were meant to change the NCLIS statute. If we change the NCLIS statute, it would be in very minor ways. For example, the old statute has language on reports to the President and the Congress that is scheduled according to the old fiscal year. So there is some discussion about whether to change the law—technical amendments. Enough of that.

Regarding the White House Conference: the state conferences are first. They are intended to do at least two things. First of all they are meant to give the states an opportunity to review the needs of the grassroots and the state program. We maintain that you cannot build a national network of services unless it is based on a strong state base. So we have said to the states: "Here is an opportunity to use the conference for your own purposes." I've attended five conferences and I've heard reports from a number others (we've had 24 to date). There are at least three states that I know of personally where that conference has resulted in positive reaction by the governors in terms of funding for the libraries in that state. This happened in Louisiana and West Virginia, just to mention two. In other words, the state conferences are having a desired effect on improving support for libraries in those states, thanks to these grassroots conferences.

If we achieve nothing at the White House Conference in Washington, it would have been a success because of the basic state conferences. That's why we're going through all this effort regarding 58 conferences. Believe me, there are easier ways to plan a national conference, but you see we believe in the grassroots approach. And we insist that if the state conferences fail, it's the states' responsibility and not NCLIS. We've had a minimal amount of regulation; the argument and the debate has been over how the state can make sure that all the segments of the library and information community in that state participate in that state conference. In addition, each state hopefully will identify issues which it feels are the proper area of concern for the national level.

Those are the issues then which we hope (sometime between April and June 1979) we can pull together into a half a dozen major issues to be discussed at the national conference.

On the comment about Mr. Becker's comment about the Commission program being already laid out: I think Carlos Cuadra has pretty well covered the fact that it is a program not a plan. I think what Joseph Becker was trying to say (maybe he said it too well and too forcefully) is that so many of the elements necessary for a good national network are described in that document. He didn't say that it is necessarily what it is going to be. He felt that the description, based on his experience over the last few years of conferences, seem to support the ideas in that program document. The White House Conference will have to determine, for example, what changes do we need in federal legislation and funding. Congressional staff have told us that Congressmen hear only from librarians about funding. But that's not good enough. Where were the people? The grassroots? Thus two-thirds of the participants at both the state and federal conferences now must be non-library related (not including library trustees, professional librarians, information specialists, etc.—only one-third can represent this group). Two-thirds must represent the user and the non-user—the individual we're trying to get to, the people who support us through taxation. We're trying to ask them what they want us to do. Let us translate that into recommendations for legislation initiatives. Many opportunities come back to you at state levels which you can implement with your existing networks, with your existing libraries, and with your existing legislation.

Gerald Sophar - Science and Education Administration, Technical Information Systems, U. S. Department of Agriculture (formerly National Agricultural Library)

I wonder how many of this audience ever heard of WINE—Western Information Network on Energy. Here is a network that started outside of the library community. They are completely unaware of the White House Conference. They know nothing about library networks. They have tried to get some of their local librarians to help them in a very crucial energy problem. I find the state of North Dakota has a $2 million system on environmental information systems without the help of libraries. They have resource information, they have data bases and they have referral systems. Not enough librarians understand what marketing is; it is not going out with a preconceived concept of what the people want and people need. "Marketing" asks what are your problems? what do you need? what do you want? Then we will start to construct on that basis.

Alex Ladenson - Urban Libraries Council

I would like to go back to an issue that was discussed earlier—equal opportunity of access. I want to call attention to the fact that the Supreme Courts in a number of states (e.g., California, New Jersey, New York) have declared that equal opportunity of education is mandatory, and I think equal opportunity of access to information ought also to be considered mandatory. Even though it is a goal that may be difficult to attain, I think that we had better retain it as a goal.

Stephen Salmon

Alex, I couldn't agree with you more; you would be interested in how that translates into practice, however, at the California Library Association. A former Presidential candidate, who is present Governor of the state of California, was asked about equality of access to information with particular reference to the growing practice of fees in public libraries. Jerry Brown came out very strongly and eloquently against that practice. He felt that it was wrong, that it would create an information elite. He came out very strongly in favor of equality of opportunity for access to information. Some weeks later I had occasion to talk to staff members in the Department of Finance which is his executive arm. They were somewhat less eloquent. They were somewhat less forthcoming and somewhat more penurious. They indicated that they had had discussions with the governor and that the whole question of equality of access and fees was "under review".

Shirley Echelman

I'd just like a chance to respond to Al Trezza. I would be interested in his answer being put together with the comments from the lady from Virginia and the gentleman from Nevada. I think a lot of working librarians shared with me the opinion that the purpose of the Governors' Conferences and the White House Conference was not to get the concerns of the librarians to the governors so that there would be more funding in state X or state Y, rather we thought that as citizens and librarians we would all have the chance to get together and to decide severally in the states, and together in Washington, what we wanted in the way of a national information resource in the United States; how we are going to organize it, manage it, and pay for it. If I'm mistaken, then I'm very sorry and I'm also very sad.

Part Three

IMPACT OF TECHNOLOGY

The fast-moving technology available to libraries presents many alternatives, with different costs and opportunities. A question is how library networks can accommodate to volatile technologies while still supporting traditional services. Required is the establishment of criteria for the evaluation of network performance, both technically and in terms of librarian and user acceptance of new modes of accessing information.

The position paper distributed in advance of the conference is given in Chapter 12. Chapters 13-16 present reactions from the panelists. Chapter 17 presents the discussion at the conference.

Chapter 12

THE IMPACT OF TECHNOLOGY
ON THE GOVERNANCE OF LIBRARY NETWORKS

William D. Mathews

Staff Associate for Information Technology
National Commission on Libraries
and Information Science
Washington, D. C.

In a country where there will soon be more televisions than people to watch them, and more unique information stored in computers than in libraries, one may well ask where information technology is leading us. Will our ability to utilize powerful information processing techniques enhance our freedoms or destroy them, make us master or make us slaves?

This chapter looks at one small slice of the information technology world. We will consider here only the concept of providing information services through library networks. In fact we will look at one specific aspect within the topic of library networks: the impact of technology on their governance. Yet this consideration merits our close attention, for it is through the governance process that we may hope to gain control over the focus of library networks and insure their social and cultural relevance.

This chapter is presented in two parts. Innovations in processing, storage, and transmission of information form a central core of technology around which library networks are built. The first part of this chapter describes the present state of affairs in these underlying technologies and looks briefly at recent trends and directions. With the relevant technologies identified, the second part of the chapter looks at some implications for the governance of library networks which arise from the close involvement of networks with information technology.

To begin with the underlying technologies, we will consider in turn three broad areas:

1. Processing, or logical manipulation and handling of information;

2. Storage, new techniques and devices for recording information;

3. Transmission, advances in our ability to transport information from one place to another, chiefly by telecommunications.

PROCESSING

In the area of information processing, the single most important trend to note is the onslaught of the microprocessor. In the past five years a tide of micro-processors of every description has engulfed us. This tide has carried with it a multitude of applications which range from the sublime to the ridiculous: from lifesaving medical instruments to better pinball machines. These ubiq-uitous devices which have for some time been the brains behind hand-held electronic calculators, are now beginning to appear in the automobile: in ignition systems and carburetors; and in the household: in electric ranges, microwave ovens, washing machines, telephones, televisions and hi-fi equip-ment. One suspects that, to coin a phrase, they will soon be popping up in toasters. In commercial and military transportation, microprocessors are finding a use in guidance and navigation systems. Manufacturing processes in the petroleum industry, in chemicals, pharmaceuticals, plastic production, and metal fabrication are all coming under the control of microprocessors. And in every area of digital information processing, especially in telecom-munications and peripheral devices, inroads have been made.

At the National Computer Conference earlier this year, there was a con-test to see who could build a mouse, roughly to scale, with enough completely self-contained intelligence to find its way through a maze. The conference was held near Disneyland; the mouse was built around a microprocessor. The winning entry was somewhat taller than your average grey mouse, but was nevertheless able to navigate through the narrow corridors of the maze, deduce which paths it had already taken, and find its way out. Probably next year the mouse will be down to scale.

The microprocessor is a culmination of a seemingly endless series of elegant design innovations in solid state physics. Densities of well over two hundred logic gates per square millimeter of silicon chip surface area are now common. We still don't know how many angels can dance on the head of a pin; but if we ask the same question about electronic components, the answer is undoubtedly several hundred. The cost/performance ratio of microprocessors has improved by a factor of ten in the last five years. A device which weighs only a fraction of an ounce can at one percent of the cost, functionally replace the electronics that used to occupy an entire room a decade ago.

The microprocessor uses very little energy and has few of the environmental requirements of older machinery. Air conditioning, for example, might not be necessary for a general purpose computer using microprocessor technology. The practical consequence of this fact is that it is now possible to bring the computer to the problem instead of bringing the problem to the computer.

To translate the advent of microprocessors into tangible consequences for library networks, four specific trends in information processing design are worth mentioning:

1. Specialized high performance auxiliary processors. Bit-slicing microprocessor architectures are being used to add specialized functions to general purpose computers. Currently, most of these functions are of the vector processing or number crunching variety—taking large matrices, for example, and carrying out operations in parallel on entire arrays. While the relevance of this may not be immediately apparent, it is probably only a matter of a year or two before similar processors are employed for text handling operations rather than exclusively for number crunching. Sorting operations come readily to mind as an area where parallel processing could be used to great advantage in an auxiliary processor attached to an otherwise general purpose machine. Sorting, of course, takes up a lot of processor time for traditional business applications as well as in library automation.

2. Processor mimics and look-alikes. Some years ago, IBM was under siege from independent manufacturers of plug compatible memories and peripherals. Now there is a frontal attack on IBM mainframes themselves, from Amdahl, Itel, Two-Pi systems and, most recently, National Semiconductor. National Semiconductor, in effect, is implementing a functional equivalent of the 370 processor on its own microcomputer chip. The chip is then incorporated into a large minicomputer, or small maxicomputer, to form a system which outperforms and undersells parts of the IBM 370 family. This blurring of distinctions between micros, minis, and maxis is itself worthy of brief note. The fact that micros are now being used as the processors in minicomputers which mimic maxis, makes it ever harder to use any of those terms definitively.

In practical terms, the ability to mimic processors fairly easily also means that even if a family of computers is discontinued—the Xerox Sigma family used by OCLC comes readily to mind—a processor that mimics the discontinued line can be manufactured at much lower costs than the software could be rewritten. To be sure, this will be a mixed blessing. Hardware elegance will be used to compensate for software inadequacies. We may well enter the twenty-first century with some of the software design mistakes of the 1970's continuing to haunt us. On the other hand, the software and operating system discontinuities that were so difficult to cope with in the shift from second to third generation hardware would be unthinkable now. So perhaps it is just as well that ways have been found to introduce radically new hardware without rocking the boat.

3. Multiple-processor systems. With the advent of relatively inexpensive processors has come a tendency to construct system configurations with redundant processors in order to achieve reliable, continuous operation. The Tandem machine at OCLC is a case in point. If the system detects failure in one of its processors, it can automatically replace the failed part with a backup processor. In general, it is now a commonplace occurrence that what seems at first glance to be a single processor system will, on closer inspection, turn out to be several closely coupled processors with distributed responsibilities and a network of data sharing arrangements within a single system.

4. The personal computer phenomenon. A booming market in affordable home computers is now very much in evidence. Home computer systems now cost about as much as home hi-fidelity systems. Not dirt cheap but not outrageous either, roughly from $300 to $3,000. This phenomenon has some interesting characteristics. It has its well-spring in the ready availability of microprocessors. But literally hundreds of small entrepreneurs, using cottage industry methods, are producing hardware, software and peripherals for personal computers. By pulling together a market from a very diverse set of interest groups—hobbyists, engineers, educators, students, scientists—reliable and inexpensive devices are being supplied to all. This has reversed a previous pattern in which innovations for the scientific and technical community were reworked and became fallout for later application by the commercial sector. Now there is a boom in construction of scientific and medical instruments built from this new strata of affordable components. Voice synthesis modules priced at a few hundred dollars are one example. Naturally, this is of some importance for library automation. Reliable, affordable, library-oriented systems can be assembled from home computer components at a fraction of the hardware cost of comparable systems using traditional commercially available parts.

But the home computer phenomenon probably has an even greater significance for libraries if we recognize it as the first step toward personal information systems. Many people have speculated, accurately I think, that home entertainment centers and personal computers will be important targets for specialized information services. Libraries will have to determine what piece of this pie will be theirs.

In fact, the innovations that gave rise to the microprocessor are still continuing. Theoretical limitations have not yet been reached. There are, however, a few ominous signs. The cost of testing microprocessors, after fabrication, is becoming a larger and larger part of manufacturing cost. The extraordinary complexity of these circuits combined with the subtlety of their failure modes, presents new challenges to reliability. This situation has also had some effect on servicing and maintenance. Where once microprocessors were looked on with great favor as a means of increasing reliability through reduction in component count and overall complexity, it now appears that some reasonable balance will probably be reached short of putting everything on a single chip. In a recent article, a hardware manufacturer ponders this very question while exploring the consequences of very large scale integration techniques. The article considers the possibilities of having more computerized intelligence on a single chip than anyone can figure out what to do with. Being a hardware manufacturer, the author of course finds a way out of the dilemma.

It seems to me that the important lesson in all of this, at least for those of us who are nurturing our paranoia, is to be ever so much more careful the next time someone hands you a martini. One must not only determine that the toothpick isn't an antenna, but must also make sure that the pimento isn't an operating system.

STORAGE

I would now like to mention some advances in devices for digital information storage. It is now time for those oldtimers who still refer to a computer's primary storage as "core" to update their vocabularies. Most of the primary storage in computers is now supplied by semiconductor circuits and has been subject to roughly the same factor-of-ten improvements in cost performance experienced by electronic circuits generally over the past five years. There have been notable developments in memory technology affecting three areas of the performance spectrum: the high speed end, the midrange, and the low speed bulk memory systems. For the first time ever there now exists what is essentially a continuum of devices across the entire cost-performance spectrum.

1. On the high-speed, high-performance end, it is now fairly common that even a small computer system might have a "cache" memory, a small associative memory retaining the most recently referenced information in a readily available place. In some cases the cache memory might be only the tip of the iceberg, or more precisely, the top of a hierarchy of memories having a wide variety of characteristics, with data shuffled from one part of memory to another to achieve some optimum in performance. Memory management, dynamic memory allocation, and virtual memory schemes, once found only on large computer systems, are now appearing on computers costing less than $100,000.

Another tendency is to incorporate operating systems and compilers into read-only memories within the computer. While this trend toward off-the-shelf machines which understand higher level languages is laudable for the most part, it makes the process of equipment purchase more complex and blurs traditional distinctions between hardware, firmware and software.

2. In the midrange, the development of charge-coupled devices and bubble memories has filled a gap which previously existed in the continuum of memory devices. These devices are faster than mechanical devices, such as fixed head magnetic disks, and slower than other semiconductor memories. Cost per bit also places them midway between these two other types of memory. These devices work like gigantic shift registers, propagating electrical charges or magnetic domains in a circulating pattern in which bits can be accessed and rewritten once per cycle of the memory train. They have an advantage over magnetic disks in that no mechanical parts are involved, yet they can be used to store a significant amount of information and can be treated like a structured file system if so desired. Someone asked me once if a bubble memory implant could cure a failing brain. Unfortunately, microsurgery hasn't progressed that far.

3. On the low performance end there has been continued improvement in recording densities of magnetic media. Floppy disks and micro-floppies provide a convenient way to ship data through the mails, just in case the mails still work. More exciting, I think, is the prospect of using videodisks for digital storage. The videodisk was developed for the consumer market as a medium for distributing prerecorded television programs.

Consumers are beginning to take their leisure time very seriously, and a few brief items should serve to indicate the magnitude of the market for home entertainment equipment. (1) Videotape units are selling at nearly double the pace of last year. (2) Home video game sales are projected to reach nearly a half billion dollars a year in 1980. This would represent about a 25-fold increase in five years. Lest the importance of that half billion dollar figure be lost, this means that in 1980 the American people will be spending more for video game hardware than the total acquisitions expenditures for all libraries of all types in the United States during that same year. (3) "It's just like hamburgers" comments the owner of a chain of franchise stores for the total home video environment. Included in his offerings are tape machines, videodisks, video games and video projectors for the total video experience. Also included are pinball and popcorn machines, microwave ovens for your TV food, and a new line of furniture specially designed for watching projection TV. Enough, one might hope, to drive sensible people off to their libraries for escape.

Used in a digital mode, a single videodisk can store the entire Library of Congress MARC file on one surface. Since it was designed as a mass production medium, copies can be made from a master for pennies—fifty-five pennies to be exact. Even adding the cost of producing the master and shipping the copy, this means that copies of a fairly large bibliographic data base could probably be made available for under $10 apiece. Playback machines which can locate any frame on the disk in less than a second are expected to cost less than $3,000—a cost comparable to that of a CRT terminal. It seems that this kind of mass storage device deserves further exploration for those applications in library automation which utilize fairly static data. The dynamic and growing portion of the data base—additions, deletions, changes—might be handled adjunctively by floppy disks.

In general, where five years ago our choices for storage mechanisms were relatively limited, there is now a panoply from which to choose. That is not to say that the choice is any easier.

TRANSMISSION

We shall now turn to advances in information transmission. This is truly an exciting area, rich in possibilities. Changes in telecommunications technology are momentous and fundamental, and move rapidly beyond the technical sphere in their implications, to involve our political and social fabric.

Here again, microprocessors are part of the picture and are being used to advantage in sophisticated multiplexing equipment which can combine many data channels operating at different speeds, packet the information, and send it in bursts down a single channel using a communications protocol to maintain an error-free link.

In contrast with five years ago, it is now possible to purchase services from commercial packet-switched communication networks. And there is a steady growth in computer-to-computer data traffic. Also, some computer manufacturers are offering network architectures which tie together multiple operating systems running on families of similar computers. But piecing together a cohesive network with dissimilar computers is still quite a challenge. And, it is worth noting that computerized networks generally have not grown quite as rapidly as one might expect.

To some extent, the microprocessor has been a countervailing force against their rapid growth. The driving force behind networking used to be a desire to share both functions and data. As small computer systems have become more powerful, more self-contained, more complete, they have also become more independent in their function. People are now buying small machines which can solve 90% of their problems and then proceed to redefine the remaining 10% of their problems as unimportant. There has been a noticeable shift away from older network designs based on functions distributed across a hierarchy of computers with the most powerful computer at the center. Instead, in more and more designs, processing functions are redundantly located throughout the network, and internodal traffic consists of data transactions. In effect, data sharing, not function sharing, is becoming the primary network rationale.

While microprocessors have played a part, they are not central to the major thrust in information transmission. The big news in telecommunications, from the technological point of view, is that a fundamental and massive shift from analog to digital modes of transmission is taking place in the industry. This shift is taking place more rapidly than most observers had expected, and it is underpinned by new transmission channels of enormous capacity. The shift is massive in that it involves the replacement of, or upgrading of, billions of dollars worth of common carrier equipment alone. The shift involves all types of communications—voice, facsimile, computer transmissions and television communications will all be affected. And the shift is pervasive—common carrier dial-up facilities, leased lines, microwave communications, radio links and satellite communications, are all going "digital."

For example, practically every major manufacturer of semiconductor circuits has begun to produce a device called the "codec"—short for coder-decoder. This circuit takes the human voice as transmitted by the standard voice-grade telephone channel, samples the signal 8,000 times per second, and encodes it into a digital bitstream. Digitized signals from hundreds of telephone conversations are then bundled together, transmitted over high capacity communications links, decoded at the other end, and reconstituted into a very close approximation of the original voice.

While this may seem to be an elaborate and excessively complicated procedure, the switch from analog to digital makes good sense from a number of points of view. First, the cost-performance of digital circuits continues to improve remarkably. Noise problems inherent in analog devices can be eliminated. Moreover, by volume, more and more conversations are occurring between computers and other digital devices. For example, typical television programming has highly redundant characteristics. Digital preprocessing of the picture can dramatically compress the amount of information that must be transmitted to reconstitute a television image. The image can be described differentially, as a series of changes, rather than repainted entirely each time.

We are witnessing then the emergence of a new entity: the intelligent communications channel. The recent success of the Chicago Experiment, (a high capacity digital link using fiber optics now in its second year of operations) and the implementation plans for Satellite Business Systems, (a corporation which will provide broadband digital communications via satellite through rooftop antennas) serve to underscore the fact that it is not too soon

to begin planning for broadband digital capabilities today. This fact also
serves to highlight the relevance of teletext, interactive cable, digitized
facsimile and electronic mail. A new neural network of interactive communication is coming into place. Inevitably, new information relationships will
result. Publishers may bypass their printers and transmit electronic text
directly to the libraries. Just as likely, publishers may bypass the libraries
and interact directly with the users. New institutions and new intermediaries
may result.

But the really big news in communications is not in the technological arena
at all, but in the legal and regulatory sphere. The emergence of intelligent
communication channels has blurred even further the fine and convoluted line
between communications and computing. At the heart of this is the fact that
the communications industry is regulated by the Federal Communications
Commission while the computer industry is, depending upon your point of
view, either a free-for-all or a monopoly, but in any event, unregulated.
The battle will not be a small one. On one side we have AT&T eager to introduce more intelligence and computational capability into the telephone network
but constrained from doing so by a consent decree. On the other side we have
IBM, one of the partners in the Satellite Business Systems consortium, ready
to supplant the existing network with a satellite-based digital network for
high-volume business use.

Early in June of this year, the Communications Act of 1978 was introduced
in Congress. It is the result of some 20 months of hearings and research by
the House Subcommittee on Communications. The bill is vast in scope, goes
into all phases of communications, and takes into account the rapidly changing
technologies in the United States. It marks the first effort in 44 years to
rewrite the communications laws of the land. Some of the provisions of this
bill are that it:

1. Abolishes the FCC, creating a Communications Regulatory
    Commission with less regulatory authority.

2. Creates the National Telecommunications Agency as a policy-
    making body.

3. Deregulates radio.

4. Prohibits federal regulation of cable television.

5. Reguires AT&T to divest itself of Western Electric, but

6. Frees AT&T to provide unregulated computational and other
    services through a separate company.

7. Replaces the Corporation for Public Broadcasting with a corpora-
    tion whose function would be solely to provide grants.

Within a few weeks of the introduction of this bill, AT&T was ready to
file a tariff with the FCC for a new communications service which anticipates
ultimate passage of the bill in some form. In fact, it is very hard to predict
how much this bill might change before being enacted into law, but it is very
easy to see that whatever happens this bill will surely have some bearing on
library networks.

Apparently, technology has dumped a grabbag full of glittering trinkets at
our door. The engineering community has given us pieces of the puzzle,
parts of the tinkertoy. But knowing that these fragments exist is only so
much intellectual clutter unless we can fit these pieces into a larger picture
and create effective applications from them. Moreover, it would be misleading to create the expectation of a rosy future brought to us by technology
without at the same time alluding to the pieces that don't exist or don't quite
fit. So I will mention some of these.

SOFTWARE

The most obvious missing piece involves the lack of adequate software and
the lack of competent people who might implement the same. While hardware
has improved each year, software has not kept pace. Yet an appreciable
amount of software is needed to shape applications for the network. Because
of the many improvements in hardware effectiveness, hardware has become
a smaller part of total systems cost while software cost has become more
prominent. Effective approaches to software implementation are more important today than ever before. Unfortunately, software engineering is just
beginning to be recognized as a science. Principles of structured programming, file management, and data base design are still foreign to a great
many practitioners. Because of the complexity of our information systems,
library networks are especially vulnerable to this weakness and lack of
formalism in software production. We truly lack people who comprehend
the hardware, understand the applications, and have the requisite software
design abilities to bring the total package together.

STANDARDS

Another missing piece is in the area of standards. There are so many different ways to implement a library network that standardization is crucial.
Standards are needed not only for the communications functions of the network but also for many details in the format of messages themselves. A
wide variety of messages will travel over the network, many of them non-
bibliographic in nature, and we must go beyond standards such as MARC to
encompass these. But present national standardization efforts are time-

consuming, unwieldy, heavily politicized and encrusted with legalisms. Moreover, standardization work is likely to consume the efforts of some of the most productive people in an organization—the top technical ambassadors who understand the guts of the problem and also possess good interpersonal skills. Further, technology moves so fast that it often obsoletes standardization work in progress. For example, the so called "S-100 bus structure," an internal communications discipline introduced by the Altair Corporation a few years ago for use with a certain family of microprocessors, has been adopted by more than a hundred other manufacturers but has not yet become a formal standard. One suspects that it will become a standard once no one any longer cares.

The political ramifications of standardization are also everpresent. In the computer industry this fact surfaced recently in a squabble between NBS and the GAO in which the NBS was taken to task for being too passive, letting industry set the pace for standards rather than championing the cause of users. In this regard it is well to recognize that the Federal Government is indeed a very large user of data processing equipment. Another political skirmish worth noting is the recent stand taken by CBEMA against adopting certain IBM practices as a standard. Historically, IBM has often deviated from national standards, some say to obtain competitive advantage. CBEMA is an organization representing a number of independent manufacturers. Yet CBEMA is also the secretariat for an important part of the ANSI standardization activities relating to computers. So the question arises, who shall be involved in setting the standards for library networks? What fox will watch this roost? How will the users be involved?

A related problem is the difficulty of developing standardized measurements for network services. Information is a perishable commodity. It must be delivered in a timely way, and in the proper form. Except for some very preliminary research on this topic, we are pretty much on our own to decide and determine what service measurements should be applied. Without these standardized measurements, any attempt at cost comparison across suppliers leaves us in a haze of confusion, comparing pineapples with pinecones.

And finally, in the area of standards, the question of quality control of the information product itself must be addressed. This does not mean imposition of a dull sameness on the product: diversity and product variety are very necessary to a network's vitality. But it does mean that products claiming to be identical, for example full MARC records for a particular item, should indeed follow some pattern of predictable behavior and quality with regard to their content no matter who the supplier might be.

MANAGEMENT

Finally, our management techniques leave much to be desired. While some notion of a systems approach seems to have influenced other areas of endeavor, the library world, including library network organizations, seems immune to harboring any taint of a systems development methodology. It is hard to see how solid systems implementation can take place unless this atmosphere is changed. We must proceed from analysis and good general design requirements, to credible design and implementation which maintains the confidence of sponsors and users alike.

Some pieces of the puzzle exist, but others do not. On balance, there is probably cause for some optimism. Never before has there been a technological convergence of such magnitude on the problems facing the information processing community.

GOVERNANCE

It is now time to look at the impact of technology on the governance of library networks in some detail. Depending on your point of view, technology has either nothing or everything to do with governance. To be sure we might be hard pressed to find any specific reason why a technologist should be involved in a library network's governance. Tongue in cheek, we might say that there is no more persuasive reason for a technologist to be involved than, for example, a librarian. On the other hand, it is hard to imagine how one might adequately govern an enterprise which uses information technology in its everyday work without having some access to a broad and fundamental knowledge about that same technology. Technology is so pervasive and basic to networks that it literally colors all the judgements one might make. Simply put, we don't need token technologists as participants in governance. Rather, we need people with a broad sense for what is possible—people who have a meaningful understanding of technology.

Before going further, let me give my own definition of governance. My intention is neither to be redundant nor definitive, but simply to establish a point of departure. Indeed my definition is likely to be at cross purposes to definitions used by others, so elusive and confusing is the topic at hand.

To me, governance is the set of processes through which an organization confirms its goals, establishes policy, selects its leaders, and insures the necessary resources to carry out its purposes. Selection of leaders is likely to be the most important role of governance, while insuring resources usually involves budgetary decisions and fund raising. Governance might be carried out simply by a board of directors acting in accordance with bylaws. But frequently, governance is carried out through a more elaborate structure with committees formed, for example, to handle policy in areas of finance, planning, operations, and so forth. Presumably each committee is related in an intelligent way to the governing board, the governance process carried forward through the harmonious action of the governance structure as a whole.

Of course, the types of people involved in governance vary enormously from one kind of organization to another. A museum might lean heavily on philanthropists, recognizing that an adequate source of donations is a sine qua non. A public utility is apt to include a liberal sprinkling of politicians and lawyers in its governance process, since legal and political constraints are so much a determinant of their environment. A small manufacturing company might emphasize people having hands-on experience with the product under development. Inside directors might dominate in this situation, and as the product emerges, the governance itself must change to reflect the life cycle of the development and include marketing and financial expertise as well.

All considerations of technology aside, it should be clear that a library network must draw on very diverse talents for input into its governance process. It must not, for example, be dominated by a luff of librarians, a mumble of moneymongers, a puff of politicians, a nettle of network directors, or a usurpation of users. Moreover, there should also be a mix of types and philosophical leanings among the governors—thinkers and doers, speculators and practitioners—but generally they should be people able to cope with a high level of abstraction and ready to help in creating a mosaic out of the crazyquilt of possibilities. No doubt there will be formal mechanisms for seeking input from users, for reassuring sponsors, or for providing representation in the very broadest sense of the term—including non-users as well as users, private citizens as well as librarians and information scientists, in some meaningful way. Finally, we should be aware that the purpose of governance is not to provide for a tug-of-war between power elites, but rather to provide a means of insuring that the enterprise flourishes and serves some socially useful purpose.

Two other points deserve brief emphasis before we return to the impact of technology. The first is that finding credible people to run the enterprise —a management team in which everyone can have confidence—is likely to overshadow any other consideration. Secondly, that once such a team is put together, it should be the firm determination of people involved in governance to stay out of their way. True, governance may countercheck or delimit management, but it should never directly meddle with management's responsibilities.

A very interesting discussion could look at the relative impact of technology versus society, economics, politics, or whatever on governance. Or we could think about the difference between library networks and other institutions in terms of such relationships. But the discussion here will instead seek answers to the single question: "What are some of the things that people in a governing position should know about technology?" We will explore the kinds of concepts with which each governor should be familiar in order to act effectively. In a way, we will be building a set of requirements for the people we should seek. Doubtless there are dozens of concepts that should be known, but we have confined ourselves here to a dozen themes that might be representative.

PROVIDING STRUCTURE

At the outset, there should be a realization that implementation of technology flourishes within a structure. The first governors will be called upon to devise and refine the governance structure for the network, and pay some attention to how these relate to the management structure as well. Those structures should be fault-tolerant in their acceptance of the fact that organizations are run by fallible human beings, and adaptable in their readiness to accommodate the unforeseen. If we wish the network to survive, our structures should not presume that heroes and miracle-workers will move the enterprise along. For the most part, library networks must rely on fairly ordinary people, sometimes brilliant one might hope, but human nonetheless.

SHOES FOR THE COBBLER'S CHILDREN

When an enterprise fails, we are accustomed to telling half-truths about its failure. We might say something like: "It was a good idea but we ran out of money," or "the timing wasn't right," or "the market couldn't sustain it." But at the heart of each failure is a lack of information. Perhaps someone has the information or foreknowledge but does not have access to the governance apparatus. Or the crucial information to make a decision is not developed and elucidated in such a way that everyone can recognize its significance. In building a library network we partake in a venture deeply committed to the task of improving the flow of information. The governors of such a network should be especially sensitive to the vital importance of creating appropriate patterns for information flow within the governance process itself.

MANAGING CHANGE

It has perhaps become a cliche to talk about managing change and coping with change. Yet the governors of a network should realize that technology is propelled by change and is indeed an agent of change. The rapid pace of change can be unnerving at times. It is disconcerting, to say the least, to realize that a single event can overturn basic assumptions and completely distort the matrix of relationships between products and the marketplace. History is replete with systems which were obsolete before they were announced. In the face of such devastating discoveries, there is a strong temptation to throw everything out and start anew. Yet there is equal danger in embracing the latest thing and waltzing too close to the cutting edge of technology. In general, library networks would do well and could count themselves successful if they could implement by using well proven and mature pieces of technology, well-cushioned to follow in the path toward integration and synthesis.

PATH-FINDING AND CHOICE-MAKING

Technology presents us with a maze of paths and possibilities that could be tried. Yet there is not time, not money, not people enough to follow even a fraction of these paths to the end. Already the discussions seem endless: remote versus local processing, distributed versus centralized storage, large versus small system integration, processing versus storage, storage versus transmission, and so on. The trade-offs are dizzying. But until choices are made and paths selected, this abundance of possibilities cannot be turned into a wealth of realities. The road not taken may leave us with a tinge of curiosity but should also impart a sense of relief and no regrets. Progress is made by moving down the paths, not standing on the crossroads reading the signposts. Realizing the strength that lies in wisely delimiting complexity, the governors of a network should support management as sensible choices are made.

ASSESSMENT VERSUS QUANTIFICATION

Something about dealing with technology lends credence to zealous attempts to carefully quantify all factors before making any decision. Yet this impulse can easily get out of hand. Often enough we set out to measure the inherently unmeasurable, take meaningless measures by rote, or spend more time building the measuring devices than the system itself. All these attempts to add extra decimal points of precision to the decision-making process suffer from Heisenberg's Uncertainty Principle. By the time the cherished measurement is made, the real world has moved to some new place. An over-quantified decision is no less likely to be a bad decision. On the other hand, a healthy tendency toward employing the techniques of technology assessment in the decision-making process has much to be said for it. Here the emphasis is not so much on quantification as it is on determining the context, weighing the direction of long-term influences, and getting some sense of the second and third-order impacts of the development work.

SUCCESSIVE APPROXIMATION

Library networks are developed through a process of successive approximation and piecemeal adaptation. Anyone who imagines that there can be a "grand plan" or comprehensive design for a system as complex as a library network misunderstands the scope of the enterprise. We are not dealing with carpentry or traditional architecture but a kind of interactive urban design for the city of information, part of the fabric of our society. The design must be built with broad margins, able to tolerate imprecision and accommodate change in a stable way. Moreover, the governors of a network should appreciate the ever-repeating, iterative pattern of the development cycle. Survival depends on a constant feedback of evaluation into new design.

DISLOCATIONS

Let's face it. Any implementation of technology creates a trail of dislocations, some good, some bad. On the positive side, these dislocations might remove some of our preconceptions. Technology, for example, is blind to political boundaries and social barriers. This might help us realize that patterns of information use which bring together people in differing political jurisdictions or in very different types of libraries can be both practical and beneficial. On the other hand, the potential for socially damaging dislocation is enormous. One has only to read the want ads for librarians to realize that people with some command of automation seem to exert greater power and influence on their respective organizations and seem to have access to different career development opportunities. The potential threat of personal obsolescence, inherent in each implementation of technology, must ever be managed with an eye toward larger social responsibilities.

INNOVATION AND TECHNOLOGY TRANSFER

The governors of a library network should appreciate the importance of innovation in a network organization, that a nurturing climate for synthesis must be sustained. Compared with other parts of the information processing world,

library networks are like underdeveloped countries. Close attention must
be given to the process of looking over the fence, borrowing developments
from related information sectors, transferring technology and adapting developments for internal use. To be sure, it would also be nice once in a while
to be able to afford the creation of some specific new piece of the puzzle.
But for the most part, library networks must survive by putting together
pieces that have already been devised for other purposes.

DISCARDING XENOPHOBIA

Libraries and library networks had nothing to do with the many rapid advances
in technology mentioned earlier in this chapter. Library networks are nearly
imperceptible as a driving force behind the technology. No one asked the
library networks what kind of microprocessor they wanted, how they intended
to store their information or who they expected to transmit that information
to. Fortunately they didn't ask, we might add, for they might still be waiting
for an answer. In fact, it is time for library networks to recognize that they
cannot "go it alone. " Our futures are closely interwoven with the concerns
of public broadcasting, community information services, interactive cable,
personal computing, electronic mail, and satellite communications systems
to name a few. Librarians and library networks should discard their accustomed xenophobia and join forces with the rest of the information community.
We must aggregate our needs with others in the larger information processing
marketplace. It is time to march together on this broad front or to be left
dusting books.

LEGAL FALLOUT

Another aspect of information technology that should be appreciated is the
delicate interplay between new technological possibilities and the growth of
legal and regulatory constraints. Practically every noteworthy innovation
gives rise to formulations of public policy designed to keep the use of that
innovation within socially acceptable bounds. In the area of biology, for example, the case of recombinant DNA research is particularly instructive.
It is now recognized that nature itself showers us constantly with millions of
times more recombined DNA than would escape from all the laboratories of
the world put together. Yet the ripple of restrictive legislation directed
against DNA research has been felt in practically every nation on earth. In
the area of information technology, it is of little merit to appreciate the
myriad possibilities at our fingertips without also understanding the relevance
of legislation relating to privacy, communications, freedom of information,
electronic funds transfer, computerized crime, and transborder dataflow, to

name just a few of the concerns currently alive in the present session of
Congress. Nor should we overlook the very real possibility that library networks themselves might become a matter of specific concern which results
in legislation regarding their use.

QUESTIONS AND ANSWERS

The final two themes that we shall mention speak to the general temperment
of governors more than to concepts they should know. For the first, we
should wish that governors of a network will see themselves as answer-ques-
tioners rather than as question-answerers. There will be an abundant enough
supply of answers from the managers, analysts, and designers putting the
network together. That's what they're paid to do, to supply answers. But
what we need in our governors is the type of person who will ask the incisive
question, who is not flim-flammed by gimmicks or befuddled by technoquacks.
Before some new solution or answer is embraced, the governors should
thoughtfully ask and understand where each new direction of the network might
lead.

SUFFICIENT WISDOM

Last and not least, one would hope that people in a governing position would
have the wisdom to understand that networks are not the cure-all for the
library community's ills. There are applications which should clearly be
included in a network, and others that should never be. One has the feeling
that a good many applications being thought of for networks today will not,
in the end, be realistic or economical. Let us hope that the governors of any
future network will have the wisdom and sensitivity to deploy networks with
a sense for their appropriate use. We should expect something more than a
scheme for automating the quill pen, but something less than a plot to net-
workize the entire planet.

Something more. If the governors of our library networks are lacking in
the qualities we may ultimately feel are important to our destinies, let us
hope we all have the collective wisdom to make our feelings known and to
seek change in the governance itself.

We have seen, in this chapter, that library networks are enveloped in the
very dynamic world of information technology and that any discussion of the
governance of such networks must take some cognizance of that bond. This
analysis has been far from complete. We have scratched the surface but
have not begun to consider, for example, specific technological issues which
might arise, the indirect impacts of technology, or the difficulty of weighing
conflicts between technology and other environmental forces.

To dispel somewhat the bias of the discussion so far, it should be clear that policymaking and governance must go beyond any kind of narrow technical consideration to embrace the understanding that information is power. That power must be unlocked and used to benefit the public good. And we should not mistakenly think that technology will ultimately determine what library networks will do. People will determine that: people of astute perception and good will.

BIBLIOGRAPHIC NOTE

New trends in information technology can be gleaned from a variety of trade and professional publications. Computerworld, Datamation, Electronics, and IEEE Spectrum are good sources for news of recent developments. This bibliographic note points to five items of special interest which should give further perspective on library networks and governance.

The Conference Board, Information Technology: Some Critical Implications for Decision Makers, New York, 1972.

This two volume monograph investigates fairly thoroughly the problems surrounding effective human management of information technology. It takes a sweeping look at the implications of information technology for business, government, politics, education, and legislation. An insightful piece.

Dalotta, T. A., et. al. Data Processing in 1980-1985: A Study of Potential Limitations to Progress, New York: Wiley, 1976.

Provides an overview of emerging developments in hardware for processing, storage, and transmission, as well as software, market structure, etc. Touches also on the need for standards and better management techniques. A very readable and well-argued book, with very helpful bibliographies.

Fortune, June 5, 1978.

Two articles are of interest here. One, on page 136, is entitled "New Technology Scrambles the Memory Market." This article puts into perspective the development of Charge Coupled Devices and Bubble Memories. The other article is an advertising section on page 22 entitled "Computing for Business into the 80's." This "white paper to management" outlines a multiplicity of opportunities with respect to business use of computers and communications.

The Futurist, Volume XII, No. 2, April 1978.

Three articles in this issue merit attention. "The Automated Office" talks about improvements in word processing and text composition. "The

Electronic Newspaper" explores the use of television as a substitute for news-
papers. Finally, "A Funny Thing is Happening to the Library on its Way to
the Future" gives a broad brush treatment of videodisk, databases, etc. From
its title one can see that this was obviously meant to be a humorous little
trifle.

Gotlieb, C. C. and A. Borodin. Social Issues in Computing, New York:
    Academic Press, 1973.

A textbook on security, privacy, copyright, trade secrecy, and many other
social and legal issues involved in the use of computers.

Chapter 13

SOME COMMENTS ON THE IMPACT
OF TECHNOLOGY ON LIBRARY NETWORKS

Donald W. King

President
King Research, Inc.
Rockville, Maryland

I would like to make a few comments on Mr. Mathews' excellent paper
(Chapter 12), and then elaborate on a possible scenario of how technology
might be employed in future communication that is now accomplished by published literature. I personally found Mr. Mathews' discussion of technology
very enlightening and the presentation on its impact on governance of library
networks quite thought provoking. In scientific and technical communication,
the area in which I am most familiar, it is clear that the technology mentioned
by Mr. Mathews could have an enormous impact in our lifetime. I say could
because there are many barriers that may limit the employment of potential
technology. Mr. Mathews has pointed out many such barriers. However,
perhaps, just as important are constraints related to lack of incentives or
motivation to change on the part of participants in the current communication
system. I will discuss some of these problems at the end of this paper.

First, I would like to expand some on Mr. Mathews' three areas of technology: processing, storage and transmission. Nearly all functions that are
performed in communications can be aggregated into five generic functions
that we have called origination, recording, preservation, end-use and transmission. [1] In the current published literature these functions are now prin-
cipally performed by authors (origination), publishers (recording), libraries
(preservation) and readers (end-use), although we find that each type of participant performs all the generic functions to some degree.

One very important point made by Mr. Mathews is that most of the potential technological advancements for library networking are available because
of the large market and use of the technology outside of this environment.

141

One of the most significant technology advancements in scientific and technical communication is found in the origination function where we find that
many authors are beginning to use electronic word processing equipment for
preparing articles and books. The low cost availability of word processors
and text editors to scientists and engineers is made possible through the widespread use of this technology in office environments.[2] We have estimated
that about 40 percent of scientific and technical articles are currently prepared on word processors or text editors and this proportion is expected to
double by 1985.[3]

The majority of automatic typewriters in service today were designed to
resemble conventional typewriters. However, more systems with video displays are being marketed and have been accepted quite well despite their
additional expense. Today, video display word processors based upon standard, "off the shelf" microcomputer systems, video display terminals and high
quality printers are available and have the advantage that they are also capable of acting as dedicated computer systems for data analysis, information
storage and retrieval, and as intelligent terminals within distributed networks.
The use of diskettes or "floppy disks" has become predominant in these systems because of their low cost, their reliability and comparatively large
amount of storage space they offer. Shared logic (i.e., multi-terminal) word
processing systems and small business computers with word processing software are finding their way into "heavy duty" applications—those where several typewriters are typically operating 75 percent of the time or more.
These systems offer the additional benefits of storing documents on-line in a
mass storage device such as a "hard" disk, thus avoiding the necessity of
filing a number of removable magnetic media (e.g., diskettes) which can be
misplaced or damaged.

Another approach to "word processing" has utilized the standard computer
terminal as a general purpose appliance to connect to various text processing
hardware/software systems. The information processor to which a terminal
is connected may be an in-house, general purpose system or a remote time-
shared service or even a specialized utility system such as the Office-1
computer which offers a wide range of information and text processing "tools."

In addition to advantages of flexibility and potential reduced costs, these
word processing systems provide book and article text in electronic form
which can be electronically transmitted to editors, reviewers and publishers.
Electronic processes are currently used extensively by publishers for editing,
redaction and composition. The possibility of direct input from authors to
publishers in digital form should increase this potential even more since the
cost of keyboarding can be eliminated. Composition is also increasingly
integrated into general text-processing in computer-based systems. As
originally designed, these systems were intended primarily for editing text.
However, the magnetic digital record can also be stripped of operating codes

and input into an electronic composer. This type of integrated system is
often used by newspaper publishers[4] and database for on-line retrieval.

In the future, electronic processes used by publishers will yield them
enormous flexibility in the form and mode of distribution of articles. Electronic technology has progressed to the point where articles can be individually printed directly from computer output. Impact printers previously
caused problems with this kind of output, but non-impact printing has resolved
the problem of rapid computer output speed. The ink jet, electrophotographic
and electrostatic systems all hold substantial promise for scientific and technical publishing.

On the other hand, computer master images can also be transformed into
microform or video disks. However, microform has many disadvantages
including too many formats, reduction ratios, and retrieval coding schemes;
poor quality film images at the reader and with paper form prints; readers
which are expensive, hard to use, and bulky; inadequate user environments
in libraries; and difficulty in obtaining paper form prints. [5] I concur with
Mr. Mathews that the new video disk technology holds substantial promise
for distribution and storage. There are some weaknesses with this technology, however, since currently video disk images are not adequate for dis-
playing a full normal-sized printed page on most inexpensive viewing devices.

As mentioned by Mr. Mathews, new technology will be directly applicable
to library operations and services. The most prominent of these are on-line
(and off-line) bibliographic searches, automated circulation, cataloging of
books and interlibrary loan processes. Technology that might make the
greatest impact on library networking is in mass storage memories. If a
National Periodicals System comes into being, one component might be digital
storage of articles input into it directly from publishers. Thus far, the most
likely such system is magnetic tape media segmented for mechanical handling.
However, there are some output problems associated with queuing delays and
the output costs are currently prohibitively high. One of the most interesting
aspects of new technology to library networking is that the preservation function could go to either end of a wide spectrum of types of storage. At one
end is a central, mass electronic storage and at the other end is completely
distributed storage made available by video disk technology.

The principal electronic processes that could be applied to end-uses are
output terminals and video displays of one kind or another. End-users can
apply these devices for full-text retrieval and teleconferences as well as for
on-line bibliographic searches which can lead to full-text. The use and success of such electronic processes depends to a large degree on telecommunication costs. As Mr. Mathews has pointed out, there are several alternative
systems in the offing that may yield very substantial costs advantages over
current processes. The telecommunication potential is enhanced by avail-

ability of minicomputers or intelligent terminals to senders and receivers which can permit rapid transmittal that will be buffered by this electronic equipment.

The technological advances mentioned by Mr. Mathews provide all the parts for an electronic alternative to paper-based publishing of the literature, particularly journals. Such a system would provide substantial flexibility since individual articles can be distributed in the manner most economically advantageous to them. Highly read articles may still be distributed in paper form, while infrequently read articles can be requested and quickly received by telecommunication when they are needed. Here, the trade-off is that resources formerly wasted in printing, mailing and storage are applied to better identification and retrieval of information which results in reduced cost, better quality and increased efficiency. Many other benefits of electronic processing can also be derived. For example, better systems integration will yield more emphasis on quality of article content, fewer articles will be repeated over and over again for updates or for different journals, and the new systems will provide better access and retrieval to information needed in multi-disciplinary research.

In an electronic alternative, articles will be prepared by authors using sophisticated text editing systems. Article preparation may include text writing jointly through teleconferencing systems in which immediate peer review is possible, comments made, and specific research questions answered. Many of the citations used in the article will come from those found in on-line bibliographic searches. When citations are identified they can be immediately retrieved by telecommunication in full-text on CRT or in paper form. The digital form of the unreviewed manuscript will be directly transmitted electronically to a publisher. The publisher will, in turn, electronically transmit the manuscript to a subject editor who will read the text by CRT or printout and make electronic notes concerning editorial and content quality. The subject editor may choose an appropriate reviewer(s) using a computer program that matches the profile of potential reviewers with the topics covered in the article. Other computer-stored information will also be used to help screen reviewers such as by affiliation and relationship to the authors, status of most recent review, frequency of reviews, timeliness of response of previous reviews and quality of reviews. The reviewers will respond to editors and editors in turn to authors by telecommunication, similar to current teleconferencing processes.

An accepted article will be redacted through a text-editing terminal and the computer-based text will be output in several forms, including full text as well as in bibliographic form. The bibliographic form will be transmitted electronically and used directly by search services or input to abstracting and indexing services to be further analyzed and processed. The full text will be sent electroncially to some individual scientists designated by the author or by request to scientists based on its topic, author or some other bibliographic identifier. In some instances articles will be telecommunicated through an SDI-like system. The scientists may receive the text on their own personal terminals or on their libraries' terminals. Articles will also be sent directly by telecommunication to a National Periodicals System consisting of a central archive(s) and several decentralized computer or video disk stores. The National Periodicals System will await telecommunicated requests for copies of articles and will respond with full text telecommunicated to the requestors.

Mr. Mathews, in his presentation, noted that computerized networks have not grown as rapidly as expected because of microprocessing accomplished on-site. A similar phenomenon may occur with electronic distribution of full-text of articles. Here widespread use of video disks by libraries may make centralized storage unnecessary. However, one of the problems of video disk technology for storing journal articles in libraries is in keeping current with new articles as they become available. It may be that the National Periodicals System will complement publishers by processing new articles and preparing these articles for the video disks to be distributed periodically to libraries. Apparently, it will be less expensive to redistribute the entire updated file than to add new materials to the old video disks in the libraries.

Mr. Mathews alluded to the possibility that libraries may not be necessary for distributing materials in the future. I don't believe this to be the case. I think that reference and storage in library-like organizations will always be required by users. In the first place, it is estimated that about 12 million scientific and technical articles have been published in the United States and access to some of these will continue to be necessary. Presently, about 73 percent of the readings of scientific articles come from individual subscriptions.[6] These are mostly newly published articles. Older articles are obtained through authors (12%) in the form of reprints or libraries (15%). The need to obtain older articles will always be required which suggests the need for storage by publishers, the National Periodicals System, libraries or users. Publishers have resisted distributing separates in the past and may continue to do so in the future. End-users appear to maintain their own files less frequently than in the past. Furthermore, recently graduated scientists simply do not have their own copies of past journal issues. Finally, the increase in multi-disciplinary science and availability of on-line searching would seem to make access to many more journals necessary.

The electronic processes also provide a great deal of flexibility of output which can enhance reading and assimilation of the information. For example, end-users could request alternative formats of the text that would suit their particular needs, for example for rapid scanning or in-depth reading. Rapid scanning can be facilitated by highlighting certain elements of text, narrowing column widths, widening space between lines and so on. Human factors considerations can also help in-depth reading through other alternative format structures. Electronic processes can also aid in combining mathematical formulae, data presentations and text in a way that meets alternative needs.

An electronic alternative system for journals is highly desirable and currently achievable through the technology mentioned by Mr. Mathews. It is believed that a majority of articles will be handled by at least some electronic processes throughout the origination, recording, preservation, end-use and transmission functions, but that not all articles will be incorporated into a comprehensive electronic alternative system in which no articles are distributed in paper form. Some articles will be processed electronically in different ways depending on the electronic capabilities of the senders and receivers involved.

Mr. Mathews has mentioned some major constraints in adoption of new technology. He dealt nicely with issues of regulatory controls and governance of library networks. Another principal constraint is the lack of incentive to change on the part of system participants. For example, authors are said to publish partially for prestige and recognition which results in professional advancement. Certainly, the "publish or perish" environment that exists in some fields of science and in some organizations creates incentive to publish and, therefore, any alternative communication system must meet this perceived need. Many publishers lack a financial incentive for drastically deviating from the current journal publishing practices. While many book and small journal publishers appear to have financial problems, most publishers of widely distributed journals are doing quite well financially. They make a comfortable margin on income or profits and they require much less capital to publish journals than books since the income from subscriptions is received before most costs are incurred. Therefore, the return on investment for journal publishing is favorable since capital requirements are low and net profit relatively high. Substitution of royalty payments in lieu of subscriptions is going to lessen this advantage some since photocopying takes place on many older publications and, therefore, the royalty income for these publications will take place over time. Thus, any new publishing systems, such as the proposed National Periodicals System, must incorporate some financial incentives or publishers are unlikely to want to change. Another problem is that some income is derived by publishers through sale of advertisements. Distribution of separates in any form appears to obviate use of advertising.

Libraries have little incentive to change their mode of operating unless their patrons and funders find such change desirable. While many libraries currently are becoming automated for cataloging, circulation and internal recordkeeping, they still require motivation to change their procedures in dealing with users. A study, recently performed by the University of Pittsburg (Chapter 16), also illustrates some resistance to technological change by public librarians which must also be addressed in the future.

Scientists as users also present some barriers to new systems that directly impact their behavior. [7] It has been claimed for many years that scientists would quickly adapt to the direct use of computer terminals and would search bibliographic data bases on-line. However, while some scientists do this, most still rely on an intermediary to perform their searches for them. This is partially because many scientists are without easy access to terminals and partially because some are reluctant to use terminals. [8] Regardless of the reasons, if an alternative journal publishing and distribution system involves direct on-line communication, some incentives must be provided to scientists and their behavior must be altered. It is believed that, in the future, new scientists who have been trained on terminals in high schools and universities will find it unacceptable to not have these facilities available for analysis, text processing, search and retrieval and other forms of communication.

In conclusion, I agree whole-heartedly with Mr. Mathews' assessment of the importance of new technology to library networking and the entire communication system within which networking resides. However, there are many barriers to achieving optimum systems of communication, including technology advances yet to be achieved, lack of standards or compatibility, governance, regulations, human behavior and participant incentives. It is essential that we address these constraints and strive towards systems that will yield greater social benefits with fewer expenditures. We will all gain by this.

REFERENCES

1. King, Donald W. and Nancy K. Roderer. Systems Analysis of Scientific and Technical Communication in the United States: The Electronic Alternative to Communication Through Paper-Based Journals. National Science Foundation Contract DSI-76-15515, Rockville, Md.: King Research, Inc., May 1978.

2. White, Robert B. "A Prototype for the Automated Office." Datamation, pp. 83-90 (April 1977).

3. King, op. cit.

4. Frost and Sullivan, Inc. "More Printers in Use." Data Communications, p. 16 (March/April 1976).

5. Wigington, Ronald L. Introducing New Technology. Paper presented to the Engineering Foundation Conference, Rindge, New Hampshire, August 14-19, 1977, Columbus, Ohio: Chemical Abstracts Service, 1977.

6. King, Donald W., Dennis D. McDonald and Nancy K. Roderer. The
    Journal System of Scientific and Technical Communication in the United
    States. Final Draft. National Science Foundation Contract DSI-75-
    06942. Rockville, Md.: King Research, Inc., December 1978.

7. King, Donald W. and Vernon E. Palmour. "User Behavior." In:
    Changing Patterns in Information Retrieval. Edited by Carol Fenichel.
    Philadelphia, Pennsylvania: American Society for Information Science,
    1974.

8. Katter, Robert V. and Davis B. McCarn. "AIM-TWX: An Experimental
    On-Line Bibliographic Retrieval System." In: Interactive Bibliographic
    Search: The User/Computer Interface. Edited by Donald E. Walker.
    Montvale, New Jersey: AFIPS Press, 1971.

Chapter 14

THE IMPACT OF TECHNOLOGY ON THE
GOVERNANCE OF LIBRARY NETWORKS: RESPONSE

Roger K. Summit

Director
Lockheed Information Systems
Palo Alto, California

In his paper "The Impact of Technology on the Governance of Library Networks" (Chapter 12), Mr. Mathews has appropriately suggested that never before has there been a technological convergence of such magnitude available to the information processing community. This technology affords the library community significant opportunities. At issue is how the community will or should organize itself to exploit these opportunities. As a private sector provider of library services, and one deeply immersed in dealing with these technological opportunities on a day-to-day basis, I wish to amplify and provide alternative interpretations for several of the points discussed in the paper.

Data Processing Technology. Mathews quite fittingly describes the onslaught of the microprocessor. He tends to neglect, however, the impact of large-scale integration (LSI), the technology which brought us the microprocessor, has had on large-scale computers. That today's microprocessor can functionally replace what used to occupy an entire room full of electronics a decade ago should not suggest that large-scale, centralized computing activities are declining in favor of the microcomputer or that the large-scale computer has not in its own right utilized LSI. LSI in large computers has enabled a room full of electronics to increase its processing potential by a factor of 100 over the past decade. The fact is that each of these areas of technology is developing along semi-independent and largely non-competing application lines.

The microprocessor has introduced data processing to the home and small office, areas largely unserved by large computers. Together with develop-

ments in telecommunications and data storage, large-scale computer technology has enabled centers such as those of SDC and Lockheed to provide a
worldwide network of librarians and other users access to a universe of
references and abstracts of a magnitude which was unanticipated as recently
as five years ago. Historically there has been a long standing debate in data
processing circles regarding the merits of centralized vs. decentralized (or
more recently, distributed) processing. The tradeoffs now as before concern
economies of scale associated with centralization, with attendant high utilization offset by telecommunications costs; versus the cost and convenience of
direct hands-on operation of local equipment, some elements of which might
be vastly under-utilized. Furthermore, it is seldom noted the cost of data
storage using floppy disks on microprocessors is 10-15 times the cost of the
latest large-scale disk storage. Couple this economy with the greater utilization of large-scale processors possible through telecommunications, and you
can see why information retrieval applications which require vast amounts of
data storage are cost attractive as centralized applications. Perhaps the
video disk will change these economics, or perhaps it will provide an opportunity for the large-scale center to provide access to more data.

If there is a trend to be discerned, it is that data processing in its several
manifestations is coming to be more familiar to and more widely accepted in
the community. Recognition that this increased use and acceptance represents an even greater market for the technology leads application developers
to respond by providing even more choices for the end-user.

Economics of Technology. Too frequently the major emphasis given to a
new technology is its cost-saving aspect. Although less measureable (and by
some standards thereby less important), the new opportunities for service
to library customers provided by a new development in technology are likely
to be far more significant than the cost savings, if any, they may provide.
In computer-based information retrieval services, for example, the trend
has not been to replace several reference librarians by a terminal (though
this was one of the early fears expressed by librarians). Quite to the contrary, the retrieval efficiency and comprehensiveness afforded by this technology has led to a dramatic increase in the use of secondary information by
the information user and an increased demand for librarians skilled in the
operation of these systems.

Telecommunications. One cannot over-emphasize the importance of the
trend toward deregulation which has been apparent within the FCC over the
past five years and now takes legislative form in the Communications Act of
1978. Previous deregulation has enabled the United States to spring ahead
of the rest of the world in computer-communications applications. Nowhere
else in the world, for example, can you communicate with a computer 3,000
miles away for a cost of $5.00 per hour (or even $50.00 per hour). As the

rest of the world struggles with issues long settled in this country, we are moving ahead to the even more exciting possibilities afforded by the broadband, digital datacommunications suggested by Mathews.

Governance. Let me concur in Mathews' point of discarding xenophobia. The library community can either be shoppers or developers, but probably not both. The plethora of choices available in the consumer market place is because consumers are shoppers. The choices available to libraries such as information retrieval services, shared cataloging, and automated circulation control result from the perception of the library as a market. To the extent that this market is perceived, there will be an army of application technologists who are willing to absorb research and development costs to provide the library community with choices. Should the provision of services tend to become monopolized through centralization or centralized control, choice is likely to disappear.

The governance of library networks should thus act to insure a lively and competitive supplier community and to insure an avoidance of dependence on any single supply authority. The new technology should be looked to for new opportunities for service to the library user, as opposed to strictly saving cost on existing service. It is through the library becoming ever more a first choice for information services that it gains strength in its community and presents a market for system designers. The library as an institutional shopper will be offered choices to evaluate, select from, or discard as appropriate. Xenophobia can only lead to a loss of choice and an ever greater dependence on a centralized governance authority for decision making.

To paraphrase an ancient wisdom: beware of bureaucrats bearing gifts.

Chapter 15

THE IMPACT OF TECHNOLOGY ON THE
GOVERNANCE OF LIBRARY NETWORKS: REACTIONS

Robert M. Hayes

Dean
Graduate School of Library and Information Science
University of California, Los Angeles
Los Angeles, California

INTRODUCTION

In his position paper, Mr. Mathews provides us with an excellent vision of
technological capabilities and opportunities. The advances in computers, in
data storage media, and in communications continue to amaze even those
who have been deeply involved for years in utilizing them. Perhaps the most
remarkable phenomenon today, however, is the extent to which they are now
represented in consumer products. Computers, fully the equivalent of the
most sophisticated and advanced devices of just twenty-five years ago, can
be purchased and consumed as though they were television sets.

The long range results of this consumer revolution are certain to be far
greater than merely the distribution of computing power in cheap, easily
accessible form. It will bring a familiarity with these devices on the part
of the general public that will make use of them in every aspect of life far
more accepted and expected than even television has been.

Even more importantly, it will result in massive increases in the number
of people able to work with these devices. Already we see the hobbyists
trading programs—marketing programs—of increasing sophistication.

All of which goes to say that the picture presented by Mr. Mathews is
realistic in its projection of capabilities and opportunities, even conserva-
tive.

Mr. Mathews has also identified areas in which there are problems, deficiencies and lacks if libraries and library networks are effectively to utilize these capabilities. The problems in developing software are evident, and even the growth of sophistication in the public's use of these devices is unlikely to change them. The problems in establishing generally accepted standards are likely to increase, not decrease, as the technology continues to explode. And management and governance? We are just beginning to learn how to cope with the problems involved.

Mr. Mathews discusses some of those problems and, since I am going to focus on some specific issues involved in them, I want briefly to summarize them. He comments on the need for structure, although he doesn't talk specifically, so I will refer to this problem in some detail and with a specific bias. He comments on the need to manage change, innovation, the transfer of technology; and he comments on the need to deal with the dislocations they create. It is primarily the dislocations that I want to explore in somewhat more detail. He comments on the need to assess and to evaluate, to make designs in a context for which there is no grand plan. It is the problems for governance posed by making those choices with which I will be primarily concerned.

Thus, Mr. Mathews has provided an extremely valuable context in which I now want to deal with some specific problems for governance of library networks that are either created by or exacerbated by technology. I also want to deal with some specific opportunities in governance that are provided by the trends in technological development, especially with respect to network structure.

Before turning to specifics, however, I must set the stage with another set of preliminary comments concerning the nature of governance. Governance is essentially a political process in which the conflicting or, at least, the divergent views of various groups are, we hope, reconciled—not eliminated, not overridden, not glossed over or ignored, but resolved. As Ervin Gaines so elegantly stated (Chapter 4), there is indeed value in diversity, and the role of governance is to assure the preservation of diverse objectives while achieving jointly perceived objectives.

The problem, as Tom Galvin epitomized yesterday, is that all of the participants hold stakes which they may be willing to invest but are reluctant to lose. So the process of governance must recognize all of the stakeholders and provide the means for reconciling their differences. Those who are served by the library network, those that represent existing institutional participants, those who will manage the network, those who will provide the funding, those who will sell their products and services—all will in one way or another participate.

I have explicated this view of governance because I want the problems I will identify to be seen as points or issues of reconcilable conflict. I cannot guess what the basis of resolution will be in any specific situation, much less in general. I can say that these problems have arisen in the past; they will arise in the future; and they are the impact of technology on governance.

THE PROBLEMS

These problems are each illustrative of typical issues that arise in governance. They are therefore not unique to technology, although they have some specific aspects due to technology. I am going to try to avoid repeating Mr. Mathews' own coverage, including areas such as legal problems.

Conformance to Standards. In every network to date and I'm sure in each of those in the future, the issue of conformance to standards has been a critical problem. The development of the MARC II format required the most careful process of governance, of balancing needs perceived by widely variant groups. It continues to plague us, and each network must resolve anew the issue of how much it requires in the way of conformance to MARC II format and content.

Standards for equipment compatibility continue to plague us and while, on the one hand, we get machines that are virtual duplicates of other machines, on the other hand, the technology continues to spew out new devices that create new problems in compatibility. And I can't use the same terminal to talk to all of the data base systems without modification.

Standards for software compatibility represent especially difficult problems. Are they to be set at the level of least common denominator among network participants, with the consequent problems in adapting them to larger needs, or are they to be set at the maximum level, with the consequent costs of overdesigns for some participants?

Standards for authority files are an initial problem forced upon us by the opportunities in the technology, but with no easy basis for reconciliation. The decision to close the catalog, to opt for AACR 2, almost by fiat, presents every participant in the national network with internal decisions. And the use of technology makes those decisions harder to make, if diversity is wanted, not easier.

Commitment of Resources. I want now to turn to another set of problems exacerbated by technology. They arise in a variety of ways, each of which appears to be a technical decision but each of which reflects the underlying issue of how existing resources have been committed and of how future resources will be committed.

The problem is created because of the differential way in which network participants have implemented systems. They have proceeded at different rates in implementation and have emphasized different functions to be implemented. Decisions that appear simple in isolation become exceedingly complex because of the capital resources already committed. Costs of conversion of files, installation of equipment, training of staff, changes in operation—all represent a vested interest, a stake in the decision.

Those existing investments can become the underlying basis for irreconcilable conflicts, unless the network governance handles them with clear awareness. While they are significant in any context of governance, they are especially so when technology is involved. Each of the kinds of cost I've identified is a direct result of decisions to implement changes in system to take advantage of a technology. If the network chooses an incompatible technology, or even simply another one, those investments may be lost.

When new investments are involved, of course, the problems become even more involved, especially if the systems approach is involved. What portion of costs represents network objectives in contrast to participant objectives and who pays for what? The technology permits us to take advantage of cataloging systems that will serve both kinds of objectives, but how do we decide on the system to be used when those objectives are in conflict?

Functional Objectives. Which brings me to another set of problems, ones that arise even if costs are set aside. Each participant in a network has its own set of priorities, its own constituency to be served. Those priorities are likely to be divergent from those of other participants and of the network. This is the reason that differential implementation is a reality, and will continue to be so.

Is the cataloging system, required if the network is to produce a union catalog, more important at this time than the circulation control system required to assure ready access to the library's own holdings? That's not a hypothetical conflict. It has occurred.

Is the implementation of a system at this time going so to disrupt existing services that it would damage the library's credibility with its own readers?

Each library will, of necessity and not out of arbitrary recalcitrance, evaluate the answers to such questions differently. Even those developing network capabilities make different decisions about priorities. Just look at the differences among the several available on-line cataloging services.

Expectations and Credibility. The technology is such a wondrous thing. It promises so much—but of course it sometimes delivers so little. In a world of great expectations, even small failures can result in disastrous loss

of credibility. People evaluate the likelihood of success with different criteria of what is important. They have differing levels and kinds of exposure
if failure comes, so they evaluate the effects of failure differently.

If those providing funds for installation of equipment have done so with
expectations of cost savings or of functional gains, the governance of the network had better have means for reconciling those expectations with reality.
And there is a siren-like attraction to technology that seems to call to everyone concerned with funding. It offers so much potential for saving in future
operations, doesn't it? It provides such fantastic capabilities for future service, doesn't it?

THE OPPORTUNITIES

If that all sounds bleak, please forgive me. It wasn't intended to. My aim
was simply to bring out some of the sources of specific conflict with which
networks, as cooperative structures involving institutions and people with
divergent views and needs, must deal.

But the technology is a source of opportunity as well as of potential conflict, so I want to conclude with a brief discussion of what I see—with emphasis not on "gee whiz, look what we can do" but on governance, and especially on network structure.

Each network faces a central technical issue with immediate effect upon
its governance. It's the choice between centralization and decentralization.
Democratic though the governance may appear to be, the nature of centralization is that it places power over decisions in the hands of those with day to
day management responsibility over operations.

Ten years ago, the great theme in evaluation of computer installations was
centralization. Grosch's law, that computing power goes up as the square of
the cost, clearly supported that choice. Systems were predicated upon its
validity as a technical and economic fact of life.

I think the technical discussion yesterday, as well as the substance of Mr.
Mathews' paper, clearly demonstrates that such a picture is no longer valid.
The technology permits us to decentralize to an extent never before dreamed
of. The microcomputer, the inexpensive mass storage system of immense
capacity, the communication network—all provide network governance with
a clear choice. Carlos Cuadra and Charles Benton clearly identified it.

The opportunity is there not only for the networks but for the entrepreneurs
developing technological packages. Every functional goal in network operation

to which technology may clearly be applicable can be achieved without creating monolithic structure, great network centers, or straitjackets of network specifications. Doing so is a great opportunity.

As a life-long believer in decentralization, in local autonomy, and in the cooperation implied by networks, I believe the technology has more to offer us than simply more functional capability.

I encourage you to consider those aspects when you are evaluating the impact of the technology on governance.

Chapter 16

TECHNOLOGY AND THE HUMAN FACTOR

Sara Fine

Associate Professor
Department of Library Science
University of Pittsburgh
Pittsburgh, Pennsylvania

The world of technology is a complicated one for many of us. As a psychologist involved and committed to the library profession, I am forced to confront the problems of people as they struggle with the effects of high velocity change. It is from this viewpoint that I react to the position papers of this conference.

Each of the papers recognizes that we are dealing with two interwoven themes: the technology that makes networks possible, and the human factor which is both the inventor and the user of that technology. The purpose of this conference is to talk about ways to bring the two together, to establish a linkage between machines and their creators. There is never a question that these two factors are interlocking and interdependent and equally significant. But one of the ways that we reveal how we really think and feel is by how much we say, or how little we say; by what we include and what we don't include; by how we choose to describe something and by how much value we place on it; by what we emphasize, and by how we balance our words and phrases. I'd like to point out the way in which these two themes, the technology factor and the human factor, are balanced and treated in these papers.

Technology is seen as complex and sophisticated, capable of endless variation and possibility, as constantly changing and maturing, as dynamic and endlessly interesting, as dramatic and awesome, and perhaps a little frightening. When there is a problem with technology, it is analyzed and weighed, solutions are proposed and tested. If there is a functional breakdown, it is probed, diagnosed, and repaired, and each time we go through the process of coping with a problem, we have learned something new. Time and re-

search, patience and experiment, bring us a deepened understanding of technological functioning, and therefore make more things possible. No one
labels technology as resistant, irrational, stubborn or insubordinate. We
see an insoluble technological problem as caused by our miscalculation or
lack of understanding; it never rests with a flaw in the mechanism.

Not so with the human factor. Human behavior is treated simplistically.
Human actions and reactions seem to have a simple and single cause; dis-
sent, disagreement, resistance are seen as inexplicable, and therefore irrational. Human problems are never seen as caused by our miscalculations
or lack of understanding, but rather by a flaw in the way people are constituted. There is an off-handedness in our discussions. Behavior that we
don't like or don't understand is labeled or diagnosed; then it can be dismissed. We seldom say, "We haven't learned to cope with this dimension."
We therefore tend to believe that we are coping with it.

I believe that underneath it all what we are really saying is that the human
behavior factor is so complicated that it is beyond our reach to understand it
and affect it. But there's the dilemma—we can't afford not to understand.
The technology, the network, the information are only one side. If we minimize the other side, we fail. I'd like to propose a hypothesis: that human
behavior is always rational, even though when we look at someone else's
behavior we don't always have enough information to understand the rationality. Sometimes we don't even have enough information to understand the
rationality of our own behavior. I am suggesting that if we are ever to truly
develop the linkage between machines and people, we may need to consider
the irrationality of technology and the rationality of people. Technology is
of course logical, but this doesn't mean it's always rational; after all, technology doesn't have personal and social needs to fulfill. People, of course,
are not always logical, but they are always rational, rational enough so that
they will always act to maintain the balance of their lives.

When I read through the position papers as a whole, I was struck by the
contrast—the depth and sensitivity with which progress and potential in technology are treated versus a limited and narrow view of human potential. I'd
like to talk about some of the ways in which this impression was created for
me.

The first paper (Chapter 1) sets the tone and direction of this conference.
It is a clear and positive statement on networking—where we are, how far
we've come, where we need to go next. We no longer meet to discuss
"whether to" but rather "how to." It alludes to some of the behavioral factors
that have been and must yet be resolved. But just beneath the surface of this
paper lies a riddle: Why won't people do what's good for them? The answer
to the riddle is also implied: Everyone knows that people are resistant to
change. Next question: What is resistance to change? The answer circles

right back: Resistance to change is when people won't do what's good for
them. I wonder how far technology would have progressed in the face of such
reasoning.

There is a second riddle: If people are indeed resistant to change, then
perhaps resistance is a normal function, essential for physical and psychological and social survival. On the other hand, if an organism does not adapt
and change with a changing environment, it will die, become extinct. It
would seem, then, that we need to distinguish healthful resistance to changes
that are damaging or happening too fast from unhealthy resistance to beneficial change. Question: How can this be done?

The second paper (Chapter 6) picks up the thread. In discovering that
current networks engage in educational and training activities, Williams and
Flynn accurately interpret this as training for the purpose of changing attitudes toward networks and their functioning. But they unrealistically suggest
that the "initial period of networking will no doubt require 'training in attitude'
which hopefully will be a one-time task, with the next generation of users and
librarians taking (the concept of networking) for granted." Question: Does
this mean that librarians and users will come to accept and love networking
as a result of this "training in attitude"? Does it mean that if we just point
out the beneficial trade-offs to libraries and librarians that they will come to
realize that it's for their own good? Does it mean that trainees will finally
realize that networks are here to stay whether they accept them or not, so
they might as well accept them? And for us, another question: Are we really
concerned with why a new concept is accepted as long as it is accepted?

I'd like to pose a second hypothesis about human behavior: there is no
system that managers can create that workers can't beat! Perhaps it is important that we know why what's happening is happening or we may find out
that what we thought was a functioning system just won't work. I don't believe
that the training in attitude which is proposed—consisting of "personal communications, meetings, and brochures," even if sessions in how to use the
system are included—will begin to impact on the real factors that generate
resistance. I think that training in attitude is an extremely valuable kind of
intervention when people or organizations are experiencing rapid change.
But I think we may need to question—who needs the training? Perhaps it is
us, the innovators? And perhaps we should consider that attitude training,
if it is truly that, often changes the attitudes of trainers more than the attitudes of trainees.

Training for change is a creative notion and a valuable one for easing the
stress of transition. I'd like to point out, however, that it is a highly complex activity and that the development of a model for attitude training requires
at least the same kind of complex analysis of the factors involved as does the
development of a network itself.

The paper on Purposes and Expectations (Chapter 18) adds further insight into the treatment of the human factors of resistance. Leon Montgomery and Ed Dowlin rephrase the riddle. Instead of asking "why won't people do what's good for them?" a question is posed that continues to rankle: "There have been many developments (toward the feasibility of a national and international network), but library networks are still in their infancy. Why?" According to Orin Nolting, there are nine factors that constitute the psychological barriers to "cooperation" (translation: acceptance of a proposed concept):

1. The custodial mentality of librarians
2. Fear of loss of local autonomy
3. Clash of personalities
4. Jealousy and stubbornness
5. Complacency and self-satisfaction
6. Mistrust between librarians
7. Inertia and indifference
8. Unwillingness to experiment
9. Assumption that each library has unique rather than common-place needs.

I'd like to add a few characteristics to that list. On behalf of librarians and library administrators, who incidentally are categorized as possessing all nine of these characteristics, I'd like to say that in addition to those characteristics I am now also hostile, defensive, angry, resistant, and outraged.

The authors of the paper then point out that although Nolting has catalogued these factors, "he has not provided a point of attack for surmounting these barriers." I believe that Nolting has not mounted an attack on these factors because they don't exist, and because Nolting doesn't begin to understand what does exist. I'd like to propose a third hypothesis in human behavior: labeling someone else's motives is not synonomous with understanding; in fact, it is antithetical to understanding. Labeling someone, or in this case a group of someones, as jealous and stubborn, does not help solve human problems. It does not diffuse resistance; it fuels its fire.

But let's look at Nolting's points and consider that he has recognized nine kinds of librarian behavior. Perhaps instead of disregarding his data, we might reinterpret them. The nine points again:

Perhaps "the custodial mentality of librarians" is actually a sense of professionalism and pride.

Perhaps "fear of loss of local autonomy" implies the dedication to provide service to the constituency without fear of external interference or control.

Perhaps "clash of personalities" is actually a willingness to confront the inequities and ineptitudes of a bureaucratic administration.

Perhaps "jealousy and stubbornness" is disagreement about the interpretation of one's professional role.

Perhaps "complacency and self-satisfaction" is the recognition that librarianship is significant in a changing society.

Perhaps "mistrust between librarians" refers to differing values and goals or perhaps even to generational or cultural differences.

Perhaps "inertia and indifference" are the posture of last resort in an autocratic environment.

Perhaps "unwillingness to experiment" is the refusal to comply with that which someone else has imposed.

Perhaps the belief that one's library "has unique rather than commonplace needs" is the highest praise that one can bestow on a professional librarian.

There is nothing to gain by labeling valuable behavior as a barrier, except as a device for dismissing it. It seems much more constructive to call that which is good good and to move from the strength we already have to the strength we are yet capable of.

In reading William Mathews' paper (Chapter 12), I think I gained some insight, an awareness of something I had not realized before. First let me admit that I was sidetracked from that insight by three behavioral issues.

First, I was distracted by the reference to the "servant versus master" theme, which is too important for many people—both technologists and lay people—to be treated lightly and dismissed. There are too many profound implications in the growth of a technological society, too many social and political issues at stake, and too many unvoiced reservations about the ramifications of such easy access to so much information. I believe that it is not an issue to be taken lightly. A casual reference does not imply concern —it implies dismissal.

Secondly, there is a quality of unreality, of innocence, in the description of the governors who should be selected to assume leadership in the future structure of networks. Don't we all want leaders who are flexible, creative, wise, cautious yet certain, understanding yet directive? I guess I can't speak for anyone else; but for myself, I will not willingly give up the control or direction of the future—even to such leaders.

Thirdly, I'd like to read you a passage from the paper and then tell you what I think it means:

"Libraries and library networks had nothing to do with the many
rapid advances in technology mentioned earlier in this paper.
Library networks are nearly imperceptible as a driving force
behind the technology. No one asked the library networks what
kind of microprocessor did they want, how did they intend to
store their information or who did they expect to transmit that
information to. Fortunately they didn't ask, we might add, for
they might still be waiting for an answer."

I think the passage means that librarians have not specified their needs and
told the manufacturers what they want. The manufacturers have developed
technology for other markets, and together with library network designers,
have then applied the available technology to the library.

But on another level I think I hear another message—librarians don't
know what they want and need. Experts must tell them. On behalf of librarians and library administrators, those of us who had nothing to do with and
nothing to say about the many rapid technological advances, I am affronted
by being told that someone else should decide what's good for me; whether
it is or isn't good for me is irrelevant. A fourth hypothesis about human
behavior: sometimes it's the style and the source rather than the message
that we resist.

But now, I'd like to share a thought with you. There is another message
in Mr. Mathews' paper that is loud and clear and refreshing. There is a
quality of expertise mixed with excitement, vision mixed with enthusiasm.
One has the sense of movement and progress, and a profound impatience with
impediments to the progress. Mr. Mathews' paper reveals a thorough understanding of the technology that may be applicable to our field and the impatience of an expert who, as a member of the NCLIS staff, is on the cutting
edge of the future. Perhaps it is this quality of impatience mixed with vision
that separates the technologist from the practitioner. The challenge is to
bring them together.

Chapter 17

TECHNOLOGY: DISCUSSION

The discussion which follows has been transcribed from tape recordings, summarized and edited. Comments and questions have been attributed to speakers when their identity was provided. The editors of these proceedings take responsibility for any errors in fact or interpretation resulting from this process, since it was not feasible to provide proofs to discussants for checking.

Roger Summit

I'd like to try something with regard to Sara Fine's presentation, particularly that point that librarians don't know their needs, but experts must tell them what they need. Discussions of memory functions distinguish between recall, recognition, and relearning as three degrees of sensitivity in memory. If we examine recall and recognition, we can all go back in our minds but probably can't remember our fifth grade mathematics teachers; but if you are presented with a list of names which includes the name of the fifth grade mathematics teacher, you are very likely to recognize that name. Now if we apply that in this situation, whereas librarians may not have the expertise and knowledge to creatively design an innovative system using the new technology, I would argue that they are perfectly capable of recognizing applications of that technology which suit their needs, given a proper variety of choice for this recognition. I agree with Ervin Gaines that there remain a variety of choices for the librarian to select from.

Sara Fine

I suddenly realize that we are talking about two different things. I'm not suggesting that librarians want to develop the technology, even though I'm wondering why they can't be shoppers and developers. Rather, I'm talking about a posture toward librarians; I'm talking on a process level—a kind of attitude that comes across in the literature and it comes across when you hear interactions between technologists and librarians that I think creates difficulties that don't need to exist.

William Mathews

I have been interested in the tendency that we've seen here to start recognizing the human dimensions and the public policy issues that are posed by technology. The technology, in itself, is not the issue. It's how do we cope with it.

Jack Belzer - University of Pittsburgh

Several weeks ago I wanted to find out what kind of computers we are going to use five to ten years from now. I got in touch with some people from IBM and asked them what they have on the drawing board. I assumed what they have on the drawing board and what they're going to produce is what we are going to use 5-10 years from now.

Several people here have been mixing up technology and knowledge and information. I define knowledge in several ways but that which I know is knowledge. But also if I know where to find it, that's also knowledge and information. We are now moving from a technology era into a knowledge and information era. For example, the many things that William Mathews has mentioned are not technology, they are knowledge. A computer is technology, but the programming to make the computer do innovative and imaginative things is not technology. The computer playing chess is not technology. People are not afraid of the technology; they are afraid of the knowledge and information. I think that the White House Conference must address the fact that we are moving into a knowledge and information era.

During the discussion of governance, a question came up about who's boss. This boss in governance is pretty much who controls the finances, the budget, and who can punish for not doing what he wants done and reward someone else. Governance basically is creating some sort of a power base by individuals and, as a result of that, I welcome diversity.

When I have a dollar I think of a hot dog and a Coke; but when I have a million dollars I do not think of a million Cokes and a million hot dogs. My range and scope of thinking is enlarged. I think that with the new technology and the new knowledge we should enlarge our own scope and range of thinking; we should not think of the kinds of things we were doing 25 and 30 years, but rather the kind of things we might want to do 20 years from now and perhaps ask why can't we do them now and find out what we lack and maybe bridge that gap.

Maurice Freedman - School of Library Service, Columbia University

William Mathews (Chapter 12) stated: "Once a management team is put together it should be the firm determination of people involved in governance to stay out of their way. Governance may countercheck or delimit management, but it should never directly meddle with management's responsibilities." I would think governance requires a review process. There must not be meddling, that's a fair point. The operational responsibilities of management should be left to management. There must be some board or independently appointed people whose job is to provide control over management to ensure that goals are being met, as opposed to rubberstamping or no control at all. I think there's a role for policy making outside of the management and review.

Would William Mathews relate some of the technology that he discussed to the current cataloging and circulation areas?

William Mathews

Let me speak first of all about your point concerning the differentiation between governance and management. And I think your point is well taken and absolutely correct. There has to be a review process and a very close review. In fact, governance is the policy making mechanism. What I was reflecting in the few sentences quoted was the ready tendency for both sides of the equation to invade each other's territory. On the latter point, Robert Hayes pointed this out (Chapter 15) when he emphasized again that the technology now permits a much greater distributed view of what a network may be: distribution of the information, the data bases, the telecommunications, but most important the distribution of responsibilities to individual organizations and institutions.

Patricia Sachs - Cedar Crest and Muhlenberg Colleges

Several speakers have addressed, with cautionary notes, the monopolistic organization of information services and/or the vendors of those services. I understand those reservations, particularly as they apply to publishing, freedom of access to information principles, and the specter of information management that accompanies them. I am, however, concerned about elements that seem to focus on such monopolism (for example, costs) relating to the delivery of information services. In that regard, I hear the voices of some of the delegates (particularly citizens of Pennsylvania) at the Governor's Conference in Pennsylvania concerned about the increasing cost of services, including information services.

My second concern relates to standards and the implementation of effective standards such as MARC II or standards relating to equipment. My third concern is the technology itself—of distribution systems. I think of analogies such as AT&T, The Pennsylvania Power and Light Company, and other utilities with protective monopolies. I sense that in some of the comments that have already been made here that there is an undercurrent of fears and apprehension relating to the possibilities that we may be headed toward some type of monopolistic organization of our information services. And that we are headed in that direction because it is required by such elements as cost, distribution systems, and standards. I'm wondering if any panelists think that the future is really an information utility, with some types of legal controls.

Roger Summit

It is truly the dilemma: the trade off between efficiency and centralized control and the working of a marketplace situation providing diversity through competitive free enterprise. But if we take the information utility notion and we look at AT&T as a protective monopoly, I think that historically there were reasons to establish AT&T as a protective monopoly because of duplication of lines stringing around the country. And obviously we didn't want many suppliers stringing many lines in competition. However, the FCC's position of recent vintage to deregulate AT&T and introduce competition into communications (which is possible now because communications are carried on other than by land lines) has resulted in fantastic benefits through the community. This is unique in the world and many of us don't understand and appreciate this. So with regard to an information utility, although one can make arguments on cost savings and efficiencies (perhaps efficiencies of scale which might be possible through such a utility), still one must offset that with the threat of centralized control and centralized dictum. I think that the competitive forces of a free enterprise marketplace probably are going to bring lower costs and greater variety of selection than the theoretical efficiency that might be possible through centralization and centralized regulation.

John Linford - NELINET

Donald King (Chapter 13) questioned Mathews' implication that libraries may not survive. King says "yes"; Mathews says "well maybe." I have to take a view that says that libraries as they are now constituted may in fact not survive, and I refer you to Gerald Sophar's comment (Chapter 11) that many information needs are being met outside the current library structures and outside the current information base structures. I think that libraries have a decision window (a time window) for making a decision to either get into it or to stay out of it, and the effect will be the result of their decision. I share almost all of William Mathews' enthusiasms. I have to emphasize the microcomputer aspect: there is in my mind a clear analogy between microcomputer technology and the old printing technology. As soon as printing technology made books cheap enough for people to be able to afford them, it then became economical, in terms of time and their interest, to learn to read. The same has happened with the microcomputers. Now the micro-computers are cheap enough for people to be able to afford them, and it has become economical, in terms of time and interest, to learn to program them. The effect of printing on the intellectual revolution was enormous, and I think it would be a mistake to underestimate both the enormity of the mircocom-puter revolution and the speed at which it will take place. One of the major effects of printing and now with microcomputers is to distribute the imagina-tion—the ability to apply imagination to problems.

Every time I've gone into a shop and implemented a library automation project there have been four stages: (1) skepticism, (2) gradual acceptance, (3) learning, and (4) demand for advanced services. I don't think that the human element is as far behind as the technologists suggest.

Mathews says that applications in libraries follow technology, rather than being the cause of it. That may be good or bad, but we've got to accept it and begin to deal with it.

George Kobulnicky - West Virginia Northern Community College

Has NCLIS or any other organization done any legal research on the im-pact of network development on privacy?

William Mathews

I would like to make clear for the record that my paper (Chapter 12) was not an agency point of view; it was my own personal point of view. The question raised is a very important one which NCLIS recognized after con-ducting a study of computer-to-computer protocals. A task force (sponsored by NCLIS with assistance from the National Bureau of Standards) was exam-ining how to facilitate communication between diverse computer systems with different operating systems. It was only after going through much of that exercise that we concluded and understood that we did not know what the impact of our own work in that area might be. You are quite correct in say-ing more attention should be paid to the legal areas and a close look at how this is going to affect us.

Marc D'Alleyrand - Teachers College, Columbia University

I would like to address myself to one aspect of the definition of network as given yesterday: "If you say it's a network, it must be a network." I will try to see whether there are any implications for governance in terms of technology. The understanding of the implications of technology for libraries requires education and training mechanisms, with appropriate response time to allow up-to-date knowledge of possibilities and limitations of such technologies. It is obvious that if the training mechanism cannot catch up with the technology, then somebody else is going to tell you what you need and you're going to have to take his or her word for it. The question of response time is probably a crucial element. And that means very active training, training of the trainer, etc. One should be at least up-to-date if not at the forefront of understanding of the implications of technology. Therefore, the presence of such training may be a required and definitely identified component in the governance of any operating, full-fledged network; and that might help to define more clearly and more successfully what is actually a network.

David Weill - New England Library Board

I'd like to build on Sara Fine's comments on dislocation (Chapter 16). I think her comments were fairly well limited to library practitioners. I'd like to talk about the dislocation effects of library technology on our clients and our nonclients. The people who libraries now serve particularly badly or don't serve at all are in more trouble with the advent of the so-called age of information. More trouble for libraries. Shifting from the production of goods to production of services creates, as we all know, a greater loss to that large segment of the population which previously found personal and social values in work and in the production of goods. Now the products of work are growing more intangible and so are the rewards. The dislocation in our society comes from the lack of alternative reward systems, and technology cannot provide them except in terms of video games.

I have heard no one say, and I have read in no paper, that anyone believes that there is a trickle-down benefit of technology to the large segment of our population (70%) who don't use libraries at all. There is no trickle-down benefit from the continuing development of technology. This would seem to suggest that we will serve even more poorly those people whom we do not serve very well now: those people who exist in this area of information but certainly are not living in it.

Video games are the inevitable horrible expression of the impact of technology on cultural values. If Mathews is correct—that people will spend more on video garbage than on library acquisitions—we should be thunderstruck with the implications. What is the percentage of the population that is going to benefit from the theme of this whole conference? Five percent? Rather than blithely assert that video games will lead inevitably to personal computing, I think we ought to reassert our commitment to that very large proportion of the population that will not benefit from what we are doing here this week.

Sara Fine

The phenomenon of resistance is multidimensional; it means different things to different people, and it means different things to the same person under different circumstances. One of the things that Jack Belzer said that really intrigued me was that people are not afraid of the technology but of the knowledge. And I have to think about that one because I think there's some truth in it. I was interested in John Linford's model for how innovation takes place. I've now heard a couple of times a concept that intrigues me and I don't understand it. The word "dislocation": I wonder if Mr. Weill and Mr. Mathews could tell me what that really means, because I think it's a very interesting concept.

David Weill

In the mass production of cars, one could talk about dislocation, since a person couldn't see the whole car but only the part he built. When people are processing information, when they are finished there is nothing to look at except something intangible; many are not able to find rewards in such activity. I would hope that most librarians are able to find satisfaction in intangible successes, but not everyone can. So we build new things for people to do. I'm sure some have been thinking about some of the popular novels of the 1930's that predicted the horrors of the coming fifty years; to me video games are the ultimate expression of that sort of thing (perhaps something that Huxley might very well have pointed out if he had thought of it). That is my understanding of "dislocation" in this particular context.

Sara Fine

A kind of disorientation; a feeling that everything is coming loose.

James Williams

Mr. Weill stated that 70% of the people in this country don't use libraries, but I think we should make the distinction between 70% of the people not using libraries and the fact that there are not 70% of the people in this country who do not use information. Perhaps the question is how can libraries become integral to those people who need information?

William Mathews

I would like to make a brief comment on dislocation. I'm taking a cue from Sara Fine that we should view these things more positively. The materials scientist thinks about dislocation very often in crystal structures and crystal growth—when something unexpected happens and it disrupts the regular pattern or latticework of the crystal. (Most of the properties which we now come to value in the semiconductor industry are based on the fact that dislocations do occur.) Almost like the mountain climber they make progress by stepping on the little tiny fractures and dislocations in the face of a rock. So I think if we can view dislocations as opportunities, we will have progressed quite a bit.

Donald King

I think there's one form of technology that hasn't been mentioned this morning but which I believe was mentioned in Mathews' paper (Chapter 12): the technology that has been developed and is now being tested in England under the name of View Data or Prestel. This addresses the issue of the 70% of the people who are not now being served by librarians but are information users. This test is going on in England under the cosponsorship of the British Library and ASLIB; it is providing people, through their own personal television, a great deal of information about public services, availability of health services, etc. And I do think that libraries as we now know them may have a role in the kind of information that might be provided through that kind of media.

Gaya Agrawal - Robert Morris College

Three basic variables in creating a network were discussed: (1) different practices, systems and needs; (2) software; and (3) microcomputers. Given these three variables, how can we decide on interrelated network activities, software, and decentralized minicomputers?

William Mathews

Some of the diversity that we see in the libraries is functional and some of it is not. We would not want to encourage some of it. While there is a lot of diversity and pluralism to be looked for, appreciated and expanded in the development of networks, we should not take the view that all of the practices, whatever they may be, should continue unchanged. I think we are raising some of the technical questions that are going to take years to sort out. You are asking questions concerning the basic difference between centrality and distribution of function. And I think we're at a much too preliminary stage to even say how much of that problem can be solved technically and how much of it will be.

Robert Hayes

From my standpoint the answer is entepreneurial; namely, there is the opportunity for development of commercially viable packages and services which the individual institution and the individual library will acquire by its own choice, its own selection from what is available. Thus if there are different functions to be addressed, and the library has different priorities on how they should be addressed, it will choose from that vendor providing the package and service most closely approximating their needs. In contrast is the more monolithic approach which identifies a single package service and in some way or another makes that the network requirement. It is that against which I have argued and am in favor of the individual choice, given an array of available services. So I'm arguing for individual choice; I'm also saying the opportunity is there for the entepreneur to provide the services that will best meet that market.

Virginia Gleason - Bituminous Coal Research, Inc.

I'm going to address the comment brought up by Mr. Weill about the large numbers of people who do not use library or information services. Also in a way it's in relation to Sara Fine's contrast between the human element and the way we look at technology. We're a very small library at Bituminous. I'm a literature information specialist, and our librarian and I get many calls and questions for information from people who work for places like U.S. Steel and Gulf Oil Company. They call us first because they've seen that we have "coal" in our name instead of going to their own library. They are not thinking of the library first. Also, in 1972 I attended a conference that EPA sponsored on environmental information. William Ruckelshaus was the EPA administrator. He really upset all of the Federal librarians who were there because in his keynote speech he mentioned that there was all sorts of information all over the place but no one knew how to find it. You can imagine how that could upset a library and information community. As a matter of fact, the librarians all got together and developed for him a little position paper. I think this is an example of the fact that we in the information area know what's available and we know how to get it. But there are so many people out there who need to know but don't know how to get to know. The one word that has surfaced that says something to me here at this conference today is marketing. Let us try to use marketing in the sense of getting as many people as possible to know what we have to offer.

Carlos Cuadra - Cuadra Associates

I have several comments; one has to do with financial impact of the new technology. Recently a staff member of mine was conducting a training session at a company which said that they have a microcomputer and regularly log into one of the major on-line systems and copy a large portion of the data base onto their microcomputer, turn off the system, and then proceed to spend the rest of the day working with this subsetted data. I later talked to the developer of the service and asked what their policy was about this. He said they don't care. And the reason they didn't care is because they

have a large front-end fee that they charge the user for the privilege of accessing the data base, so they don't really care whether the user uses the
big computer (their big computer) or the user's own microcomputer. On the
other hand, another data base owner that was experiencing the same problem
of having people log in, copy data, and turn it off, was forced to take their
data base "off the air" because they had no way of controlling this erosion of
their income. They now distribute this data base directly on floppy disc
which they mail to their customers. So it's clear that new technology, microcomputer technology, can have and is already having a very substantial impact on some areas of the on-line reference business. We can probably see
some changes in pricing methods for those data base producers who feel that
in order to protect themselves against rip off of their data they must have a
front-end fee.

My second point: The decreasing cost and the increasing power of small
computers, and the improvements in storage as well, facilitate the ease of
entry by new services into the on-line data base business. A number of private companies have cosponsored a study to look at the whole on-line data
base marketplace (companies like McGraw-Hill, Wiley, Control Data, GE,
CBS, Bell & Howell, Encyclopedia Britannica and some government agencies).
They wish to examine aspects of being in the on-line service business. And
it may be that there will be many more choices available to libraries than
they can foresee at the present time. Some data base producers are beginning to think of being their own distributors of their data bases. I've talked
to some of them and suggested that they think very hard about what the user
is going to do if there is still one more system that they have to learn in
addition to the ones that they say are already too many.

My third point is simply to put in a good word for people who think they
know best. In 1969 I conducted a questionnaire survey to find out what the
need was for on-line services of the sort that most libraries here use. I
sent out 8,000 questionnaires, fully confident that the results would support
the need to build this kind of service in the company that I worked at. I got
about 80 returns from information-using libraries; I looked at the data and
panicked. I finally said to myself, "dammit, I'm right. I don't care what
these say—there is a need; there will be a need; the world will go on-line,
and I'm going to tuck these into my file and make my company do it anyhow."
As of this time there are probably three hundred data bases on-line through
60 different services; libraries have their choice of using any of these services, and I think some of these came about because there were fanatics who
did not wait for people to tell them what their requirements were. So I think
that even though it's important for libraries to feel that they are contributing
to the definition of requirements, they should make a little room for crazy
people, entepreneurs, fanatics, who may foresee need and be willing to work
on it ahead of time.

Frederick Raithel - Mid-Missouri Library Network

I would like to just briefly comment on the impact of personal computing. First, I think we think of personal computing as something down the road five or ten years from now. I've used a personal computer in the library network where I work for a couple of months now to prepare monthly statistical reports and also as a tremendous tool in staff development. This is the only computer access we really have. So I think it's important for all of us as a profession to remember to keep informed of the impact of this technology and where it's going, lest we find ourselves in an embarrassing position that our patrons have more sophisticated information technology in their pockets than we have access to as public supported information centers.

Part Four

THE GOVERNANCE OF LIBRARY NETWORKS:
PURPOSES AND EXPECTATIONS

The complex technical character of network design and operation, along with
the growing interdependence among libraries that accompanies increased
dependence on the networks for materials and services formerly provided
locally, calls into question the continuation of traditional forms of voluntary
participation and majority decision-making. Multi-tiered funding arrangements, sometimes short-term and precarious in character, raise new issues
of fiscal stability and optimal participation in governance by all fiscal partners. The role of the network executive vis-a-vis both participants and
sponsors, as well as in terms of managerial control of the supportive technology, necessitates reconsideration of conventional governance structures.

The position paper distributed in advance of the conference is given in
Chapter 18. Chapters 19-23 present reactions from the panelists. Chapter
24 presents the discussion at the conference.

Chapter 18

THE GOVERNANCE OF LIBRARY NETWORKS:
PURPOSES AND EXPECTATIONS

K. Leon Montgomery   C. Edwin Dowlin

and

Associate Professor   Ph. D. Candidate
Interdisciplinary Department   Graduate School of Library
of Information Science   and Information Sciences

University of Pittsburgh
Pittsburgh, Pennsylvania

GOALS OF LIBRARY NETWORKING

The intent of this chapter is to review the purposes of governance in a library network and to examine some of the expectations of those involved in network governance. Governance in the context of library networks is the sum of the relationships between participants (and their institutions) and the network organization(s). Let us begin by reviewing some of the goals identified for library resource sharing networks in the 50's and 60's.

The hopes for libraries' cooperation have been expressed:

"Libraries working together, sharing their services and materials, can meet the full needs of their users. "[1]

This statement of the public library's standards of 1956 establishes a goal that we are still struggling to meet. Another goal intended to initiate cooperation among libraries of different types was expressed:

"The point of origin for such planning is consideration for the needs of the library users. The goal is to meet these needs as efficiently and economically as possible without regard to the type of library involved and without classifying the user as a public, school, or academic library patron. "[2]

This goal, stated in the Library Services and Construction Act of 1956, is still being argued.

In 1968 Purdy admitted,

> "The ultimate feasibility of a national and international informa-
> tion network is pretty much taken for granted today, the assump-
> tion being that computers, perhaps combined with other devices,
> will be linked together to retrieve and transmit information
> which will be stored centrally, or in local or regional centers,
> or both."[3]

There have been many developments, but library networks are still in their infancy. Why?

There are many barriers which must be overcome in establishing cooper-
ative efforts among libraries. Nolting surveyed libraries in the late 1960's and identified five basic classifications of barriers.

  A. Psychological barriers
  B. Lack of information and experience
  C. Traditional and historical barriers
  D. Physical and geographical barriers
  E. Legal and administrative barriers[4]

These barriers are still relevant.

From another point of view, a Westat report identifies three coordinated parts of a nationwide library network: a resource system, a bibliographic system, and a communications system. They are defined as follows:

  1. "A Resource System designed to provide guaranteed access to all
      needed materials through designation and development of librar-
      ies or other information facilities which will provide such access,
      and through coordination or collection development support to
      insure that needed materials are collected and made available for
      users."

  2. "A Bibliographic System designed to provide a unique authorita-
      tive bibliographic description for each item held in guaranteed
      access, as well as location of such materials."

  3. "A Communications System designed to provide on-line commu-
      nication of bibliographic data and requests for data and services
      between levels of the network. The system should facilitate
      communications among the multiple components of the National
      Library Network, including provision for educational and train-
      ing programs for staffs and users."[5]

McLuhan observed in 1964 that major advances in technology influence the scale, speed, and the way we work.[6] Indeed, computers and communications technology have begun to impact on libraries and librarians. Technology permits library networks to be built, but the aforementioned barriers still exist.

In addition to the resource, bibliographical, and communication components, it is important to add one more, a behavioral component. Mitchell chooses to call this component "perceptions. "[7] The term that we prefer is "expectations. " In this case perceptions can be defined as the expectations that people and/or organizations have of one another. It is a premise of this chapter that behind each barrier to networking is an unmet expectation.

Governance then, in the context of a library network, is concerned with the relationships among the participants and institutions with respect to the resource system, bibliographic system, and communication system. Another premise of this chapter is that personal, institutional and organizational expectations play a major role in governance. It is important to distinguish between governance and management. Management is concerned with operational decisions used to achieve organizational or network goals and objectives. Governance permits those using the running networks to express their interests and concerns, in short, to establish goals and objectives as well as the policies by which these goals and objectives are to be achieved.

PURPOSES OF GOVERNANCE FOR LIBRARY NETWORKS

So we understand that library resource sharing networks exist, have goals, have a management and governance structure (whether explicitly identified or not), and a number of possible barriers that need to be surmounted. Using governance to overcome these barriers will be addressed later on. But first, what are the purposes of governance?

Stevens identifies the purposes of governance for library networks as: (1) To set a direction for action; (2) To establish basic procedures for activity; (3) To give stability in an orderly progression towards established goals and objectives; (4) To protect the participants; (5) To establish an operating entity that can be recognized by others; and (6) To establish the standard by which library network effectiveness should be measured. [8]

He explains these purposes as follows. Setting a direction for action means the establishment of written goals (and objectives) which can then be periodically reviewed to incorporate changing needs, constraints, and resources. By establishing the basic procedures, governance delimits the paths to be followed. Administrators deal with the day-to-day decisions. Governance provides stability to making a network "an organization controlled by principle and not by persons. " Governance protects the participants by establishing and upholding rights and privileges while limiting legal liabilities. For example, how are initial and continuing costs to be amortized and divided? Establishing an operating entity provides a mechanism for working with other organizations, for receiving grants, etc. Based on goals and objectives, network effectiveness can be determined.

In summary then, the purposes of governance are to provide a mechanism for identifying goals and objectives of the library network; for the establishment of policies by which the library will operate; and for the resolution of conflict. In particular, governance is also the mechanism for overcoming the barriers to networking. In a broader sense, the purpose of governance is to provide a mechanism for overcoming the barriers to any "new" organization such as a library network.

BARRIERS TO LIBRARY NETWORKING

Although Nolting has cataloged and classified the barriers to cooperation (and network development), he has not provided a point of attack for surmounting these barriers. All of these barriers are not found in every phase of network development. The first step in development of a strategy of attack is to identify the cast of characters and their relation to these barriers. Under each of Nolting's five categories a number of examples are listed.[9] In Tables 1-4, these examples are categorized as to the people involved in each: network administrator, network staff, library administrator, library staff, and library users.

Barriers in the first four tables have been related to individuals as members of a network organization, individuals as members of a library and its institution, and individuals as library users. However, not all barriers are related to individuals, some are related to our legal environment. Table 5, Legal and Administrative Barriers, categorizes barriers in terms of: multistate networks, state networks and local libraries.

Dealing with the legal and administrative barriers spelled out in Table 5 seems to be based on the formal relationships that must exist between institutions and, where applicable, local and state levels of government. These relationships are, of course, evolving. There seem to be two major thrusts needed here. First, the appropriate environment must be developed for cooperation. Second, there must be proper incentive.

Table 1
Psychological Barriers

	Network Administrator/Staff	Library Administrator/Staff	Library Users
1. Custodial mentality of librarians		X	
2. Fear of loss of local autonomy	X	X	X
3. Clash of personalities	X	X	
4. Jealously and stubborness	X	X	
5. Complacency and self-satisfaction		X	
6. Mistrust between librarians		X	
7. Inertia and indifference	X	X	
8. Unwillingness to experiment	X		
9. Assumption that each library has unique rather than commonplace needs		X	

Table 2

Lack of Information and Experience

	Network Administrator/Staff	Library Administrator/Staff	Library Users
1. Lack of knowledge of needs of users	X	X	
2. Lack of information about the true functions of different types of libraries		X	
3. Unpredictability of demands on the library by its legitimate users	X	X	
4. Lack of public interest and concern for total library service			X
5. Failure to inform the public on library collections and services		X	
6. Lack of knowledge by librarians on new interlibrary loan code			
7. Failure of small libraries to realize the value of resources of larger libraries		X	
8. Unawareness of successful cooperative efforts in other states			

Table 3
Traditional and Historical Barriers

	Network Administrator/Staff	Library Administrator/Staff	Library Users
1. Lack of adequate funds		X	
2. Fear by large libraries of being overused and undercompensated		X	
3. Lack of understanding by laymen of library needs			X
4. Institutional competition between school and public libraries		X	
5. Inadequacy of libraries to serve their own needs		X	
6. Conflict between the boards of public libraries and those of private libraries		X	
7. Limitations on access to academic and special libraries		X	
8. Thinking of only one type of cooperation	X		
9. Reluctance of independent libraries to relinquish any responsibilities		X	

Table 4

Physical and Geographical Barriers

	Network Administrator/Staff	Library Administrator/Staff	Library Users
1. Distance between libraries and distance of users from the library		X	X
2. Difference in size of library collections		X	
3. Difficulty of providing service to sparsely settled rural areas		X	
4. Lack of space in public library to serve students		X	
5. Delays in satisfying needs and requests of users	X	X	X
6. Overemphasis by librarians on housekeeping activities		X	
7. Lack of a good public transit system			X

Table 5
Legal and Administrative Barriers

	Multistate	State	Local Library
1. Too many local government taxing units	X	X	X
2. Large number of institutions providing library service	X	X	X
3. Lack of appropriate state enabling legislation		X	
4. Lack of creative administrative leadership	X	X	X
5. Cumbersome fiscal practices of local governments	X	X	X
6. Lack of effective public relations programs	X	X	X
7. Inability to accept (or opposition to) state and federal aid	X	X	X
8. Lack of communication across jurisdictional lines at the policy level	X	X	X
9. Lack of contacts with voluntary and governmental agencies engaged in area-wide cooperation	X	X	X
10. Lack of bibliographic tools and controls	X	X	X
11. Failure to utilize technological equipment		X	X
12. Incompatability of equipment, procedures, and rules between libraries	X	X	X
13. Lack of properly trained staff		X	X

GOVERNANCE STRUCTURES

Stevens divides library network governance into three categories: governance by government; governance under a quasi-governmental body; and governance by the membership under a legal charter and by-laws. [10] To these categories might be added: governance by a for-profit organization; governance by a not-for-profit organization; and governance by a network supplier organization.

The governance structure adopted may vary depending on the category selected. Unfortunately, the formulae for choosing among these structures are not yet developed. The principal differences among these categories

Table 6
Governance Structure Categories

	Policy Approved By	Incentive
1. Government	Government Agency	Political/Service
2. Quasi-government	Government	Political/Service
3. Membership	Membership	Service
4. For-profit	Organization	Service/Profit
5. Not-for-profit	Organization	Service
6. Network suppliers	Suppliers	Service/Profit

involve the organizational environment and its relationships with member libraries as expressed by policies; and in the incentive for cooperation. Table 6 attempts to link governance structure with policy approval body and the incentive for making the library network work.

OVERCOMING THE BARRIERS

Reorganizing the data presented in Tables 1-4 permits us to cluster the barriers involving the network administrators/staff, the library administrators/staff and the library users. Overcoming these barriers may be facilitated by categorizing these barriers further into personal, institutional and organizational, where appropriate. These reorganized data are presented in Tables 7-9.

From data presented in Table 7, it appears that the network administrators/staff from a personal point-of-view should have expectations of working closely with people; of being able to change, to try new things; of seeking data about their ultimate users, library patrons; of exploring how library functions differ for different types of libraries; and of solving the libraries' problems rather than limiting network activities. As a service organization, a library network must have expectations of working with institutions and libraries as well as other networks so that there will be a minimum or at least agreeable loss of autonomy on the part of libraries.

Table 8 clusters the barriers for library administrators and staff. Table 8 also categorizes these barriers in terms of personal, institutional (i. e., the institution within which the library exists) and the associated network.

Table 7
Network Administrators/Staff

	Personal	Organizational
Psychological Barriers		
1. Fear of loss of autonomy	X	X
2. Clash of personalities	X	
3. Jealousy and stubborness	X	
4. Inertia and indifference	X	X
5. Unwillingness to experiment	X	X
Lack of Information and Experience		
1. Lack of knowledge of needs of users	X	X
2. Lack of information about the true functions of different types of libraries	X	X
3. Unpredictability of demands on the library by its legitimate users		X
Traditional and Historical Barriers		
1. Thinking of only one type of cooperation	X	
2. Delays in satisfying needs and requests of users		X

Data from Table 8 show that a major portion of the barriers revolve around the goals and objectives of a library as established in an institutional context. Library administrators seem not to be convinced that networks can really help them to achieve their institutional goals and objectives or at least not in a cost-effective manner. Merits and demerits of network participation must be understood by the library staff and users. Library administrators must also perceive that network goals and objectives are reasonable with respect to institutional goals and objectives. Networks must be sensitive to the impact that changes cause in each participating institution's goals and objectives. Changes that cause a library not to be able to achieve its own goals and objectives are certain to meet with opposition. Library administrators must be convinced that the library's goals and objectives can be adapted to or changed to conform with the network's goals and objectives. Library administrators must also be convinced that the network's goals and objectives can be influenced to meet new needs.

Table 8

Library Administrators/Staff

	Personal	Institutional	Network
Psychological			
1. Fear of loss of autonomy	X	X	
2. Clash of personalities	X		
3. Jealousy and stubbornness	X		
4. Complacency and self-satisfaction	X		
5. Mistrust between librarians	X		
6. Inertia and indifference	X	X	X
7. Unwillingness to experiment	X	X	X
8. Assumption that each library has unique rather than commonplace needs	X		
Lack of Information and Experience			
1. Lack of knowledge of needs of users	X	X	
2. Lack of information about the true functions of different types of libraries	X		
3. Unpredictability of demands on the library by its legitimate users	X		
4. Failure to inform the public on library collections and services	X		
5. Failure of small libraries to realize the value of resources of larger libraries	X		

Traditional and Historical Barriers

1. Fear by large libraries of being overused and undercompensated		X	
2. Institutional competition between school and public libraries		X	X
3. Inadequacy of libraries to serve their own needs		X	
4. Conflict between the boards of public libraries and those of private libraries			X
5. Limitations on access to academic and special libraries		X	
6. Thinking of only one type of cooperation		X	
7. Reluctance of independent libraries to relinquish any responsibilities		X	X

Physical and Geographical Barriers

1. Distance between libraries and distance of users from the library	X	X	
2. Difference in size of library collections		X	
3. Difficulty of providing service to sparsely settled rural areas		X	
4. Lack of space in public library to serve students		X	
5. Delays in satisfying needs and requests of users	X	X	
6. Overemphasis by librarians on housekeeping activities			X

Table 9
Library User

	Personal	Institutional
Psychological Barrier		
1. Fear of loss of local autonomy	X	X
Lack of Information and Experience		
1. Lack of public interest and concern for total service	X	
Traditional and Historical Barriers		
1. Lack of understanding by laymen of library needs	X	
Physical and Geographical Barriers		
1. Distance between libraries and distance of users from the library	X	X
2. Delays in satisfying needs and requests of users	X	X
3. Lack of a good public transit system	X	

Table 9 lists the barriers for library users. Educational programs reflecting the advantages and disadvantages of library network participation can probably change these barriers into favorable expectations.

EXPECTATIONS

Having identified the areas in which barriers occur, it is necessary to develop a framework for identifying the nature and causes of dissonance or conflict. Aldrich and Pfeffer identify two theoretical perspectives developed in organizational research to address the perceptual component, viz., exchange theory and dependency theory:[11] Exchange theory holds that relationships develop when two or more organizations expect to receive mutual benefits. This is known as a symmetrical relationship. In a symmetrical relationship, there is goal compatability between participants, and hence, a committment to solving problems that arise. [12] Dependency theory assumes that the motivation to interact is asymmetrical, that is, one organization is motivated to interact and the other is not. There is lack of goal compatability and, hence, these relationships involve conflict.[13]

It seems reasonable to speculate that both symmetrical and asymmetrical relationships may exist within a network or within a library that finds itself involved in a number of networks. In his dissertation research at the University of Michigan, Townley proposes to investigate the perceptual component of one fully operational, multitype, multifunction library network. [14]

A library resource sharing network can be defined as two or more libraries or library-related organizations exchanging library data, materials or services for the realization of their respective goals and objectives. It should be observed that linking an organization to its stated goals and objectives provides a mechanism for determining whether or not that organization is fulfilling its own purposes and expectations. It should also be observed that cooperative activity can be assessed by determining how these activities are impacting the goals and objectives.

It is useful to distinguish between goals and objectives. Goals are statements of what an organization is trying to achieve. For example, a public library goal might be stated—to provide access to library materials for all people living within a specified geographical area. Objectives, on the other hand, are measurable statements of expected performance within a specified time frame. For example, the objective statement for the aforementioned goal might be stated—to provide access to library materials for 30% of those living within a specified geographical area each year. The objective statement, then, takes into account the practicalities of the situation. Relationships among organizations exchanging library data, material and services may be categorized along the following dimensions: resource system, bibliographic system, communications system and expectations.

Symmetrical relationships then are achieved when the stated goals and objectives for each of the participating libraries and the network are similar with respect to each of these dimensions. Asymmetrical relationships are those in which there are dissimilar goals and objectives for at least one of the aforementioned dimensions of exchange. One consequence of sharing resources between libraries is the development of dependency of one library on another library or network organization. The critical question is in what areas are dependencies to be tolerated or encouraged and in what areas are dependencies not to be tolerated or encouraged. Organizational behavior research provides a measure of dependency. Dependency of organization A on organization B can be measured as directly proportional to A's interest in goals mediated by B, and inversely proportional to the achieveability of these goals from sources other than B.[15] That is, A's dependency on B is measured indirectly by the options A has for achieving its goals from sources other than B. This measure has been introduced here to show that some of the theory from organizational behavior might well be useful in exploring library network development and assessment.

The major axiom of the resource—dependency theory is that organizations must be studied in the context of all the organizations with which they are competing and sharing scarce resources. Ultimately then, library resource sharing networks must be studied in the context of other libraries and other library networks serving the same clientele or providing the same services. The critical factor is how much does organization A become dependent on another organization B, that controls resources and/or markets necessary to organization A's achievement of its goals and objectives. Stated more precisely, the greater the incompatability of organizational goals, the more conflict there may be; and the greater the ability of one organization to interfere with the goal attainment of another organization, the more conflict there may be.

For the purposes of this chapter, compatibility of organizational goals is taken to include complementary goals which are not mutually exclusive. Thus, for example, an academic library and a public library can make exchanges, providing services to differing constituencies with goals that are not necessarily of interest to both. The presumed overall efficiency increase is the assumption upon which the multitype library arrangements can be based.

Dependency with goal incompatability or ability to interfere with goal attainment may lead to conflict. Of course, there are different degrees of conflict, some resolvable, some irresolvable. The governance structure must be prepared to deal with the conflicts that may arise in asymmetrical relationships.

In applying the exchange dependency theory to network governance, there are two main considerations: the individual and the organization. An individual will bring to any potential library network a set of personal and institutional expectations with respect to the degree of symmetry required for the: resource system, bibliographic system and communication system.

Expectations come in two categories. The first relates to performance and is dealt with in statements of goals and objectives. If well done, these statements can prevent the problems arising from performance expectations.

Less well recognized, however, are the expectations of the exchange/ dependency relationship. These are "status" goals of the individual and organization. A failure of expectations in this area are more difficult to identify and deal with. This failure may explain the demise of some library networks that seemed to be meeting the performance goals and objectives.

The key persons in a library network scheme will bring personal expectations to the network. These may require time and mutual understanding to deal within the network framework. Certain other expectations however are partly predictable because they are prompted by the historical background and the nature of the individual's position.

Here, we attempt to suggest some of the situational factors that will influence the expectations of "key persons." These are neither comprehensive nor conclusive; they are offered to illustrate an application of this behavioral analysis approach.

NETWORK MANAGER'S PERSPECTIVE

A network can't exist without management. In all but the most elementary situations an individual is given responsibility for the network decision-making process. That individual, whether a staff member from a participating library or a full-time appointee, is needed to assure that timely, feasible decisions are made and carried out to accomplish the network purpose.

The network manager is constrained in part by the characteristics of the technology and the governance structure of the network. Network members rarely have the network manager's detailed knowledge of the cost factors, the technological limits, and the potential of the computers and communications devices of the network.

> "Although libraries have banded together for decades in arrangements that are more or less formal, the use of computers dictates a level of formality and unity of purpose that has not been required until now.... libraries with idiosyncratic needs have been able to adapt national standards without disrupting relationships with other libraries....
>
> The nature of computer-assisted networks will no longer allow this luxury. Computers are expensive, and almost everything associated with designing and implementing a computer system is expensive. Therefore, in order to proceed economically, certain constraints must be incorporated into the system. If provision were to be made for every library to use all its variations of practice, the computer costs would be untenably high —and chances are that communication among libraries would be rendered virtually impossible."[16]

Few libraries have found it necessary or desirable to document objectives and practices to the precise extent required for introduction of sophisticated technology. While operations research studies shed light on the performance characteristics of the member library, the unstated expectations in regard to the exchange–dependency relationships are potential traps for technological innovation.

A network manager's performance achievements are dependent upon communications with both managerial and operational levels of library personnel. The expectations with regard to the network tend to vary through this hierarchy. The manager faces a variety of communications problems in dealing with these expectations.

These are but a few of the problems the network manager faces as a result of technical demands and the individual and group expectations of member libraries. He faces the pressures to achieve network performance expectations at the same time that he is building trust and a series of relationships that will be viewed as mutual dependency by library directors and library staff.

To repeat a premise of this chapter, behind each of the barriers listed in Table 7, Barriers for Network Administrator and Staff, and Table 8, Barriers for Library Administrator and Staff, is an unfulfilled expectation. The network administrator must be cognizant of these barriers and their associated expectations.

NETWORKS FROM THE STATE LIBRARY PERSPECTIVE

The goals, purposes, and organization of state libraries vary widely from state to state. The various state libraries are constrained by the legal and jurisdictional limits that are founded in a historical distrust of the state level of government.[17]

Frequently these limits prevent a direct operational role in state network operation. Few state libraries would be allowed to pay the salaries of systems analysts, network designers and computer programmers. In many states it is difficult for state libraries to tie network operations to centralized state service centers. Therefore, few state libraries are expected to be the operations center of state networks keyed to sophisticated technology.

State libraries have been assigned a major role by the state and federal governments in channeling funds and public accountability for results. This responsibility without operational authority promotes asymmetrical relationships. As stated earlier, asymmetrical relationships may lead to conflict. In many cases governance structures which would permit resolution of conflicts simply don't exist.

Table 10
State Library

	Personal	Institutional	Network
Psychological Barriers			
1. Insularity of states	X	X	X
2. Mistrust between organizations	X	X	X
3. Inertia and indifference	X	X	
Lack of Information and Experience			
1. Lack of understanding of expectations	X	X	X
2. Lack of skills in problem solving	X		
3. Inexperience with technology	X	X	X
Traditional and Historical Barriers			
1. Legal limitations		X	X
2. Insufficient and inadequate staff		X	X
3. Limited view of role of state library	X	X	X
4. Limited status		X	
Physical and Geographical Barriers			
1. Distance between libraries		X	
2. Difference in size of staff		X	
3. Lack of operational space		X	

State librarians are aware of this very real problem, of responsibility without authority, and it is one of the goals the networking committee of the Chief Officers of State Library Agencies (COSLA) to develop and promote contributory roles of the state library in networking. A draft position paper of this committee has focussed on the coordination of network efforts and conduct of needs assessment plus the traditional responsibilities assigned by government bodies. At this writing, negotiations are underway between COSLA and the Council for Computerized Library Networks (CCLN) to develop a mutually supportive statement of roles and relationships.

The state library faces a number of problems in addition to those identified by Nolting. Table 10 lists some of the barriers faced by the state libraries.

SUMMARY AND CONCLUSIONS

Computers and communications technology make many of the goals and objectives of library cooperation achievable via library networks. These new library organizations are experiencing a number of problems. Of these, the problems of technology may prove less formidable than those of governance.

Several authors have suggested that governance is the major consideration in library networks. Today, as the number of library networks increase and as participation by libraries becomes irreversible, attention to regional, state and national levels of library coordination is mandatory. Major questions concerning governance that must be resolved include:

• What issues should be decided at the local, regional, state and federal level?

• How should conflicts between institutional and network administrators be resolved?

• How should fiscal and governance arrangements be set up (e.g., by legislation) to permit access to the widest range of library materials by the widest range of library users?

• Library networks and interdependence among libraries is growing. The question is, will library networks and interdependence grow in a reasoned manner?

This chapter has attempted to differentiate between management, governance, and governance structures. It has attempted to identify the purposes and expectations of governance in a library networking environment. Barriers to the development of viable library networks have been identified and structured in a way that hopefully permits an approach to their resolution. Further, this chapter suggests that organizational behavior research may offer some insight into the development of library networks. After all, libraries are not the only organizations in our society undergoing change. Hospitals, for example, are now operating under the jurisdiction of regional planning boards. Maybe libraries could benefit from a similar structure.

Finally, "libraries working together, sharing their services and materials, can meet the full needs of their users,"[18] was a meaningful goal in 1956 and it still is.

REFERENCES

1. Public Library Service: A Guide to Evaluation with Minimum Standards, (Chicago: American Library Association, 1956), p. 7.

2. John C. Frantz. "The Library Services and Construction Act," American Library Association Bulletin, (February, 1966), 60:151.

3. G. Flint Purdy. "Interrelations Among Public, School and Academic Libraries," in Leon Carnovsky (ed.), Library Networks—Promise and Performance, The University of Chicago Press, 1969, pp. 52-63.

4. Orin F. Nolting. Mobilizing Total Library Resources for Effective Service, (Chicago: ALA), 1969.

5. Westat, Inc. Resources and Bibliographic Support for a Nationwide Library Program: Final Report to the National Commission on Libraries and Information Science, (Rockville, Md.), 1973, p. 27.

6. Marshall McLuhan. Understanding Media: The Extension of Man, New York: New American Library, 1973, p. 27.

7. James C. Mitchell. "Networks, Norms and Institutions," in Network Analysis: Studies in Human Interaction, eds. Jeremy Boissevain and James C. Mitchell, (The Hague: Mouton, 1973), pp. 23-29.

8. Charles H. Stevens. "Governance of Library Networks," Library Trends, Fall 1977, p. 222.

9. Orin F. Nolting. Mobilizing Total Library Resources for Effective Service, (Chicago: ALA, 1969), p. 20.

10. Charles H. Stevens. "Governance of Library Networks," Library Trends, Fall 1977, p. 222.

11. Howard Aldrich and Jeffrey Pfeffer. "Environments of Organizations," Annual Review of Sociology, 2 (1976), pp. 70-107.

12. Sol Levine and Paul E. White. "Exchange as a Conceptual Framework for the Study of Interorganizational Relations," Administrative Science Quarterly, 5 (December 1961), pp. 583-601.

13. Howard Aldrich and Sergio Mindlin. "International Dependence: A Review of the Concept and a Reexamination of the Findings of the Ashton Group," Administrative Science Quarterly, 20 (September 1975), pp. 382-392.

14. Charles Thomas Townley. The Perceptual Component of Relationships in Library Networks, (Ann Arbor, Mich., 1978). A Dissertation Proposal at the University of Michigan, School of Library Science.

15. David Jacobs. "Dependency and Vulnerability: An Exchange Approach to the Control of Organizations," Administrative Science Quarterly, 19 (March 1974), pp. 45-59.

16. Susan K. Martin. Library Networks, 1976-77, (White Plains, N.Y.: Knowledge Industry Publications, Inc., 1976), p. 72.

17. Kenneth E. Beasley. "The Changing Role of the State Library," Advances in Librarianship, Vol. 2, ed. Melvin J. Voigt, (New York: Seminar Press, 1971).

18. Public Library Service: A Guide to Evaluation with Minimum Standards, (Chicago: American Library Association, 1956), p. 7.

Chapter 19

CREATION OF A GOVERNANCE STRUCTURE FOR OCLC

Susan H. Crooks   and   Vincent E. Giuliano

Arthur D. Little, Inc.
Cambridge, Massachusetts

We will take a slightly different tack from that followed by Montgomery and
Dowlin (Chapter 16). They describe conditions which would be found to be
true for any governance structure. We shall describe the basis for creation
of a governance structure as an action process related to one specific organization. We will use as a case in point the governance study Arthur D. Little
recently completed for OCLC. We shall not spend much time on the actual
governance structure we recommended. A copy of the governance report is
still available from Scarecrow Press. Nor will we discuss the experience
thus far in implementing the governance structure, for we believe it is early
to comment on whether or not the design is working. Rather, we will discuss our process for development of this governance structure. We are
pursuing this approach because the process we used says some very important things about the nature of the governance structure.

We shall introduce a discussion of our methodology by describing the
value framework with which Arthur D. Little approached the problem of
creating a governance structure for OCLC. We believe the selection/creation
of a governance structure is a basic and all-informing decision process which
must be individualized, externally-oriented, and iterative. We will then discuss the events that occurred in the creation of the governance structure for
OCLC. This includes reference both to our charter from OCLC as to how the
task was to be performed and the method we used to implement the work.
Finally, we will comment on the applicability of this approach to development
of governance structures for individual library networks. This discussion
will indicate the degree to which the governance structure is a living, creative part of the organization and, in fact, will help realize the potential represented by library networks.

VALUE FRAMEWORK USED BY ARTHUR D. LITTLE

In the discussion of the methodology below, we take as a given that the organization for which a governance structure is created must know where it wants to go. It is rarely the case, however, that the desired end point is explicitly clear to the organization at the start of the process. As a result, the methodology must provide a mechanism for determining where the organization wants to go at the same time it develops the governance structure. This introduction describes the need for creating a governance structure on the basis of the known desires or end points of the target organization. We believe that effort devoted to structuring a governing body will be an academic exercise if some or all of the following points are not understood and accepted by the planners.

First, as background, we strongly believe that governance, like organizational structure, is not merely a technical matter of an arrangement of boxes on a sheet of paper. Nor is governance merely a group of premises agreed to by participants in an organization which enable the operations of the organization to be carried out. You can see that this is true when you review for a minute your own concept of monarchy, a city state, or a traditional corporate organization. In each case, what immediately comes to mind is not an academic understanding of the power relationships of those societies. It is more likely that the image evoked by each is one of people living in the societies and the actions they performed in the social positions which they held —in other words, the kings on the Field of the Cross of Gold. The point here is that, as expressed by the activities of human beings, governance or organizational structure creates the arena which restricts and defines subsequent action to a particular set of relationships. Yet governance, when embodied in the realization of personal ambition, of personality, and of interaction with social trends, brings to life an actuality of greater power and emotional reality than would be suggested merely by the technical elements of the structure.

Given the fact that the governance structure of an organization has an all-informing relationship to the events befalling that entity, the issue of determining a desired end point for the organization has an intimate relationship with—and must be carried on simultaneously with—creation of its governance structure. To deal adequately with the question of the desired end point, the organization for whom governance is being created must identify as fully and as honestly as possible its—and no one else's—desires for itself for the future.

Identification of an organization's unique objectives is an important and sensitive issue in the library field because of aspects of our professional ethics. This became clear to us during our work on the OCLC governance structure. In the course of interviewing old friends, we realized that a few

felt that we were in serious danger of doing the profession as a whole a dis-
service by seeking to determine what was desirable for OCLC rather than
what was desirable for the library profession as a whole. Cognitive dissonance was created in the minds of these friends because they perceived that
appropriate objectives for OCLC might not be identical to and entirely conso-
nant with objectives for a national library network. And yet, it was customary to believe either that what helps one organization move forward in the
library world helps others to do the same, or that libraries choose only
courses that are mutually beneficial.

Indeed, there was a dissonance here: what was best for OCLC and best
for a national library network did not necessarily reduce to the same thing
in the short term. Yet our profession's serious and long commitment to cooperation risked masking divergence of one organization's goals from the
profession's as a whole as organizational ego or selfishness. Yet, it is a
fact, as Montgomery and Dowlin recognize, that different organizations in
cooperative endeavors will not always have the same desired ends. You will
recall their reference to the spectrum of interdependencies under cooperation. Their point is that, at the extremes of this spectrum, one organization
can constrain another from achieving its ends.

The approach we are describing is one you might designate as the self as
client. In this approach, the dissonance between one's own ends and ends of
other significant outside organizations is acknowledged and faced as honestly
as possible as a real dissonance. There are many indications why this is
the best approach. First, other behavioral sciences literature on cooperation
and on the generic form of cooperation, the exchange relationship, suggests
the same conclusion as was drawn by Montgomery and Dowlin. This literature shows that interdependence can almost be approached as a computable
item rather than as a matter of faith.

There is also, however, a second and perhaps more important reason for
making an effort toward self-understanding the touchstone of the process of
creating a governance structure. In exploring, bringing to the surface, and
finally being able to state clearly one's own desired ends, an organization
identifies and capitalizes on the energy which has supported its development
thus far. This internal direction will out, whether or not the public utter-
ances of the organization acknowledge or belie it. In the case of OCLC, we
had an organization determined to be responsible for significantly changing
the way libraries operate. We took as our charge identifying a governance
which would simultaneously release that powerful energy and protect it—by
assuring that OCLC kept a responsible tie with the elements of its environment on which it needed to depend. In this sense, understanding of OCLC's
truly desired direction was critical to enable an accurate assessment of both
opportunities and dangers.

For all of these reasons, the organization for whom governance is being planned must be considered as the client; that is, as the body whose ends the planners are primarily responsible for optimizing. Those creating the governance may misperceive an organization's character or ends, and mistakes can thus be made, but the planners will be sowing confusion—for the target organization and for its associates—by taking any other approach.

In pursuit of this approach, as many beliefs that are in fact merely articles of faith should be questioned as possible. In our work for OCLC, this need to question articles of faith to help define and realize the organization's energy required a confrontation with two sets of beliefs which Dr. Giuliano describes as prevailing mythologies in the library world today. The first of these was that the cooperative spirit is more important than any one's own individual requirements. The second, probably derived from the first, was a belief that one nationwide national library network would spring full-formed from the heads of a few library planners. The currency of these two beliefs, had they not been questioned by the Arthur D. Little team, might have led in directions which would not have withstood the light of reason.

In 1977, when our study was performed, papers on the National Library Network postulated a relatively minor and regional role for OCLC in present and future networking plans. This failed to reflect the reality of the day. Nor did it suggest a credible outcome if OCLC had been to decide artifically to slow its rate of growth in order to wait for the development of operable systems from potential competitors. We surmised, rather, that competition among public sector library-service organizations would promote valid and important alternatives for library customers—and would do so far more effectively than would artificial constraint of any organization's individual action in order to express adherence to the cooperative ethic.

Thus, seeking for knowledge of desired end points is the precursor of any other intellectual effort in creation of the governance structure. Intellectual effort is also required, however, to amass relevant information and understand the organization's environment. Governance development must be environmentally-oriented, since governance positions the organization to make the internal responses to external stimuli. Furthermore, trends in the outside world, their direction and speed, represent the arena in which the organization pursues its ends. Understanding of the dynamic relationship among environment, structure, and role does not come all at once, however, and the attention to environmental impacts must be iterative. Consideration of likely developments in the external world allows speculation as to which external events will make or break the organization. The appropriateness of different structures is gauged in response to the prospect of these future contingencies. Depending on the role performed by the organization, certain events are more or less probable and more or less important as opportunities or threats. Roles, futures, and structures must thus be postulated and then varied so as to point toward common themes that will then be realized in specific recommendations.

Thus, the governance structure is developed on the basis of what is suspected or known about what the organization desires to be, what opportunities and dangers the environment will present, and what particular strengths and capabilities the organization has developed heretofore. For all of these reasons, a governance structure is an individualized as a fingerprint. While the question of governance structure can be considered as an abstraction for theoretical work, it is an absolutely specific question for the organization for which a governance is being developed, and it is folly to approach governance as a generic sort of problem solving tool which will enable the organization to address non-specific generic kinds of challenges.

STUDY, APPROACH AND METHODOLOGY

When Arthur D. Little was engaged by OCLC to develop a governance structure in the face of the enlarged participation of networks and their library members in OCLC, many of the critical bases described above were touched in the description of the required work. The request for proposal directed the consultant to recommend the governance structure with respect to the following different criteria:

- The role which OCLC could most appropriately play in a National Library Network;

- The activities and plans of many stakeholder organizations;

- The recommended systems network architecture; and

- Possible governance structures.

To implement this charge, Arthur D. Little utilized a methodology in which we iteratively considered the environment, possible roles, and ways various governance structures enabled fulfillment of those roles. Figure 1 lists the five subjects and steps in the methodology. We shall not describe each step in detail but will comment about interesting and important elements of the methodology.

Driving forces we considered included libraries' economic plight, centralized network planning initiatives, the availability of subsidies, actions of for-profit sector firms, new technological developments, the ethic of library cooperation, and OCLC itself. We defined a driving force as a technological, social, or economic force that is so robust that no single participant or group of participants can affect its impact. After identifying the forces, we examined possible dynamic relationships among them. This analysis first yielded a description of <u>possible</u> futures, from which we derived <u>possible</u> roles for OCLC. Then we selected the most <u>likely</u> future from among the possible futures and from it derived <u>practical</u> roles for OCLC.

In making the preliminary analysis of governance structures, we considered four possible structures—a not-for-profit corporation, a for-profit corporation, a government organization, and a quasi-governmental organization. From the outset it was apparent that some roles were not good choices. Given OCLC's origins in a cooperative endeavor, for example, a for-profit corporation would not have been an effective selection. Yet, even the obvious reasons for dismissing particular forms helped to highlight key characteristics which the governance structure should emphasize and project. In describing network architecture requirements, we made another important decision about governance structure when we distinguished between the structures dictated by needs of technology and of governance. The future possibility of distributing part of the data base did not imply that OCLC's governance should also be decentralized. On the contrary, the need for planning to meet changing user requirements in the face of probable technological change meant that the responsiveness provided by a centralized organization would be particularly important.

We next refined our understanding of the interplay of the driving forces and the possible governance structures. Our purpose was to determine what could go wrong in various futures and to examine the position in which each structure placed OCLC for dealing with it. To obtain this understanding of the interaction between events and structure, we used scenarios. A form of sketches of the future we have often used before, scenarios are composed not to predict the future but to better understand the possible interdependencies among events in the future. Depending on what is to be learned, scenarios are written either by setting an end state and creating events necessary to reach that state or by focusing on certain events and seeing what end states are most likely to develop. In this study we postulated different types of governance and then experimented to see what would happen to OCLC under each form of governance in different environmental conditions.

    1. DRIVING FORCES

    2. GOVERNANCE STRUCTURES

    3. INTERPLAY OF FORCES, STRUCTURES AND ROLES

    4. CRITERIA GOVERNANCE MUST SATISFY

    5. STRUCTURE—AS A FUNCTION OF GOAL

Figure 1. Methodology.

- REQUIREMENTS OF RELATIONSHIP TO PRIMARY CONSTITUENCY

- REQUIREMENTS OF RELATIONSHIPS TO SECONDARY CONSTITUENCIES

- KEY CAPABILITIES REQUIRED IN FACING ANTICIPATED FUTURE

- VERY PERSONALIZED REQUIREMENTS BASED ON THE ORGANIZATION'S UNIQUE HISTORY AND CHARACTER

Figure 2. Subjects governance must cover.

Figure 2 lists subjects the governance structure must include. At this point we had determined that many features of OCLC's success were closely tied to elements of its relationships to its members and environment. We wanted to assure that these needed capabilities were built in for the future as structural elements. One important secondary constituency, for example, was the financial community, from which OCLC expected to have to obtain funds in the future. It was necessary, therefore, for OCLC to have credibility with that community. As a consequence, we recommended selection of a member of the financial community as an OCLC Board member to help assure financial sources that their perspective was represented in OCLC's governance.

Similarly, OCLC wanted to continue to be a technical innovator, and wanted to participate in experiments such as QUBE because of OCLC's possible interest in having more direct relationships with library users in the future. Because we had determined that the driving forces in the environment meant a future of potentially rapid change, we identified flexibility to respond in the environment as one of the key capabilities to be provided by the governance structure.

The final step was to derive the OCLC governance structure as a function of what the structure must do and make possible. At last we were ready to consider and make specific recommendations concerning the specific bodies to be involved in governance and the interrelationships among those bodies. Rather than commenting on the specific recommendations, I want to convey our underlying attitude in approaching this part of the process.

At this stage, future changes in the composition and nature of the governing bodies which will result from replacement of individuals filling the initial slots can, to some extent, be anticipated and guarded against—by careful consideration and description of roles and qualifications. Nonetheless, the structure will take on a life of its own when the governance slots are filled with human personalities. The purpose of the careful process of creation up to this point is not so much to preclude this occurrence as to specify underlying objectives and expectations against which to compare actual progress. That is, after proceeding through these planning stages, it is less necessary to envision and protect against all eventualities. Key vulnerabilities and opportunities have been identified, and it is these which must be carefully monitored.

APPLICABILITY TO NETWORK GOVERNANCE

Now we will discuss the applicability of the methodology described above to individual library networks. The principal question was whether the methodology applies to a network organization with a scope not necessarily as broad, but perhaps deeper, than the nationwide provision of automated cataloging services. The question was thus, are the options, the driving forces, and the roles which individual library networks face varied and numerous enough to merit this kind of planning exercise? Our answer was a strong "yes, " as we are certain that those who represent the country's networks would agree. In the following comments, therefore, we are not so much arguing for the complexity of your environment, but rather using the discussion of governance to describe the potential of networks as promised in the introduction.

Perhaps the most obvious question of whether a network faces the range of options that was faced by OCLC, is whether there is any counterpart for the different governance structures which were considered by OCLC. While in general the choice is more limited for most networks, the main important variables are present even though the same range of distinct structures is not. These key variables include the organization's relationship to its funding sources, its relationship to government on the relevant level, and the tradeoffs which derive from the size, the composition, and the mode of operation of the governing body.

Relationship to sources of funds is a narrower choice for an individual network than for OCLC. It is not unlikely that revenues could be generated, and the revenue-producing component could be spun off as a separate organization. It is unlikely, however, that the mainline of a network's activities could be for profit. The more difficult and possibly more important funding issues are therefore linked to issues of the relationship with state and local governments. In the case of networks serving all or parts of several states, the relationship with those governments is key because the networks are anomalous with respect to the existing structure for distributing federal monies. Recent dialogue between the Council of State Library Agencies and the

Council of Computerized Library Networks would suggest that the multi-state regional networks have begun to explore this terrain.

For networks whose boundaries are coterminous with a single state's boundaries, the issue of relationship to the government is quite closely tied to libraries' associates in human services delivery. That is, libraries are likely to be able to link or to be forced to link to other providers of service as a function of the relationship among libraries, education (K-12 and higher), and other human service organizations within state government. Once again, the network's future is to be determined in part by directly facing and exploring the problems and opportunities that arise from its unique history and identity. This centrally includes the network's bedfellows in the eyes of the state legislature and the general public. We shall devote a few more sentences to this linkage, as a driving force which can be used to open new areas of program and support, in conclusion below.

Finally, we suspect that the trade-offs deriving from size, composition, and mode of operation of the governing body will be most crucial to individual library networks—as they were most crucial in our deliberations for OCLC. It is here that critical issues concerning the network's identity as perceived by its users raises basic questions—questions of degree of participation by members, range of relevant interest groups to be involved, and the degree of priority placed on efficiency of operation as a function of the stakes for and direction of greatest likely future success.

We are thus suggesting that the same three sets of issues we considered for OCLC—structure, environment, and role—should be considered in creating any network governance. The stakeholders and driving forces making up a typical network environment are shown in Figure 3. Possible driving forces arising from policy initiatives in government are shown in the upper lefthand quadrant; important initiatives launched by organizations in the other three quadrants will be a matter of the unique character of events in different regions. To help suggest possible roles, we refer you to the great breadth of organization shown among the stakeholders and our assertion above that governance is a dynamic enough element of organizational identity to be used to help realize—and alter—role.

Think for a moment of the many interests, some of which are related closely to network interests, of the organizations shown in Figure 3. With that perspective, examine Figure 4. This figure represents the fact that a single secondary, but important constituency of OCLC, was first identified, then involved in governance, and finally began to influence the way OCLC makes decisions. Inclusion of this stakeholder is helping to confirm OCLC's orientation to using management tools available from the private sector to increase effectiveness. A similar alteration in the organization, and eventually in either kinds of services offered or orientation to delivering services, could be attained if one or several of the types of organizations shown in Figure 3 were identified as potential allies for the future and gradually involved in governance. (Ally here includes both ally against future trouble and ally for future gain.) The final Figure 5 generalizes the process.

The determination of the organizations and interest groups to be embraced as secondary constituencies in governance is an individual matter. It relates to the organization's specific past, strengths, and unique relationship(s) with other organizations in its environment. (This is why there cannot be a generic answer to network governance.) Thus, whether or not today's state and regional networks play a roughly similar role vis-a-vis national, private, and public service providers, their strengths and weaknesses, their origins, the styles of their leadership, and key adjacent stakeholder interests—all are different enough that we would hope not be see great similarity among networks below the level of their national systems interfaces.

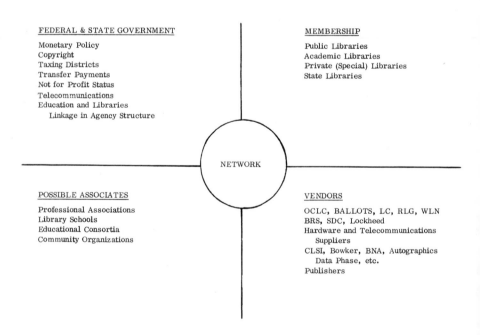

Figure 3. Network environment.

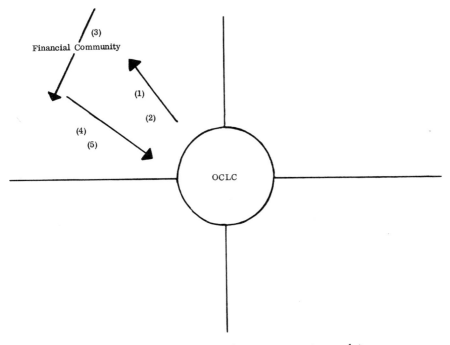

Figure 4。 Evolution through governance (example).

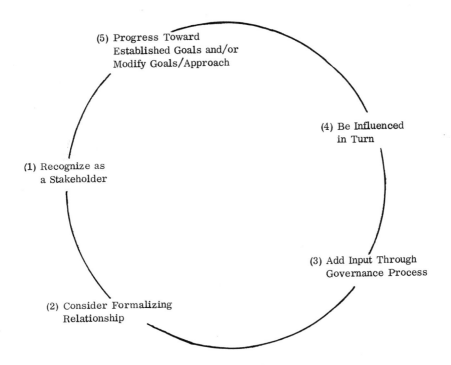

Figure 5. Evolution through governance.

Chapter 20

COMMENTS ON THE GOVERNANCE OF LIBRARY NETWORKS: PURPOSES AND EXPECTATIONS

Beverly P. Lynch

University Librarian
University of Illinois at Chicago Circle
Chicago, Illinois

The Montgomery/Dowlin paper (Chapter 18) offers a surfeit of issues upon which to comment. The issues I have chosen are those related to interorganizational relationships, the theoretical terms being the impact of the environment upon the internal structure and operations of the library. The paper thus gives me an opportunity to explore ideas relating to my own research, an opportunity I am very pleased to have.

At this conference we have talked about the structure and governance of networks on several different levels, the level of the individual and his or her behavior within the library or within the network, the library and its relationships with other libraries, and the network consisting of libraries or groups of libraries interacting with one another. We have not spent as much time as perhaps we should on analyzing the impact of networks upon the internal structure and the organizational behavior of the library. The issues pertaining to these matters are not simple. They are extraordinarily complex.

Montgomery and Dowlin propose that the unenlightened librarian constitutes a barrier to library cooperation. You will recall such barriers in their paper as "custodial mentality of librarians," "unwillingness to experiment," "thinking of only one type of cooperation," "over-emphasis by librarians on housekeeping activities." These barriers, which are characteristics at the individual level of analysis, are not the only impediments to successful networking, nor may they be fundamental impediments. Though I am always disappointed to have these characteristics assigned to librarians, I do concede that people are people, and people may indeed present barriers to

213

organizational change. We shouldn't forget that people also make change occur. There are organizational barriers, organizational elements which influence the structure and governance of networks and which influence the structure and operations of libraries. An analysis at the organizational level may help us understand that barriers will remain after all librarians have agreed to experiment, or have de-emphasized housekeeping, etc. We have little research to guide organizational analysis, so our comments mainly are in theoretical terms.

Some tantalizing hypotheses already have been suggested by earlier speakers:

* The lower the autonomy of the library, the greater the library's interest in decision-making.

* The greater or more complete the participation of the library in a network, the more internal conflict within the library.

* The greater the impact on the library by outside forces, the more interest on the part of the library in controlling those forces.

Librarians who have the greatest interest in the governance of networks seem to be from libraries already involved heavily in cooperative ventures, are planning innovative technical changes which they see as interlocking with other libraries, or perhaps those with the greatest vision of the future. The interest of these librarians in designing governance structures stems from a self-interest in making certain they or their libraries are included in these structures. Thus as librarians perceive a greater diminution in their library's autonomy, the more they will attempt to influence the decision-making of the cooperative venture. (Thus, the lower the autonomy or the perceived autonomy of the library, the greater the library's interest in decision-making.)

Internal conflict occurs in libraries when a library is involved heavily in networking because library members at levels below that of director become engaged in inter-organizational activities, in coordination and in communication—in boundary-spanning roles if you will—bringing new and uncontrollable elements into the library, generating conflict of ideas, of goals and objectives. (Thus, the greater or more complete the participation of the library in a network, the more internal conflict within the library.)

Because the library wishes to reduce uncertainty, it will seek ways to control these outside forces; interorganizational relationships will become formalized, certain library jobs will be designed for control purposes, interlocking directorships will emerge. (Thus, the greater the impact on the library by outside forces, the more interest on the part of the library in controlling those forces.)

For purposes of enhancing the development of library networks, we view all libraries as having the same basic purpose, that of service to users. By speaking in global terms and identifying a purpose with which we cannot disagree, we tend to avoid analysis of various types of libraries in terms of environmental or organizational differences. For instance, the influence of the controlling organization (e.g., in the case of the academic library the controlling organization is the university) will vary from one type of library to another, from one size of library to another, will vary across time, and will influence internal affairs to the library. The response of a particular library to network participation may vary accordingly. The library's reward structure, the locus of its principle source of funding, the demands of its primary constituency, promotion and salary structures, hiring and firing policies and procedures are carried out within the individual library and will influence to a certain extent the library's response to interorganizational cooperation. Even though the purpose of service to users is basic, organizational variations in terms of environmental differences, technological differences, differences in size and scale as well as structure will lead libraries to respond differently to the structure and governance of networks and of interorganizational arrangements.

Montgomery and Dowlin develop a framework to help us understand the nature and cause of conflict in library networks. They suggest exchange theory and dependency theory as useful approaches in furthering our understanding of networking. These theoretical perspectives presently dominate the research on organizations. The general research thrust is to examine the focal organization in the context of its organizational set in order to sort out power relationships and situations of conflict.[1]

According to exchange theory, an interorganizational relationship occurs when two or more organizations decide to interact for the purpose of deriving mutual benefits. Each organization perceives that by interacting with another it will be better able to attain its goals than by remaining autonomous. The motivation for forming an exchange relationship most often occurs during periods of scarce or declining resources. Exchange theory, while explaining some of the motives for the development of interorganizational relationships, also suggests that the organizational interactions are characterized by a high degree of cooperation and problem-solving; conflict and bargaining are diminished in an exchange relationship. By and large, the organizations are motivated to coordinate their efforts in order to maximize joint benefits.

If two libraries enter into an exchange relationship, a cooperative agreement, or some kind of networking arrangement, each assumes the other will make demands upon it. Libraries will display reluctance to continue an exchange relationship if demands require sacrifices which exceed the perceived reward. Under a norm of reciprocity which is implied in an exchange, the exchange should be mutually beneficial and roughly equivalent.[2] The voluntary system of interlibrary loan is an example of an exchange relationship developed so that libraries would share resources in a roughly equivalent way. If reciprocity is to occur, the needs of both participating libraries must be filled by the exchange. In some instances involving the voluntary interlibrary loans arrangement the norm of reciprocity is not met, so some libraries which are heavy lenders and not heavy borrowers have designed systems of payment so that the exchange will become more nearly reciprocal.

The system of exchange through traditional interlibrary loan was inhibited by a number of factors but perceived lack of reciprocity certainly was a major one. Each autonomous library is accountable to its own authorizing body and is evaluated primarily in terms of specific services rendered to a primary clientele. Exchange relationships indeed are influenced by this perspective.

Dependency theory assumes that the interorganizational motivation is asymmetrical. One organization is motivated to interact; the other is not. A relationship is formed only when the motivating organization is powerful enough to force or to induce the other to interact. For at least one of the organizations the motivation or pressure to interact is generated externally; if free to choose, that organization would prefer to remain autonomous. According to dependency theory, interactions are characterized by bargaining and conflict. Each organization seeks to attain its own goals at the expense of the other.[3] On the face and without extensive analysis, exchange theory and dependency theory do seem to explain some interlibrary behavior, particularly in terms of motivation and conflict. These theories may help us understand some conflict regarding library networks. But additional analyses also are useful.

The analysis of the library in relation to its environment begins with the observation that the library responds to constraints imposed upon it. Different environmental conditions and different organizational relationships lead to different organizational structures and accommodations. Some theorists[4,5,6] suggest that the greater the variability and the uncertainty in the environment the more the organization will be adaptive, the organizational roles will be open to continual re-definition, and coordination will be achieved by frequent meetings and considerable lateral communication.

If the organization's environment is characterized by a high degree of complexity, there will be greater role specialization particularly in those areas of the organization which deal directly with the environment; and problems of coordination among these specialists will increase.

Complex, heterogeneous, and unstable environments impose more constraints and contingencies upon the organization and create greater decision-making uncertainty than do environments that are simple, homogeneous, and stable.[7] In a study of industrial firms, those departments with more uncertain environments relied less on formal rules and procedures, had fewer reviews of job performance, and were generally less formal than those departments in organizations with more certain environments.[8] In a study of health and welfare agencies, those organizations that had more formal exchanges with other organizations reported more decentralized decision-making structures, were more innovative, and provided more formal mechanisms of communication.[9]

The use of environmental analyses to further our understanding of organizational relationships stems from the growing use of the open system theory in the study of organizations. There is an important qualification which we should make however, lest we become too enamoured by the argument that the environment in which the library operates determines its organizational structure and processes. Not only are there other important variables which will influence organizational structure and process, for example, technology and size, there are several manifestations of what we might call strategic choice.[10] Library decision-makers do have an opportunity to select, at least to some degree, the type of environment in which they will operate. (It is in recognition of the ability to choose environments and to make strategic choices which leads us to Pittsburgh to talk about library networking.)

Librarians, particularly leaders of libraries, have certain objectives they intend to meet. The leader can decide which functions the library will undertake to achieve those objectives. Depending upon the immediacy of objectives, different segments of the environment will be distinguished and emphasized. The observable boundaries between the library and its environment can be defined to a large degree by the kind of relationships the decision-makers chose to enter into with the decision-makers in other organizations. Decisions as to who the clientele shall be or the kind of employees to be hired also will influence the organization's behavior.

Library leaders identify the expectations of those providing the organization's resources. (In the case of libraries these expectations might be provided by the administration of the university, the Board of Trustees, the state board of higher education, the state library.) The library decision-makers seek to determine trends in the environment. (In the case of libraries these trends might be assessing where networking is going, whether there can truly be adequate delivery systems, whether the library's clientele care about networks, how well the library is performing.) After these evaluations, goals and objectives are formed and are reflected then in the organizational choices which are made. With respect to the external variables, the environmental issues, the decision may be to move in or out of a cooperative arrangement, to add or to reduce classes of clients, etc. With respect to the internal variables, choices will be made which seek to place personnel, technology, and structural arrangements in an internally consistent design.

Libraries work in an environment of complexity, ambiguity and constant change. Each library manager seeks to reduce the complexity and ambiguity, since it is very difficult to manage a library which is in a constant changing environment. We seek to routinize the non-routine, to structure the unstructured, to make certain the uncertain. The strategic choices librarians make regarding the structure and governance of networks will depend upon whether the library is perceived as being in an exchange relationship or a dependent one; whether the library's reduction in autonomy goes past some critical point, how the library will move to control or reduce conflict, how the library responds to the impact of forces outside it.

Reluctance or hesitation to agree on a grand design for a national network may be due, at least in some part, to these organizational factors. It is useful to have this opportunity to explore them.

REFERENCES

1. Lynch, B. P. "The Academic Library and its Environment." College & Research Libraries, v. 35 (March 1974), pp. 126-132.

2. Negandhi, A. R., ed. Organization Theory in an Interorganizational Perspective. Kent, Kent State University, Comparative Administration Research Institute of the Center for Business and Economic Research, 1971.

3. Schmidt, S. M. and T. A. Kochan. "Interorganizational Relationships: Patterns and Motivations." Administrative Science Quarterly, v. 22 (June 1977), pp. 220-234.

4. Burns, T. and G. M. Stalker. The Management of Innovation. London, Tavistock, 1961.

5. Aiken, M. and J. Hage. "Organizational Interdependence and Intraorganizational Structure." American Sociological Review, v. 33 (1968), pp. 912-930.

6. Lawrence, P. R. and J. W. Lorsch. Organization and Environment. Boston, Harvard Business School, 1967.

7. Thompson, J. D. Organization in Action. New York, McGraw-Hill, 1967.

8. Lawrence and Lorsch, op. cit.

9. Aiken and Gage, op. cit.

10. Child, John. "Organizational Structure, Environment and Performance
    —The Role of Strategic Choice." Sociology, v. 6 (1972), pp. 1-22.

Chapter 21

THE GOVERNANCE OF LIBRARY NETWORKS:
A CALL FOR ACTION

Henriette D. Avram

Director
Network Development Office
Library of Congress
Washington, D. C.

As I read the position papers for this conference, it appeared to me that nowhere had we developed a network concept with a statement of network properties and basic functions around which to discuss the topics of the conference. I find it difficult to understand how we can home in on the identification of problems, to say nothing of finding solutions, without a statement of a network concept around which to begin to shape our thoughts.

The staffs of the Library of Congress Network Development Office and the National Commission on Libraries and Information Science (NCLIS) recently "retreated" for the day away from modern inventions such as telephones to identify networking issues and problems of joint concern and to postulate approaches and solutions. In order to set the framework for that day's activities, we came to an agreement on the characteristics or properties of an information service network: the network is an information store (the materials themselves and all the records related to those materials); is pluralistic in make-up; has a well-defined organization; is capable of incremental change; has a broad-based user population (the network would not prejudge patterns or purposes of use, preclude special interests, or exclude systematically any group of institutions and concerns); and perform many functions. We defined the basic functions as: collection development management; placing materials under bibliographic control; finding and delivering the materials; and using the materials and related records for their information content.

This statement is offered for your consideration, and I shall assume a network with these properties and functions as the basis for my paper.

I understand this section of the conference as dealing with the purposes and expectations of the governance of the national library and information service network, i.e., what is the reason for which the governance is to exist and what do we expect the governance to accomplish. It is not clear to me that Montgomery and Dowlin (Chapter 18) interpreted expectations in the same context, i.e., they seem to be concerned with what we expect the network to accomplish rather than what we expect the governance to accomplish.

Having admitted to my confusion, I also admit to difficulty in separating consideration of the purposes of governance from what we expect governance to accomplish.

Nevertheless, I will respond to some of the authors' views as stated in their paper, present some of my own thinking, and call for some action.

Every organizational entity must be managed and at some threshold of organizational complexity a policy-setting body above operational management is required. We refer to this higher management as governance. Montgomery and Dowlin state "...the purposes of governance are to provide a mechanism for identifying goals and objectives of the library network; for the establishment of policies by which the library network will operate; and for the resolution of conflict. In particular, governance is also the mechanism for overcoming the barriers to networking. In a broader sense, the purpose of governance is to provide a mechanism for overcoming the barriers to any 'new' organization such as a library network."

In my opinion, the purpose of the governing body can be stated as the exercise of authority to set policy and objectives that serve the needs of the network's constituency and to direct management to attain these objectives. (Here I define constituency as all levels of the network hierarchy.) In so doing, governance must insure that the policies and objectives adopted and the actions taken are for the benefit of the network organization per se which must have priority consideration over any individual organization making up its constituency.

The bottom line of governance is the production of unambiguous decisions regardless of any opposing views of individual members of the governing body.

We expect then that governance will seek funding and exert financial control, will develop an organization that will assist the network constituency in meeting their own service requirements, produce a management structure capable of meeting the stated objectives of the network organization, and hire the management to see that the objectives are met.

Given these purposes and expectations for the governance of the network, let us consider the barriers to networking as seen by the authors. These barriers may or may not be applicable to the topic of governance.

Leading with the discussions of barriers, Montgomery and Dowlin state that library networks are still in their infancy. Although we are nowhere near the implementation of a full service network, I cannot fully agree with the authors in this assessment. There are over two thousand institutions in this country using the computer-based utilities such as OCLC, Inc., the Washington Library Network, and BALLOTS. These computer-based utilities provide different levels of service, satisfying a variety of library functions.

However, we do in fact have a long way to go and there certainly are many barriers to progressing in an orderly fashion and at an increased pace toward full service network development. Many of the barriers given by Nolting and cited by Montgomery and Dowlin can be categorized as fear resulting from a lack of common understanding of what networks ought to be, what they will require of the staff and of the management of libraries, and how they will help to better serve the clientele of libraries. To the Montgomery/Dowlin list of psychological barriers, I would add uncertainty and insecurity with respect to estimating costs and acquiring necessary funding.

Another impediment to progress is the tendency in some quarters to pay lip service to coordination and cooperation. At all levels of network endeavor, competition between individuals reflects lack of confidence in ability to cope with situations in an environment they do not control and concomitant fear of loss of status.

Since our major problems seem to stem from the fact that many people do not have a sufficient understanding concerning the different facets of information networks, are we not faced with the requirement for a concentrated educational and marketing effort? There is no doubt that mounting this effort is a challenge, and I would recommend that we put the best minds to work and let this be the subject of next year's Pittsburgh conference. We need to get across the idea that participation in networking will mean a certain loss of autonomy, which will be compensated for by the use of the bibliographic work done by others and by greater access to materials outside one's own library. We need to emphasize that indeed there will be a cost to following standards, but there would also be a cost to not following standards, in duplication of efforts and in failing to get maximum benefits from the network. Library staff should be exposed to the network possibilities for innovative services. Administrators must understand the impact of the network on their staff, the resources required to fully use the network, and the implications of the major organizational changes that will result from networking. I realize the magnitude of such a task, but there are already in being certain entities that could assume some of the responsibility. For example, the Management Review and Analysis Program of the Association of Research Libraries, supported by several foundations, is partially responding to this educational requirement by addressing the needs for managing change created by technological advances. And we also have in place the Continuing Library Educational Network Exchange (CLENE).

The public must also be included in this educational and marketing effort. They should understand the costs and benefits of resource sharing, the role of the technology, and the problems of funding and governance. The White House Conference on Library and Information Services is expected to produce direction for legislation for information networking. Therefore, it is urgent that we educate the delegates to the problems libraries have in serving public needs. How else can we expect to elicit their support?

In addition to the need for further understanding through training, we should seek to also learn by doing. Information systems such as the national library and information service network are far too complex to be fully understood and designed as one grand plan. The final system will involve the integration of many modules and we will modify and augment many of these modules, based on knowledge gained from developmental and operating experience.

The impossibility of building the entire system at one time and the benefit to be gained from experience has already been recognized. In an attempt to come to grips with something less extensive than the entire NCLIS program, the Library of Congress Network Advisory Committee proposed the development of a library bibliographic component as the first stage toward the full service network.[1] This component encompasses segments of the communications system and the bibliographic system discussed in the Montgomery/Dowlin paper and is the mechanism whereby a member of any one computer-based utility will have available the data base and services of the other utilities in the network.[2] Although more limited in scope, the library bibliographic component is based on and is in accord with the NCLIS program document.[3] Recognizing the complexity of attempting definition of the entire information network, the Network Advisory Committee considered that the library bibliographic component would demonstrate networking viability in the shortest time frame.

Based on the work of the Network Advisory Committee and through efforts by staffs of the Council on Library Resources and the Library of Congress Network Development Office, a program document was prepared and used by the Council to request monies from several major funding agencies. Most of this money has been committed and will be funneled through the Council for a development effort. The management of this development will be vested in a committee involving the Library of Congress, the National Commission and the Council. The Council will assume responsibility for administration of the development effort. Advisory teams will review objectives, technical plans, and operating policies. Thus, in the not too distant future, it is hoped that a part of the system will be completed and ready for operation.

It is expected that we will learn a great deal from building and operating this part of the system that will serve us in good stead in planning, building, and operating other parts of the system. Likewise the actual costs of the development and operation of the network cannot be usefully estimated at this time because we do not have precise definition of the system or knowledge of the resources required for development and operation. We will be able to get a firmer grasp on costs as we progress toward the development and operation of certain aspects of the network and more detailed specifications of others. We already know that at least part of the development effort of the network will be supported by private granting agencies, and it is anticipated that the operational network will be economically viable, capable of sustaining itself. In order to help realize this goal, libraries must reorganize their own operations so that networking capabilities will not be an add-on but will become an integral part of the operations of each library, otherwise the cost of the network would be superimposed onto the costs of member library operation. In addition, the networking capabilities becoming part of the library's operation provides the vehicle through which the library contributes to the network.

Working toward the development of the library bibliographic component, the Network Advisory Committee report recommended that certain tasks described in its paper receive the highest priorities for action. Among these tasks was a study to specify the legal and organizational structure for the library bibliographic component, i.e., its governance. A subcommittee was formed to write the requirements for such a study in order to put that statement of work into a request for proposal for contractual services. This subcommittee has met for a period of over a year, and I regret to report that there is still no agreement on the content of that work statement. I consider this most unfortunate since, like the bibliographic component itself which, when developed, will provide empirical data toward the building of the larger information network, a study to recommend a governance structure of the bibliographic component would provide background data to help understand the requirements of the capping agency for the full service network.

Why should it be so difficult to agree on the content of a work statement leading to a study? Could this be evidence of some of the psychological barriers at work? I submit that we need the substantive results that such a study would provide and that the study will have a secondary benefit as a learning process for us all.

In reviewing what has been considered to date concerning a governance structure for an information network, it is clear that here we are truly in our infancy. We have just begun to develop the requirements (not how the requirements will be met, but what they are) and the objectives (not how the objectives will be achieved, but their definition). We do not know the shape of the full service network well enough to evaluate which governance structure would be the most appropriate.

The study by Arthur D. Little, Inc., leading to a new governance structure for OCLC, supports my position.[4] Compared to the full service network envisioned for this country, OCLC, though anything but insignificant, is limited in its functions and small in its membership constituency. However, OCLC operated under one set of conditions long enough for the results, when studied and understood, to provide criteria upon which to recommend the next generation governance structure.

The recently published technical development plan for a National Periodicals Center probes into the organization and management for one network component whose functions are fairly well documented and understood, and suggests an approach to the governance of multi-components.[5] The national library board that it proposed developed out of a need for a structure that would permit the simultaneous development and growth of related systems, in this case the National Periodicals System and the library bibliographic component. These components must eventually be linked and function together in an orderly fashion. Without commenting on the pros or cons of the proposed board, because alternative governance structures are the province of the next section of the conference, I would consider that such a board would at least enable us to get started. Perhaps the board could be considered interim and from experience with it a longer term governance structure could be developed. The main point here is to again place emphasis on learning by doing.

John Bystrom's paper (Chapter 25) calls for a plan which includes the establishment of a Public Corporation to manage the Nationwide Library Information Service and he cites two examples—the Satellite Communication Act of 1962 which authorized the formation of COMSAT (Communications Satellite Corporation) and the Public Broadcasting Act of 1967 authorizing the Corporation for Public Broadcasting. Casual investigation into both COMSAT and The Corporation for Public Broadcasting reveals at least the following:

> COMSAT, although established under public law, is a private corporation—its Board of Directors made up of those elected by the shareholders and those appointed by the President of the United States with the advice and consent of the Senate. COMSAT is subject to regulation by the Federal Communica-

tions Commission. COMSAT consolidated reports available to me show that COMSAT has been profitable in every year since at least 1972.

In contrast, The Corporation for Public Broadcasting has a board of directors appointed by the President and is supported by public funds. Public broadcasting has constantly been plagued by internal turmoil and inadequate government funding. The January 14, 1978 issue of Congressional Quarterly reviews the present unhappy situation, and reports on Presidential and Congressional activities to rectify the situation.[6] After ten years of operational experience, public broadcasting can be said to have made a significant contribution to society but the program is seriously threatened by a lack of funding and a bureaucracy.

These two very different corporate financial structures indicate that the recommendation to establish a nonprofit public corporation should be carefully studied before we settle on it as the structure for the U.S. information service.

We already know the purpose and the expectations of governance, but we cannot define the governance structure when we have not yet fully defined the network. We cannot define the network completely due to its complexity but we have made progress defining modules of the network which, when developed, should assist in the definition of other modules. As the structural form of the network develops, optimum governance structures should become more apparent.

What is going on at this conference focuses our attention, if only briefly, on governance. But I would like to see us go much further. I would like to think of this as the beginning of a discussion and the first step in an earnest effort to come to grips with the many issues surfacing at this meeting. I would like to propose that a governance development group, perhaps sponsored by NCLIS, be established and meet frequently to address these concerns. But whoever sponsors it, the need for such a forum is clear: we need to begin to think and to apply systematic attention to this problem of governance. And we need to do it now!

REFERENCES

1. Henriette D. Avram and Lenore S. Maruyama, eds. Toward a National Library and Information Service Network: The Library Bibliographic Component. Prepared by the Library of Congress Network Advisory Group. (Washington: Library of Congress, June 1977).

2. The three systems discussed in the Montgomery and Dowlin paper—the resource system, the bibliographic system, and the communications system—are not three discrete entities. The communication system is the use of the technology to link together the various information resources and thus permit greater resource sharing. The resource system and the bibliographic system are interdependent—the bibliographic system existing to place the collection under control in order to find the item or to give information about the collection. The National Commission, in its study, Resources and Bibliographic Support for a Nationwide Library Program (Rockville, Md., Westat, Inc.; Washington, D.C., U.S. Government Printing Office, August 1974), describes these systems as making up the network.

3. Toward a National Program for Library and Information Services: Goals for Action. Prepared by the National Commission on Libraries and Information Science (Washington, D.C.: U.S. Government Printing Office, 1975).

4. Arthur D. Little, Inc. A New Governance Structure for OCLC: Principles and Recommendations. Case Team: J. Harrison [and others], (Cambridge, Mass., November 1977).

5. Council on Library Resources. A National Periodicals Center: Technical Development Plan, (Washington, D.C., 1978).

6. Congressional Quarterly, 36: 67-70, (January 14, 1978).

Chapter 22

NETWORK GOVERNANCE: PURPOSES AND
EXPECTATIONS — COMMENTS

Charles H. Stevens

Executive Director
SOLINET
Atlanta, Georgia

When I was growing up, I used to listen to the stories my dad told me. One of his favorites comes to me to share with you now.

Two men were working on a WPA street repair gang (that tells you when I was growing up). One of the men said, "I hear a lot of talk these days about communism. Is that just another name for resource sharing?" "Well," said the other, "I don't know about resource sharing, but communism is when you've got two Packards and you give me one because I have none." "Oh," said the first, "that sounds okay." "Communism is when," continues the other, "you've got two yachts and you give me one because I have none." "That's okay too," said the first. "Finally, communism is when you have two shirts and you give me one because I have none." "Beans," said the first, "I don't like it. I've got two shirts. I don't think I want anything to do with resource sharing."

Now, let's consider what to do about the Montgomery/Dowlin paper (Chapter 18). Since he quotes me from time to time, I think that if I praise him I'll be self-serving, and if I criticize him, I'll be panning myself. Instead of trying to swim between Scylla and Chrybdis, I'll try to wade in some other waters.

To do so, I'll have to go back to the topic and scope of the conference. The topic, you recall, is The Structure and Governance of Library Networks. The scope included these sentences, "a host of unresolved problems centering on management and organization, standardization, criteria for network membership, choices among complex technological options, interrelationships among network, measures of network performance, and financing demand immediate attention. Among the most compelling issues are those of network design and network governance. "

My contention is that the governance considerations we have been talking about are worthy of a different look than they have had here in other sessions. Carlos Cuadra touched on the issue when he mentioned that Allen Kent had omitted the brain in his comparison of network governance to body systems. The point that I want to add is that practically all animals and all human organizations have a governance. Yes, they have it. It is not added later or tacked on as an afterthought. It is organic—it grows with the original product.

Even dinasours had a governance mechanism—that's how old it is. Just about everyone has a chuckle when someone mentions dinasours. The laugh starts because everyone realizes that there are no dinasours around in Pittsburgh today. The comment is that they became extinct because they couldn't adapt to changing conditions; they didn't have the brain (governance) that would help them to adapt.

I hope we can do as well as the dinasours. They were around for 70 million years, give or take 2 million! Some flew, all survived, tramped the earth, and proliferated. If you want to compare, the earliest libraries were new not more than 5,000 years ago and the oldest network has only two decades at the outside. Wish me a dinasour, please, as far as governance is concerned.

Speaking of old, I gave some attention to the word government from which governance is an ungainly derivative.

"Governance, " says the author, "is the sum of the relationships between participants and their institution. " So if the Montgomery/Dowlin paper is to examine the purposes and expectations of networks, it is to look at the sum of all the relationships between the members and the network. In that connection, government has a history going back to the primitive.

No less an authority than the Encyclopedia Britannica contributes this to the discussion: "The characteristic feature which differentiates primitive government from the later forms is the lack of any kind of regularized or institutionalized administration. . . Primitive government in its most general connotation may be described as a government incidental to tribal life and informally linked to its general patterns of behavior and belief. "

Now, for the words "institutionalized administration, " I think you should hear bureaucracy because that's what it is. When you are in a bureaucracy, you had better know the facts and these are facts of library governance.

1. There are two forms of governance—one is participatory and
    it stems from the Greco-Roman tradition; the other is totali-
    tarian and has its roots in the tribal arrangements of a dozen
    so-called civilizations.

2. In the two forms of governance, the controlling element is
    not whether it is participatory or totalitarian. Instead of the
    form of the governance, it is the people in it that matter.
    People of good will can make a network function. Middle
    management carries the day; it always carries the day.

My contention based on just a little experience is all that stands behind the
conclusion, but as I look around, I can reinforce it. Find a successful network and you will find people of good will in management and especially in
middle management. It takes a worker to make a net—work.

Now there are other points to make in regard to the purposes and expectations of networks. Some years ago I enrolled in a fine course with the euphe-
mistic name of Aesthetics—(I would have taken Party 101 but it was full).
Professor Parker made this point: In good architecture form follows function;
at least it does when the artist, architect, sculptor or whatever gets his or
her act together. Given that the function of governance is to get the parts of
an organism or an organization moving together, the best governance uses
the KISS system. Yes, KISS, Keep it simple, stupid! The more complicated
the task and the working elements needed to do the task, the more important
it is to keep the governance simple and task-oriented.

Mr. Gaines reminded us that service to the library user is the reason for
the library and for the network supporting that library. The network must
contribute to the central activity, the main mission, or it is worthless and
useless. Once again the expectation, the purpose is service. Give service
and no one from the user community will look too closely at the system or its
governance.

One final point matters and matters very much to the successful operation
of any network. That point is scale. Not a musical scale, not rust or barna-
cles, but size. Did you ever see an institutional cookbook? The recipes are
not multiples of family recipes in the Better Homes cookbook. Scaling in
cookbooks or networks matters very much.

One interlibrary loan—no sweat!

10 minutes, $1.00 in postage

Ten interlibrary loans

100 minutes, $10.00 in postage

One hundred loans

    1,000 minutes, $100.00 for postage

One thousand loans

    10,000 minutes, $1,000. Sweat!

If a network is to fulfill its purpose and function, it must stay within scale.
I visited last week with Ed Shaw at RLIN-Ballots. He said that RLIN will try
to attract 40, 60, and perhaps 100 or so out-of-state libraries and reach
equilibrium. Scaling is his concern and he will avoid the trap, he says, of
exceeding reasonable expectations for growth.

    Let me summarize my points.

    1. Governance is organic.

    2. Service is the reason for governance.

    3. The form of governance is less important than the personnel
        who make it work.

    4. Simplicity in governance is probably a key to successful
        operation.

    5. Scale is the quintessential element in service structure.

Chapter 23

RESPONSE TO THE GOVERNANCE OF LIBRARY
NETWORKS: PURPOSES AND EXPECTATIONS

Patricia B. Pond

Associate Dean
Graduate School of Library and Information Sciences
University of Pittsburgh
Pittsburgh, Pennsylvania

I was tempted in this response to the paper by Leon Montgomery and Ed
Dowlin (Chapter 18) on the purposes and expectations in the governance of
library networks to steal a title from Charles Dickens' Great Expectations,
for reasons which will soon become clear. My comments are based not only
on issues raised in their paper but also in the opening paper by Allen Kent
(Chapter 1) on the objectives of networks and the appendix to that paper by
Margaret Mary Kimmel, children's specialist on the faculty of the Graduate
School of Library and Information Sciences.

NETWORKS: GREAT EXPECTATIONS OF RESOURCE
SHARING THROUGH NETWORKING

Montgomery and Dowlin trace the great expectations of resource sharing,
initially through library cooperation and more recently through networking,
to the statements of goals in the public library standards and in the Library
Services and Construction Act of 1956. While the public library standards
of 1956 envisioned a world in which public libraries "working together, sharing their services and materials, can meet the full needs of their users, "[1]
the Library Services and Construction Act moved beyond public libraries to
other types of libraries "without classifying the user as a public, school, or
academic library patron."[2] It is the user that is the focus of the 1975 goal
of the National Program for Library and Information Services of the National
Commission on Library and Information Science:

"To eventually provide every individual in the United States with
equal opportunity of access to that part of the total information
resource that will satisfy the individual's educational, working,
cultural, and leisure-time interests, regardless of the individual's location, social or physical condition, or level of intellectual achievement."[3]

The reality, however, of resource sharing networking is considerably
different from such great expectations. As Allen Kent notes in his opening
paper for this conference (Chapter 1):

"Typically, resource sharing networking has been directed to
disciplines and types of libraries for which material costs are
high and/or where there is a vocal clientele. Many areas have
not been touched and yet deserve attention."

Areas which deserve attention, but lack a vocal clientele—children and
young people—are the focus of this paper.

NETWORKS: THE REALITY OF LACK OF ACCESS
TO RESOURCES BY CHILDREN AND YOUNG PEOPLE

Children and young people, traditionally, have been heavy users of public
libraries, and today they also use the more than 74,000 school library media
centers located in public schools. Yet if children and young people sought to
fulfill any "great expectations" of equal opportunity of access to that part of
the total information resources that will satisfy their needs, they would soon
enough discover, as Theordore Hines suggests in a seminal paper on children's access to materials, that access is an adult right and such networking
as does exist, exists for the grownups. Hines believes that barriers to
access arise "either from a failure to perceive properly how children's intellectual development does require access to a very wide range of titles, or
from a setting of priorities which places children and young people very low
indeed on the totem pole."[4] I believe that both reasons Hines lists are operative. The average adult's knowledge of the intellectual development of
children is limited, and librarians often show little inclination to move outside one library's collection to another in order to meet the information needs
of children and young people. And yes, children do rank very low on the totem
as leaders in the current children's rights movement point out. One of these
leaders, Richard Farson, devotes a chapter in his book, Birthrights, to children's right to information and claims:

"The most serious denials of information to children come from
our perceptions about the nature of childhood. For the most
part, we don't think much about children's needs for information

and don't believe that we should make special provisions for them to enter our world. As a result, children are being denied information by being denied access to adult life, and in turn are denied access to adult life by being denied information. "[5]

Because children and young people lack the legal rights and status shared by adults, they lack effective means of voicing their concerns about basic institutions and organizations, including libraries and networks. Thus, it falls to librarians who serve children and young people in school and public libraries to voice concerns for access to resources and services of networks that their clientele cannot voice. As Margaret Mary Kimmel advocates in a recent paper on children's rights:

"In schools and public libraries, we must ask whether children deserve all the privileges and services given to adults—access to a total collection or interlibrary loan—or do we define children as those who need protection, education, guidance? Does their status alone demand different treatment for children?"[6]

If children and young people are not represented in the governance of library networks directly, and this is unlikely for they do not now typically serve on library boards, then they will need to be represented indirectly by librarians who serve them in school and public libraries. And if access to library resources through networking continues to be limited merely because of a patron's status, there is little hope for inclusion of children and young people in a national information policy. I have concentrated on the rights of children and young people to physical access to materials through resource sharing, and will not here explore the further limitations of bibliographic and intellectual access to print and nonprint materials used by children, and not infrequently by adults, which Kimmel summarizes in the appendix to Kent's opening paper for this conference. I do wish to note, however, that films, much used in school and children's libraries, are precisely the type of materials for which costs are high and towards which resource sharing efforts are typically directed. While bibliographic control of films leaves much to be desired, school and public libraries have a long history of sharing film resources which merits consideration in planning full-service networks.

NETWORKS: THE REALITY OF LACK OF
INCLUSION OF SCHOOL LIBRARIES

Also meriting consideration is the inclusion of school libraries in networking. For one reason, a large proportion of the 23 percent of this nation's population enrolled in public elementary and secondary schools could be served through school libraries; for another, it is likely that a school librarian may be the only professional librarian in a large geographic area and, in such areas, a school library may be the best service point for meeting the needs of users, whatever their age or status.

There are difficulties, of course. Network linkage to school libraries is indirect, that is, the contracting agency is a school district, not a library. Also, school libraries are only one of a myriad of concerns in a school district, and even if contractual agreements can be reached between library networks and school districts, their differing and often incompatible objectives lead to conflicts of the types delineated by Montgomery and Dowlin. Furthermore, the belief that school libraries would benefit from but contribute little to networks seems to prevail and provides little impetus to exploration of school library participation in networking.

In short, it is not easy, as Kent points out in his opening paper, to mix types of libraries in networking. Alice Fite, Executive Secretary of the American Association of School Libraries, supports this view, particularly as it relates to school libraries:

> "The cohesiveness which is apparent in the single-type network
> is not easily transferred to the organization bases of multitype
> library cooperatives. Although the goals of service may be the
> same for multitype library networks as for the single type, the
> legal bases and operational procedures are largely predicated
> upon those established for public library systems with the focus
> coming from the state library agency. This is a totally different
> structure and mechanism for operation for the school component
> in a multitype network...."[7]

While less than a tenth of the states cite the planned participation of schools in multitype library networks, the beginning of participation of schools in such a network can be cited in Colorado, California, Illinois, and Washington. Washington, particularly, indicates the potential for school library participation in networking: one-fourth of its 200 member libraries are school districts where cooperation and coordination of library services is occurring at the local, regional and state level.[8]

NETWORKS: GREAT EXPECTATIONS FOR
INCLUSION OF SCHOOL LIBRARIES

At the national level, the report of the Task Force on the Role of the School Library Media Program in Networking, accepted at the September 1978 meeting of the National Commission on Libraries and Information Science, provides the most exciting—and useful—guide to fulfilling "great expectations" for inclusion of school libraries in resource sharing networks. The goals toward which all recommendations in the report are directed, and one which is particularly relevant to a paper on the governance of library networks, is simply this:

> "...library networks in which school library programs are full, participating members be established and operational in every region, state, and area of the nation. "[9]

Implementation of recommendations in the report will require action not only by national associations such as the American Library Association (ALA), the American Association of School Librarians (AASL), and the Association for Educational Communications and Technology (AECT), to name but a few, but also by national councils, such as the Council of Computerized Library Networks (CCLN), the Chief Officers of State Library Agencies (COSLA) and the Council of Chief State School Officers (CCSSO). Last, but not least, school librarians who wish to participate in network governance will need to be more than "token technologists, " to steal a phrase from William Mathews' position paper (Chapter 12); they will need to be people with a broad sense for what is possible.

The Task Force report reviews the state of networking in school library media programs nationwide, including (in an appendix) an inventory of existing networks involving school libraries. This is valuable since there is so little available in print on such involvement. Much more valuable, however, is the clarification of the role of the school library media program in a national program for libraries and information services. Specifically the report covers:

- a rationale for inclusion of school libraries in networks
- contributions to networks by school libraries
- benefits to users of school libraries from participation in networks
- problems or barriers in school library participation in networks
- recommendations for overcoming problems or barriers to school library participation in networks

The rationale for inclusion of school library media programs in networks strongly supports the NCLIS goal of access to information for all users, because if schools are not involved as full participating members of library networks, a substantial segment of the population will be restricted and discriminated against in access to information and the resources of strong school library media programs cannot be shared fully with the general public. [10] The report also suggests, as do Montgomery and Dowlin, that goals of various types of libraries may include complementary goals which are not mutually exclusive. For in addition to their specialization as teachers as well as librarians, school library media specialists have much in common with other librarians:

> "They share the concerns of academic and special librarians in dealing with a collection designed to support the specific needs of their users. School, academic, and public librarians also share similar problems with regard to providing adequate budgets and professional staff. When school library media specialists have had contact with other types of librarians, the awareness of a common role has emerged."[11]

The contributions of school libraries to resource sharing networks are generally unrecognized and underutilized, according to the Task Force report. The reports identifies materials, services, and human resources which might be shared. Most likely of these to be shared are materials. Beyond the collections of literature for children and young adults, school library media collections include audiovisual materials of all types (with film resources particularly strong at the district and regional level), professional materials for teachers, career education materials, and high interest/low vocabulary reading materials.

The primary users of school libraries are, of course, students, but other users would benefit from school library participation in networking: teachers, school specialists such as counselors, school administrators, parents, and the general public.

The "problem areas" related to school library media program participation in networking identified in the report closely match the "barriers" to cooperation among libraries which Nolting described in 1969[12] and Montgomery and Dowlin analyze in their position paper. Both Nolting and the Task Force cite psychological factors first. In their study of participation of school libraries in networking prepared for the Task Force's use, Johnson and Hines found the major obstacle to successful networking seemed to lie in attitudes of librarians.[13] While Montgomery and Dowlin recognize that attitudes are difficult to change, they stress that governance provides a mechanism for overcoming barriers to networking. Nolting lists as a second barrier to cooperation lack of information and experience. Perhaps the psychological barriers and the barrier of lack of information and experience might be relieved considerably if school librarians were more systematically involved than is now the case in the governance of multitype networks.

Nolting and the Task Force also list political and legal factors as barriers to cooperation and networking. School library participation in networking is subject to a variety of state laws with two states, Colorado and Washington, having laws which clearly define a structure for interlibrary cooperation, and two states, Oklahoma and Connecticut, which specifically exclude school library participation in library cooperative or networking projects. At the local level, the school library decision-making process is slowed down by the necessity to pass through successive layers of structure, where principals and superintendents are intermediate authorities between school library media specialists and the school board. Barron, in a recent Library Trends issue on trends in governance, warns that the trend toward decentralization of control in schools with increasing autonomy at the school building level and the fragmentation among schools within a system and among systems themselves will have a negative effect on school media program planning.[14] Obviously, such a negative effect would extend to planning for school library participation in networking.

One other problem area in school library participation in networking, identified in the Task Force report—funding—Nolting lists with traditional and historical barriers; the other, communication factors, he lists with physical and geographic barriers. Regarding the latter, communication factors, the Task Force notes that in an era when on-line telecommunication links are essential to full school library participation in networking, some school libraries still lack a telephone!

The last problem area listed in the Task Force report, planning factors, is particularly related to governance. The Task Force suggests that "careful planning by a well-defined group of principals is needed to bring about effective participation by school library media programs and other kinds of libraries in a library network"[15] and that "pre-existing library networks that do not include school library media programs can themselves act as a barrier to the planning process. It is often more cumbersome to alter accepted patterns of cooperation, than to involve all potential users from the beginning."[16]

Whether school libraries become part of library networks when they are first organized or sometime later, Montgomery and Dowlin note that participation in "governance permits those using and running networks to express their interest and concerns, to establish goals and objectives as well as policies by which these goals and objectives are to be achieved."

Only by participation in the governance of networks by school librarians and other librarians serving children and young people can the interests and concerns of this group of young citizens be considered in network resource sharing. Such participation is now a rarity, but it is essential. One can only agree with Montgomery and Dowlin's conclusion that, in networking, the problems of technology may prove less formidable than those of governance!

REFERENCES

1. Public Library Service: A Guide to Evaluation with Minimum Standards, (Chicago: American Library Association, 1956), p. 7.

2. Frantz, John C. "The Library Services and Construction Act," American Library Association Bulletin, (February 1966), 60:151.

3. National Commission on Libraries and Information Science. Toward a National Program for Library and Information Services: Goals for Action, (Washington, D. C., U. S. Government Printing Office, 1975), p. xi.

4. Hines, Theodore C. "Children's Access to Materials," p. 625 in Zena Sutherland and May Hill Arbuthnot, Children and Books, 5th ed., (Glenview, Ill: Scott, Foresman and Company, 1972).

5. Farson, Richard. Birthrights, (New York, Macmillan, 1974), pp. 83-84.

6. Kimmel, Margaret Mary. Unpublished manuscript, 1978, p. 8. (Note: This manuscript will be published in a festschrift, edited by Kimmel and Galvin for ALA publishing, to appear in 1979.)

7. Fite, Alice. Untitled manuscript, 1978, p. 6. (Published in revised form as "Networking: An Old Word Goes Back to School," American Libraries, [November 1978], 9:603-4.)

8. Ibid.

9. Report of the Task Force on the Role of the School Library Media Program in Networking, (Washington, D. C.: National Commission on Libraries and Information Science, 1978), p. 34.

10. Ibid., p. 5.

11. Ibid., p. 11.

12. Nolting, Orin F. Mobilizing Total Library Resources for Effective Service, (Chicago: American Library Association, 1969).

13. Johnson, Mary Frances K. and Theordore Hines. School Media Programs and Networking: A Position Paper, (Greensboro, N. C.: University of North Carolina, 1977).

14. Barron, Daniel. "The Control of Public Education and School Library Media Programs," Library Trends, (Fall, 1977), 26:280.

15. Report of the Task Force...., p. 57.

16. Ibid., p. 59.

Chapter 24

GOVERNANCE, PURPOSES: DISCUSSION

The discussion which follows has been transcribed from tape recordings, summarized and edited. Comments and questions have been attributed to speakers when their identity was provided. The editors of these proceedings take responsibility for any errors in fact or interpretation resulting from this process, since it was not feasible to provide proofs to discussants for checking.

Henriette Avram

I would like to ask Susan Crooks whether I understand that she was suggesting that the OCLC methodology could be used for the entire national library and information service network?

Susan Crooks

One of the points that we made in the governance recommendations was that the national library network was an evolving activity. I've been concerned during this conference that the span of objectives of a network as we talk about it ranges from the immediate needs of the local library, through sophisticated national service needs, through electronic communications. This will lead to a situation (in 10 or 15 years) where everybody is a "have"; now it is a situation of "haves" and "have nots." In data processing one would never have anticipated a time when everybody would be a "have," maybe even five years ago. But now I think, through a lot of the developments that were described this morning, electronics will have infiltrated everywhere in another 5 or 10 years. So applying any methodology would not lead to the same kind of discrete and relatively easily described structure that we did for OCLC. We would not be that discrete, probably, for a national network.

Mary Ellen Jacob - OCLC, Inc.

I wanted to correct one comment that was made by Ms. Pond regarding children and young adults in schools not having access to networks. It's certainly not true in the case of OCLC—we do have school systems using the network now. I was just told of a project that the SUNY network has, involving multitype cooperations, with schools giving children access to the system. Further, I'd like to say that I just recently did a survey by telephone of all the institutions using the public access terminals, and I'm very pleased to report that some of the most enthusiastic users of the terminal are in fact the children and that all of the use is not just playing games, and all of it is not foolish. In some cases they're actually using it for information needs. I'm surprised, but they're doing it. There is also use among academic institutions, use of terminals by the public, and some of that public includes the high school students coming in looking for additional information. So there's certainly evidence, at least as far as OCLC is concerned, that children and young adults have access and in fact are making some use of the resources available.

Patricia Pond

My point was not that they're not using the terminals, rather that they're often not represented indirectly or directly on governance.

Mary Ellen Jacob

With the new governance structure they're not excluded.

Beth Hamilton - Illinois Regional Library Council

Mrs. Pond, I'm very happy to have you say that participative management in network decisions is desirable by school librarians. I had hoped to hear it a lot earlier this afternoon, and I assure you that ours is one network which does have a school library representative. I would like to register a few comments about the paper by Montgomery and Dowlin (Chapter 18) as well as the panelist papers.

First of all, there is some discussion in the Mongtomery paper of the managerial decision process and the network managers performance in eliminating and overcoming barriers to networking. I would urge, however, a distinction be made between policy and managerial decision-making and the impact of each on network development. I know there's a school of thought that says the network manager can get around the board members, the policy makers, and get them to do what he or she wants. I do not think this is the way we want our networks to develop; I think we want full participation by representatives of all types of libraries.

Second, hardly any attention has been given this afternoon to the golden
rule of networking and that is whoever has the "gold" gets to "rule." That's
not just a funny saying—there is some serious examination needed here.
For example, the problems facing state libraries are reviewed by Montgomery, but they are reviewed from a state library point of view and not from
the point of view of those of us out here in the field. No attempt has been
made to deal with the problems of policy decisions by nonusers of networks
as required by many state statutes. For example, there has been no recognition at all of the contradiction between the logic and the need of governance
by network users and the fact of life of governance of statutory networks by
lay boards and by nonlibrarian bureaucrats.

Russell Walker - Upper Arlington Public Library

I have a question in regard to school participation in networks. One thing
we really haven't covered here is the great disparity existing between the
expenditures of public libraries and school libraries and the funding of public
libraries and school libraries. Obviously if a public library spends 25-27%
of its budget for resource materials and a school library spends one-half of
1% for library resources—and if a public library spends 50% for personnel
and a school library 80-90% for personnel—then obviously somebody is dig-
ging coal and somebody else is getting paid for it. That's a great problem
that has to be rectified. The public libraries are out there in limbo as far
as governance and finances are concerned and the school libraries have an
entirely different structure. And I think that kind of situation has to change.

Patricia Pond

I'd argue on one point. The disparity in the amount going for resources
(material resources versus personnel resources) is not as wide as you suggest. Most of the school libraries are not paying 90% for their staffing; it's
very similar to the public library and the academic library—somewhere in
the neighborhood of 75-80%.

Russell Walker

Well I'm familiar with the figures in our area and that's where I'm quoting
from. But again, if a public librarian is to share in the educational scene,
a public librarian cannot work evenings and weekends and start at a much
lower salary than a school librarian. If in fact the resources in a community
are available to public libraries, obviously when we talk about sharing we
should be talking about sharing resources—which means money as well as
materials.

Patricia Pond

The task force report I mentioned in my paper speaks about sharing three kinds of resources: services and human resources as well as materials. There are a lot of questions asked in a tight money time—could you not use materials more efficiently by making school libraries into public libraries and visa versa? After all, public libraries are open a great number of hours a week. The average school library works five days a week, nine months a year, and it's not generally available to people in the community during the summer months. There are exceptions to that. Through resource sharing you could make those materials available throughout the year. Those materials are housed on a shelf and are not being used. It is not very good fiscal management.

Harold Baker - Indiana State University

Just adding to the testimony of participation in school libraries in networking, we're very proud of the fact that in Indiana in our networks and in COLSA and in our ALSA regions, they are a very important part of our governance. We make every effort to make sure that they are on our executive committees and that they are well represented. In the very near future the Department of Public Instruction is starting a project to get the AV materials of the school and the libraries into our networks. We do consider them vital to network development.

Sally Drew - Division of Library Services, Wisconsin

I'd like to change the subject just a little bit. Throughout the discussion of governance, there has been very little discussion of the point of view of the users. As a nonprofessional in networking, it seems to me that most types of libraries have some kind of governing structure which does include lay people (not librarians). Public libraries have a lay board, schools have a school board, universities have a board of regents. And yet it seems to me that when you are talking about governance of networks and using the term user, you are usually referring to a professional. It would seem to me that there either needs to be some consideration given to the incorporation of lay people into this type of governance or some sort of composite of the lay/professional.

Patricia Pond

I couldn't be in more agreement with you than I am. One of the things I find is rather ironic in the White House Conference plan is that we have two-thirds lay people and one-third librarians, and many of the librarians complain that the lay people have too much control.

Henriette Avram

I made the statement that the network constituency and the clientele of libraries should be included. I also feel strongly about having to educate those lay people that will be going to the White House Conference, so they will know what the problems of the libraries are and will be willing and able to support us.

Susan Crooks

There are people out there who are laymen who are not being served in any kind of targeted way. The people I mean are public interest groups, citizens movements, decision makers, who are concerned today with cross-cutting problems— technology, science, economics, business, narcotics, occupational safety, health, energy. Those people have information needs that cross-cut disciplines. Many different kinds of information intermediaries are growing up to serve those people. They represent a more targetable population than many of the population we have felt we were missing in libraries. So these are the kinds of lay groups that I think also ought to be involved.

Adele Zenchoff - Virgin Islands Bureau of Libraries

The last speaker on school libraries made a very interesting point. The Virgin Islands' demonstration library network does include the school library agency as a central component of its emerging local network. As a matter of fact, our first project was a union list of 16-mm motion pictures, most of them educational films owned by the state educational library agency. But I think that it's also important to note, both in the discussion of school library participation and in the discussion of lay participation, that there are many libraries all across this country, all across the United States, including libraries that are in the off-shore territories in the noncontiguous states, as well as in the western states of the United States, which so far have not had any role in the governance of an emerging network or in being consulted on an emerging national network. Our resources are small, we would be the dependent libraries in any network; however, our people have need of information; we need to be consulted when it comes to development of technology, development of systems for delivery. Our people have more need perhaps than those who are in the large metropolitan areas. We do need enormous amounts of support, I believe, from the Federal government at the Federal level. We do need to be consulted about which way the networks will be developed. We are a small market. If we are talking about a market economy, we can never be considered; and yet, if we are talking about equal access to information, we must be considered.

Marc D'Alleyrand - Teachers College, Columbia University

In order to add to the few speakers or commentators about the ongoing programs, I want to say Teachers College Library is undergoing a complete renovation project—one of its aspects being the construction of an open education library, open to anyone who needs to have access to educational information. One of the features being contemplated now and being in the active development or planning stage is an access center—a development center, demonstration center which will include multi-media and educational material. Anyone who has needs, anyone who has suggestions, anyone who may wish to contribute would be more than welcome, and the person to contact would be the director of Teachers College Library, Teachers College, Columbia University.

Part Five

THE GOVERNANCE OF LIBRARY NETWORKS:
ALTERNATIVES FOR THE FUTURE

The growing significance of multi-type and multi-state networks suggests a potential federal role in terms both of support and regulation in order to assure equality of access to network services and resources. What are some of the realistic considerations in formulating governance for a nationwide network? How do we go about the difficult process of institution-building, insuring participation from appropriate parties, accommodating the ceaseless changes wrought by technology, learning lessons and moving forward from the networks that already exist? What institutions already exist, what new ones must be built?

The position paper distributed in advance of the conference is given in Chapter 25. Chapters 26-30 present reactions from the panelists. Chapter 31 presents the discussion at the conference.

Chapter 25

A PROPOSAL FOR NEW FEDERAL LEGISLATION

John W. Bystrom

Professor of Communications
University of Hawaii at Manoa
Honolulu, Hawaii

INTRODUCTION

The focus of this chapter is on Congress and on new legislation. Proposed is
a Federal strategy for the further development of library information services. Space limits allow only a bare-bone outline and attention is given to
the explanation of the components of a National Program with little opportunity to discuss the alternative choices considered and rejected. The basic
elements of the proposed legislation are drawn from a longer paper prepared
at the request of the National Commission on Libraries and Information
Science.

With legislation, Congress can effect several changes. It can authorize
the establishment of management to carry out stated functions. It can make
available Federal funds for stated purposes. And it can prescribe acceptable
and unacceptable behavior. However, Federal legislation cannot do it all,
and this is sometimes disappointing. In the case of the decentralized American library information system, Federal legislation can offer only limited
initiatives. Nevertheless, these can have important effects on operations
and services throughout the country. Federal legislation is essential, in
fact, if we are to make a solid effort in providing equal opportunity to citizens. Congressional action is required if we are to assure the rapid flow of
information on which national development—and probably national survival—
depends. The goal of making available to citizens, with reasonable effort on
their part, the world knowledge record is one that requires the active participation of the Federal government.

In their document <u>Toward a National Program for Library and Information Services</u>, the National Commission on Libraries and Information Science lists eight major objectives for action. Two of these objectives are addressed directly with this proposal. The Commission saw the need for establishing (1) a "locus of Federal responsibility" and (2) the development of a nationwide network of library and information services. These two effect the remaining six objectives, since they shape the management structure of central services for a highly decentralized national library information system.

When considering the Federal role, it is important to remember a central fact of the American library information system. Although the Federal government owns the operates an enormous number of libraries and information centers, most of the nation's information resources are the property of non-Federal organizations, not under the direct control of the Federal government. If broad nationwide objectives are to be achieved, it will be through the work of thousands of independent organizations with non-Federal facilities and without Federal employees. A cooperative approach is essential with Federal participation designed to achieve goals that are generally desired but not obtainable without some degree of central management.

There is a growing realization in our society of the importance of information and what its availability can mean in determining the future of individuals and the nation. In the past, control over information has won battles, destroyed cultures, and changed the course of human affairs. The founding fathers in the First Amendment sought to restrict government influence over channels of communication, man to man and man to God. Any approach to Federal library information legislation has to recognize the basic proposition that the flow of communications within society should remain free from central control. A National Library Information Program should increase the availability of information, and expand the individual's access to what he determines he needs. At the same time, management structures should clearly provide protection from Federal influence.

DEVELOPMENT PLAN

The Federal legislation outlined in this chapter embodies only three management changes:

(1) Development of a locus within the Federal government equipped to determine policy and carry on policy research but divorced from implementation and operational management.

(2) Gradual growth of a nationwide management structure in which central direction machinery is the product of the diverse knowledge sources and requirements of a pluralistic society.

(3) Development of an efficient and effective Nationwide Library Information Service that seeks to provide effective transmission from all library information institutional sources to all library information institutional receivers.

The proposed legislation is designed to retain all the basic elements of the current decentralized library system. No central agency within the Federal establishment is envisaged to coordinate the many Federal libraries, information services, and categorical programs, as is sometimes advocated. Rather, legislation would strengthen the National Commission on Libraries and Information Science as a national locus of policy development. The current Federal library information operations and categorical support programs would continue to follow established directions as authorized and funded by Congress. The two major structural changes involve cooperative action by the States and the Federal government in firmly establishing a regional level in the national library information structure and the establishment through Congressional action of a National Library Information Service.

The addition of the Nationwide Library Information Service, a network for sharing materials, is an opportunity to establish a national structure of management that allows the elements of the decentralized American system to cooperate in achieving national information objectives, such as encouraging equal access to all individuals wherever their location or whatever their income, maintaining the nation's lead as a technical power, and contributing to an informed electorate.

As envisaged, the system would provide for telecommunication interconnection of libraries and information services within a multi-level system allowing operating libraries to obtain materials on demand from designated state, regional, and national centers. In this context, a center refers to a management point in the system, not necessarily storage and other facilities. In most instances operation would be contracted for from existing institutions. Modest additions would be required, but major new facilities would probably be necessary only after traffic had developed. The system would use high quality telecommunications and computer systems under contract. In addition, the National Service would develop special services, such as a national periodical service, and specialist and research networks of various types.

The legislative proposal, when passed, would result in the establishment of a public corporation to manage the Nationwide Library Information Service.

The structural elements that are introduced in support of central responsibilities would depend on the depth and variety of experience that exists within the present decentralized system. Central goals would be achieved through mutual interaction of organizations managed and largely financed independent of the Federal government. The proposed management structure would engage the functioning units of the present system in support of nation-wide purposes and withhold from the Federal government a line management organization necessary to create a national system operated by central directive. Together the proposed structural elements would perform the functions that might alternatively be performed by a newly created central Federal agency or by delegation to an existing Federal agency or library. These two alternatives have been rejected.

It will be observed that Federal funds are largely directed to functional services performed by those who interface with the user, thereby strength-ening working units. Reliance is not placed on the decisions of central review boards, as in a Federal grant program. Services performed for users by operating units are reimbursed from Federal appropriations within an established cost schedule. Proposed financing is primarily from Federal tax sources with some application of user fees. Federal cost in the early stages will be small with gradual increases. This will avoid sudden un-announced modifications in existing categorical programs. The total develop-ment period covers 12 to 15 years.

We now turn to the basic elements of the program and the steps needed for early action.

STRENGTHENING THE NATIONAL COMMISSION

It is important to guard against giving to the National Commission high-sounding responsibilities without the tools for the job. The authority assigned to it by legislation and the resources provided should relate to the environ-ment in which it will function. Purposes should be clear and achievable.

We have nearly a decade of experience on which to base the authority appropriate to an effective National Commission. Opinion will differ on some matters, but most will agree that the resources allowed the National Com-mission have been insufficient. The modest changes outlined below are suggested by the writer as a method for more clearly defining the purpose and function of the Commission, increasing the financial and management resources available to it, and strengthening the cooperation needed with Federal and State agencies, and the public and private sectors, to actually achieve objectives.

What is not changed is the National Commission's position in the Executive Office of the President and its role as the nation's principal source of policy in library information.

In reading P. L. 91-344, the act that established the National Commission, it is apparent that the Commission has substantial leadership authority today, far more than it has exercised with the limited appropriations obtained thus far. The National Commission was conceived to provide policy guidance primarily to the Federal government. Operating authority such as that needed to build a Nationwide Service is lacking, and assigned powers are limited to those required for national policy determination.

No change in this general conception is envisaged. Building on past Congressional actions, it is proposed that the National Commission be strengthened as a center for policy and planning through specific statutory directives that enlarge the abilities to influence future development without changing the spirit of the current act.

Despite the importance of the subjects with which they deal, policy units in the Executive Office of the President often have a frustrating time. When established by administrative directive rather than Congressional action, they can find themselves dependent for effectiveness and survival on the operating agencies they are meant to lead. They often lack a popular base, close relationships with Congress, and essential ties with the change makers within the government. Often required to go to the line agencies, hat in hand, for needed manpower according to the rules of the game, they receive short rations to keep their energies at manageable levels.

It is important to guard against this condition. The National Commission would stake out its ground above the operating goals of Federal units, avoid inverted involvement in Federal programs and view itself as the principal source of nationwide leadership and the best hope of the citizen and the professional.

These changes are suggested as a means for strengthening the role of the National Commission as a locus within the Federal government badly needed to plan and coordinate national development of library information services.

(1) Reconstitute the National Commission as a public rather than a professional body. Membership will be representative of the public and will not include employees of Federal, State, or local governments, nor those with interests in the private sector which might be affected by decisions of the board.

(2) Establishment of an Advisory Council to the Commission made up of representatives of the library profession, the knowledge industry, and major user groups.

(3) Improvement in the Commission's capacity for policy planning with the establishment of a Center for Policy Studies under the Commission.

(4) Assignment of responsibility to the National Commission for the Federal Library Committee.

(5) Legislative authorization for a study of Federal government requirements for information services and networks to be carried out by the National Commission and a moratorium on further implementation of Federal government networking pending completion of the study.

(6) Congressional directives to Federal agencies to support and participate in particular phases of national program development.

(7) Separation of the National Commission from its administrative ties with the U.S. Office of Education.

(8) Develop relationships with field at policy level.

Added appropriations and authorized positions will be required to implement these changes.

The purpose is to enhance the National Commission's reputation as an informed, disinterested agent, representative of the citizenry as a whole, which draws on advice from all sectors of the field, and has the organizational capacity to determine ways and means for the better use of national resources.

The National Commission will become a leadership force only when it uses its new tools effectively and establishes itself with Congress by demonstrating its value in obtaining improved services or reduced costs. The National Commission will have gained the status needed for effective national planning when it begins to effect worthwhile changes with the cooperative support of operating institutions and without major offense to large sectors of the established library information order.

SELECTION OF COMMISSIONERS

Currently, the President is limited in his selection of Commissioners by carefully drawn statutory language that makes the National Commission a professional board. While keeping alive the suspicions that the legislation is the product of professional pressure, this provision reduces the credibility of the Commission when addressing questions of broad public policy. Any group that stands to benefit from public expenditures can be easily suspected of serving their own and not the public interest, or at least cannot convincingly answer the charge. Professionals and representatives of the information industry have a self-interest in greater appropriations, expanded authority, and larger programs. More effective advocates are those representatives of the general society.

It is proposed that P. L. 91-344 would be amended to strike the following language:

> "Five members of the Commission shall be professional librarians
> or information specialists and the remainder shall be persons
> having special competence or interest in the needs of our society
> for library and information services, at least one of whom shall
> be knowledgeable with respect to the technical aspects of library
> and information services and sciences."

The National Commission would be made up of citizens appointed by the President with approval of Congress. The new makeup would cast the National Commission in the role of protector of the public interest. It can appeal to Congress from the posture of those concerned with national goals: economic, social and international.

ADVISORY COUNCIL

Wide representation from the information community would be provided through a statutory Advisory Council, following the patterns of the United States Postal Service which has an Advisory Council of 11 members. Any one of a number of methods of selection would be workable, and it may seem desirable to set some membership conditions in the statute. The job of the Advisory Council is to improve the quality of national planning and to increase the sensitivity with which new programs are developed and applied. A strong tie with the professional is essential if National Commission policies are to be reflected in system behavior and concurrence by the field.

REGIONAL DEVELOPMENT

Regional library organizations are providing a variety of functions today that require a cooperative relationship among the States. A strengthening of regional organizations, defining the region as a distinct working level of a national system, is desirable. A strong regional level can serve as a buffer against arbitrary Federal dictation, as well as a fall-back base for continuing coordination of service if there is a failure of Federal leadership.

The regional organization should have responsibility for specific functions, clearly recognized by Federal law, and be identified as an integral part of the national system. It is proposed, for example, that regional organizations nominate one-third of the Board of Directors of the Nationwide Library Information Service. Many regional authorities will operate regional clearing-houses and nodes in the Nationwide Library Information Service. It is

essential that regional authorities have a clear legal relationship, both with
the States and with the Federal government, that is uniform nationwide.

Strengthening of the regional level counsels careful consideration of the
Federal-interstate compact. It is proposed that legislation include language
in which Congress agrees to compacts between States and authorizes Federal
involvement. The act would determine a procedure for setting up a Federal-
interstate compact agency. We could anticipate that most, if not all, existing
regional organizations would become compact agencies.

Under the United States Constitution, Congress is required to agree to
compacts between States. The action of approval by the many State legislatures can take several years. For this reason it is desirable for the Congress to give prior approval and set up a procedure that facilitates prompt
actions by the States. Congressional agreement to a compact arrangement
and the procedure to be followed for concurrence by State legislatures would
be spelled out in the act authorizing the new National Program.

Large scale enterprises—such as the New York Port Authority—have
been able to function effectively within the Federal-interstate compact arrangement. The importance of the compact is that a legal entity is established with
distinct rights. There is a legal and functional basis for several states to
operate cooperatively, share facilities and jointly work to achieve objectives.
This strengthens the agencies' relationship to the State legislatures involved
because the agency is approved by the State bodies. Federal authority is
limited, by the compact, both legally and because a functioning organization
is created with purposes and objectives growing out of the interests of the
library information community.

The Federal-interstate compact agency provides a middle level between
a Federal center and a large number of State and local units. Properly
designed, the new regional level can be a mechanism that brings into the
decision-making process the private libraries and urban libraries. The
traditional direct relationship between the Federal agency and the counterpart
State agency is not only insufficient to cover the range of productive organizations, it has the almost certain consequence of overweighting the importance
of government-owned facilities at the expense of the private institutions.

PUBLIC CORPORATION

In two important instances in recent years Federal statutes have authorized
a corporation in order to develop new communication services. If for no
other reason than the history of successful legislative action, careful consideration must be given to the public corporate form. In both instances

public and private interests were able to accommodate differences and legislation was passed with substantial majorities. The Satellite Communication Act of 1962 authorized COMSAT, the Communication Satellite Corporation. COMSAT combines elements of both public and private corporation. The Board is made up of public appointments by the President and appointments by leading domestic common carriers. Its stock is on the New York Stock Exchange.

The Corporation for Public Broadcasting was authorized by the Public Broadcasting Act of 1967. Its Board of Directors is appointed by the President and funds for its operation and use are provided by Congress.

The public corporation can be created only by an act of Congress specifically authorizing such action. Congress has allowed its greater flexibility of operation when compared with Federal agencies, and it enjoys privileges associated with private business operation. The public corporation is designed to combine the flexibility of private corporation enterprise with the ability to use the resources of the government. The corporate form for public or quasi-public purposes goes back to 1819 when in McCullock vs. Maryland it was ruled that the United States possessed the constitutional powers to grant charters of incorporation. The first government corporation owned entirely by the Federal government was not initiated until World War I. In 1945, the passage of the Government Corporation Control Act was recognition by Congress of the public corporation as an accepted instrument of government.

The corporate form has been judged to be applicable for Federal purposes when an activity is (1) predominantly of a business nature, (2) revenue producing and potentially self-sustaining, (3) involves a large number of business type transactions, and (4) requires greater flexibility than the customary type of appropriation budget permits. A good case can be made that these correspond to the characteristics of a Nationwide Service, with the exception that the service cannot become self-sustaining. It will require Federal financial assistance. The corporate form has been used, however, when some of the conditions above were lacking. The Corporation for Public Broadcasting, for example, was recognized from the beginning as an activity which would receive its primary support from taxes. Only supplementary financing could be obtained through private contributions.

Textbook descriptions of benefits available with the public corporation include the following: (1) it can utilize Federal tax dollars easily; (2) it has been effectively used in State-Federal relationships; (3) it provides flexibility of management; (4) it permits a sharp focus on objectives within a unified management structure; (5) it is separated from the direction of the Executive Branch; and (6) it may enjoy a high degree of freedom. All these advantages are desirable for an effective Nationwide Service.

HYPOTHETICAL PUBLIC CORPORATION

Unlike the Federal agency, the powers and procedures of each public corporation differ, shaped by its authorizing legislation. The public corporation
is a form which is susceptible to design based on functional requirements,
and is less limited by the directives and constraints applied generally to the
agencies of government. As a result, the degree of corporate independence
from the Executive Branch varies from entity to entity. The important distinguishing characteristics of a particular public corporation are the product
of the organization structure and the specific grants of power defined in the
enabling statutes as amended.

For discussion purposes we will outline a hypothetical public corporation
established to oversee the development of a Nationwide Library Information
Service. This organization is shaped by the intention that it has a high degree
of independence from Federal control and works in close harmony with autonomous libraries and service units; that it functions to increase the availability of knowledge and operates effectively. What tasks will the corporation
be authorized to undertake? Who will direct the organization? How will it
be funded? These are the key questions.

AUTHORIZED FUNCTIONS

As projected, the public corporation is a mechanism to plan and organize a
Nationwide Service. Its job is to receive Federal and private funds, use
them to obtain the necessary operations, and arrange for the participation
of eligible libraries and information centers.

The principal functions envisaged for the public corporation are: (1) to
oversee the operation of a nationwide service, (2) to encourage the extension
of service to all possible areas and groups, (3) to assure a comprehensive
national collection, (4) to attack and reduce barriers to the free flow of published materials, and (5) to obtain funding from a variety of sources, non-
Federal as well as Federal.

Among powers specifically authorized for our hypothetical corporation by
enabling legislation are the following:

To facilitate the full development of information dissemination in
the United States and with foreign countries.

To assist in reducing barriers to communication and to protect and
develop the several stores of information in the United States so as to
assure that copies of all published and circulated materials are available to United States citizens.

To assist in the establishment of a nationwide library and information service by one or more systems of interconnection of libraries, information services and related institutions or facilities.

To assist States, areas, and regions in establishing or developing systems of interconnection and information dissemination activities.

To increase efficiency and access to information by contracting for the operation of new special services.

To increase equitable access to information by all citizens.

To encourage utilization in support of scientific and technical pursuits, economic and social welfare, defense, commerce, agriculture, the arts and humanities for individual and national development.

To obtain gifts and grants from and to make contracts with individuals and with private and public agencies, organizations and institutions.

To determine and make reasonable payments to authors for use and publishers of materials and for copying associated with circulation, without regard to requirements of copyright or other laws and agreements.

To make payments to libraries and information services for costs associated with locating and providing loan materials.

To conduct planning, research, demonstrations, training and dissemination activities of value to a nationwide information and library interconnection service.

To encourage the creation of new libraries and information services and the improvement of existing services so as to enhance local, state, area, and regional developments.

To carry on studies, experiments, demonstrations and pilot projects which encourage the application of technology to library and information services for purposes of greater efficiency, increased and more equitable access to information, and improved use by the sciences, arts and humanities.

To carry out purposes and functions and engage in activities in ways that will assure maximum freedom of access and expression and will act to protect libraries and information services from interference with the content of materials in their care and from limitations imposed on circulation.

What the public corporation does not do is as much a part of its personality as what it does do. It does not compete with existing Federal functions such as categorical programs and Federal libraries and information services. It

does not encroach upon the national policy and planning function reserved to
the National Commission, which remains separate from the Nationwide
Service operations.

A FUNDAMENTAL CHARACTERISTIC

The most important characteristic of the hypothetical corporation outlined
here is that it is prohibited from operating the Nationwide Service or any
part of it. Its role is that of planner, organizer, financier, and evaluator.
The Nationwide Service is created by contract and the corporation, rather
than compete with existing operations, public or private, will promote and
expand them through contracts in support of national objectives.

Here we borrow from the Public Broadcasting Act of 1967:

> "The Corporation may not own or operate any television or radio
> broadcast station, system or network, community antenna tele-
> vision system, or interconnection or program production facility."

Not only is the provision basic to the character of the Corporation for
Public Broadcasting but it was undoubtedly important in obtaining support for
that legislative program from various private and public media organizations
who would be uncomfortable with competition from a Federally subsidized
government corporation.

The passage of the act would establish a market relationship in which
suppliers can enact by contract with the corporation, use creativity and yet
remain confident that the fruits of their labor will not be taken over by the
corporation if it decides to assume an operating role.

Good reasons can be offered for leasing services. The corporation is
able to keep up with technological change. Rather than remain bound to
capital equipment for too long a time, because of the difficulty in finding new
equipment, the corporation is able to specify the latest technology with each
new lease. Lower costs can result when the contractor is able to group
corporation requirements with those of other users and reduce per unit costs.
The cost of unnecessary competition can be avoided. The Library of Congress, for example, can contract with the corporation to provide services
into which they have put many years of development, but which may not have
become operational for lack of funds.

In the legislative process, reliance on leased services means that large
appropriations for capital investment need not be made early in the game.
It is clearly desirable to avoid burdening Congress with a large capital investment for the Nationwide Service at the very beginning of the program, when

advocates lack the system experience with which to demonstrate social benefits. For the legislative strategist, a relatively modest appropriation that covers operating costs is far easier to defend than a large capital investment.

The corporation should be viewed by the variety of institutions and commercial firms as a straightforward effort to assemble and pay for an important public service, not as a competitor. The Nationwide network can have the pleasing result of bringing together suppliers, operators, and users.

THE BOARD OF DIRECTORS

The method for selection of the board must meet the political test of acceptance by Congress, as well as promote the effective functioning of the system. Although potentially there are many ways of going about the selection of members, the methods used in practice today are limited. Members on Federal boards and commissions are usually nominated by the President and confirmed by the Senate.

Habit would have selection of the board members for the hypothetical public corporation made by the President. Undoubtedly this would be the preference of the legislative tactician looking for the smoothest path through Congress for the enabling bill. However, we assume that the President will appoint members of the National Commission. Selection by the President of the public corporation board members can lead to confusion. Those who fear excessive Federal dominance or possible political influence, or who emphasize the need for close interaction among the autonomous units of the Nationwide Service, will look for another approach.

For discussion purposes, this hypothetical corporation would have a mixed board reflecting the fundamental conditions required of a successful operation. Prescriptions as to the makeup of the board of the public corporation is one method for limiting central influence and for assuring close cooperation between the network and operating library information centers.

While the National Commissioners are Presidential appointees, the board of the hypothetical public corporation is proposed as a mix of three appointment processes: one-third of the board is to be nominated by the National Commission on Libraries and Information Science, one-third to be nominated by regional Federal-interstate compact agencies, and one-third to be nominated by the board itself. A board of twelve members, with six-year terms, would see an average of two names a year being sent by the President to the Senate for confirmation. Control of such a board by any small combination of interests would be difficult under this procedure.

For activities designed to serve a special field, selection of board members by the professional association is sometimes advocated—usually by the associations in question. The control of tax-supported services by professional associations with a direct interest in the operations will not meet with public favor. Congress is not likely to warm to the idea. Even organized professionals will soon have second thoughts. The appointment powers assigned to some groups can give them a dominant position relative to the unfavored organizations. In a field such as library information with varied and often competing interests, there will probably be more outs than ins.

FINANCING

Why should the Federal budget support the Nationwide Service without matching from States and localities? First, it assures that there will be no discrimination among libraries, public and private, State and Federal. It is easier to administer; is not burdensome to the Federal treasury; and is equitable in that the larger share of investment in library services has already been made from non-Federal sources. The U. S. citizen wherever he resides will receive more equitable treatment when Federal funds are used. And a powerful national requirement is served. The whole of the nation benefits from an informed electorate and a more highly educated population in peace and war.

If at a later date Congress wishes to require some form of matching, it has the option to do so. User fees may be recognized as a potential source of income, but to become involved in State and local matching formulas will raise many complications that should be avoided as long as possible. At any rate, the figures shown here reflect full participation by the Federal government.

ALTERNATIVES

Undoubtedly, in the minds of many, the first choice to handle a Nationwide Library Information Service is the Library of Congress. Other candidates are the National Commission, the U. S. Office of Education, perhaps the Smithsonian Institute, or even the selection of a favored instrument from among private corporations.

In my view, LC management is not in the interest of the library, nor will it result in the most effective network. The LC is directly under Congress, it is important to remember, and is a unit of the legislative branch. The appropriation item for the Nationwide Service would compete with library functions, some of which are certainly closer to the heart of Congress.

Furthermore, the annual appropriation for the Library of Congress can be seriously limited by ceilings Congress places on its own operating budget, of which the LC is a part, such as the recent limitation of $1 billion; this in turn could limit growth of the Nationwide Service. The policy and decision-making responsibilities of the LC extend into many areas. In the copyright area, for example, it is extremely important that the Nationwide Service should take an aggressive and independent position. In any event, the LC will continue to perform work for which it is especially suited. The public corporation will contract out all operations. What the LC receives from the corporation will not limit operating funds received from Congress.

The U. S. Office of Education and all other government agencies lack the flexibility in financial, personnel and business matters available to the public corporation. None except the LC have any special operating experience that might carry over into the new situation. Not to be forgotten is the independence gained through a public corporation. While there is no guarantee that the effects of "political influence" can be avoided entirely under any system, the corporation is more exposed to view than is a division or agency within a government department.

If the National Commission was designated to operate the Nationwide Service, the Service and perhaps the Commission itself would not remain long in the Executive Office of the President, but might be found in the U. S. Office of Education or in the new National Telecommunications and Information Administration of the U. S. Department of Commerce.

It is not likely that Congress will act to select a "chosen instrument" from among private corporations. Congress is not going to take on such an administrative task, which it would properly leave to the Executive Branch. The private sector would disapprove of the selection of a particular private corporation since a public corporation will be compelled to contract more widely, involving many more industries.

SAMPLE LEGISLATION

The bill outlined below summarizes the discussion thus far. The purpose of the statute is to create a basic structure to deal effectively with the problems that will accompany the development of an effective national system. Congress must authorize the Executive Branch to proceed and appropriate Federal funds to carry out the work. Legislation must be written and passed by Congress and signed by the President.

It is not the purpose of the statute to solve all problems. The objective is to establish a structure that can deal with them effectively; one with the authority and the economic resources necessary to systematically bring the nation's enormous information resources to bear on the nation's expanding need for information.

This structure includes: (1) the National Commission, reorganized and with resources necessary to become the locus of national planning; (2) a new non-profit corporation with the task of arranging a Nationwide Service, channeling Federal funds into interstate use of materials, and achieving full acquisition nationally of the world's knowledge record; (3) regional agencies to assist in the direction and implementation of the program; and (4) Congressional directives to established Federal agencies in support of functions needed to advance the Nationwide Program.

Title I: National Commission. It is in effect an amendment to P. L. 91-344, the act of establishing the National Commission. The charges are designed to strengthen the Commission as a locus for national planning and development. It establishes a national policy direction designed to release potential at all levels of a national system that will continue to be made up of independent, client-focused units. Provisions of Title II, III, IV further strengthen the National Commission leadership role.

To establish the Commission as representative of the national interest, the members of the Commission are to be nominated by the President and approved by Congress from among outstanding citizens. Current membership requirements are dropped.

An Advisory Council selected by the Commission from among representatives of the library and information community is authorized to provide professional and technical advice.

The Federal Library Committee is given statutory authorization and placed under the Commission with responsibility for recommendations on Federal library policy.

The Commission is directed to establish a Research Center for Planning and Development to engage in policy research, to advise with public and private agencies on the development of new knowledge and to utilize the findings of research and pilot projects as necessary for the development of an effective national information system.

The National Commission is directed to maintain a comprehensive Nationwide Development Plan to assure an understanding of projected needs, services, costs, sources, and institutional responsibilities. The purpose is to advise the President and Congress, the Federal, State and local governments and public and private organizations as to the allocation of resources for national information services and to assist the nation's autonomous institutions in estimating and planning for their responsibilities.

Administrative functions of the Commission will be under a director and a staff selected by the National Commission. No functions are delegated to any other agency of government under the act, although the National Commission may contract for services from private and public organizations.

Title II: Public Corporation. A non-profit corporation is authorized that is not an agency or establishment of the United States government. Powers are those conferred on a non-profit corporation by the District of Columbia non-profit corporation act. Basic objectives are to expand and protect knowledge resources in the United States, broaden and improve accessibility to them, and increase opportunity for rapid use.

Principal tasks are to arrange for (but not operate) a Nationwide Service to provide equitable use of the nation's information store and to support programs of acquisition that will assure full access to the world's knowledge. Objectives include: (1) the equitable treatment to remote areas as well as populated areas without regard to social standing or economic ability; (2) the advancement, through information systems, of science, technology, and industry on which the constitutional functions of defense and general welfare depend; and (3) the protection of freedom of information and defense of free flow of information.

A board of directors with responsibility for management is to be selected for terms of six years. Four of thirteen members are nominated by the Commission for Libraries and Information Service, four by the regional Federal-interstate authorities in rotation, and five members by the board itself. The President would appoint the initial board and thereafter forward names to Congress for approval.

Research, training, and pilot services specifically related to the development of a Nationwide Service would be included among authorized activities.

The corporation is to be supported by annual appropriations from Congress, payments for services, and gifts from private and public sources. Appropriations are based on reimbursement for services by libraries and on operating costs of the Nationwide Service.

The corporation is authorized to enter into contracts with Federal, State, regional and other public and private agencies for the purpose of developing a Nationwide Service network to facilitate interstate and interlibrary exchange of materials and to engage in international exchanges of benefit to the nation.

268 JOHN W. BYSTROM

The corporation is directed to plan a Nationwide Service in consultation with the nation's libraries and information services, and to undertake pilot experiments.

A major pilot demonstration of library networking is authorized, including regional interconnection of libraries, to obtain the data needed for prudent nationwide development.

Title III: Regional Agencies. Authorized is the establishment of Regional Library and Information Authorities under Federal-interstate compact and the processes necessary to Federal approval of Regional Authorities are established.

The National Commission is authorized to set up specifications, including the division of the nation into regional areas. When the States had organized to meet these conditions, they would request approval as a Regional Authority.

Regional Authorities are eligible for corporation and Federal funds for development or operation of information centers that conform to nationwide standards and may share in reimbursements for actual services under nation-wide formulas.

The boards of each Authority would be representative of the area served and selection would follow a general procedure prescribed for all regional bodies.

Regional board members are to be selected from among citizens residing in the region, one half of which shall not be employed or associated with libraries or the information industry.

Title IV: Agency Coordination. Congress can facilitate the National Program and avoid possible overlap of function by specifying supporting actions for agencies such as the FCC, the NSF, and the NTIA.

FEDERAL COSTS

Included in the enabling legislation is an authorization to allow future Congresses to appropriate funds for the purpose and the time period of the act. The authorization sets a dollar ceiling. It is estimated that the full National Program proposed here would require an authorization of $200 million (1976 dollars shown throughout) for the first five years, or an average of $40 million a year. This would rise to a steady state level of $145 million annually at the end of ten years, when the full scale program would be operational.

Compare this with recent Federal expenditure levels. In 1973, the highest year for Federal support for libraries, Robert Frase totalled appropriations of $222 million. Levels have fallen since. This is for a program that has not changed in essentials since 1965 and the Great Society. A case can be made that unless something new and directly related to improved service is brought to Congress, Federal support for libraries will continue to diminish. In the past a distinctive new program has sometimes been able to salvage the remains of a tired old one.

The program cost figures developed here are speculative, but more than shirtcuff estimates. They help to establish the general levels of financing and, in my judgement, show that program costs are no bar to legislative acceptance. Major benefits are obtained with a relatively small outlay. No great detail on costs is possible here, but expenditure levels can be provided.

When the enabling bill is brought before Congress, the stress is on obtaining the needed authority with which to begin. If this is achieved, it will become possible to go back for more money later. Initial costs should remain as low as possible. The first year appropriation requirement is estimated at less than $10 million, with half going to the new public corporation and half going to the National Commission.

Fiscal requirements fall into two categories: funding of the National Commission's program, and support for the network operations of the new public corporation. A five-year authorization in support of the National Commission's program would approximate $40 million. Included are the operation of the new National Commission, a program of research and development, and development assistance to regional agencies. Total appropriations would range between $4 and $9 million annually over the period.

The program of the public corporation, during the first five years, would develop gradually and involve testing applications and determining demand. Strategy calls for a limited pilot test project initially. Congress will appreciate that it is not being asked to buy "a pig in a poke." By starting small, risks are limited and the field test evidence is produced against which later larger investments and expanded services can be judged.

A National Service pilot project, covering a region that included a half dozen states, would require $17 million annually after five years. The Periodical Service, proposed by the Task Force on a National Periodical Service, is estimated at $10 million annually. Cataloguing and acquisition were estimated at $15 million annually by the National Commission. The public corporation, its pilot project, special service demonstrations, cataloguing and acquisition contracts, and grants for regional development would require approximately $140 million for the first five years.

The second five years would see the expansion of the network nationwide so that at the end of the second authorization period a steady state condition for the system would be approached. At that time annual costs are estimated at $145 million, of which $10 million would go to the National Commission and the remaining $135 million would go into network operations and other services managed by the public corporation. Of this amount $35 million would be required for the operation of a National Service Center and eight regional centers, drawing on the estimates of Palmore, Bellassai and Roderer (Resource and Bibliographic Support for a Nationwide Library Program).

Figures such as these require far more study and are not included with any thought of being final. They suggest that costs will be modest enough to support program feasibility while raising a question as to the impact on existing categorical programs. Because of the small appropriations required initially, the question need not be faced for some time.

OUTLINE OF ACTION

To obtain legislation and carry out a program that has the support of Congress calls for a strategy extending over many years and passing through several phases.

Phase One: <u>Preparation</u>   Estimated 18-month period

Determination of policy and principal mechanism to advance policy. Support data are collected. Important interest groups are organized. Favorable relationships are developed at key points in the executive and legislative branches of government. Professional and public support is generated.

Phase Two: <u>Legislation</u>   Estimated 18-month period

The introduction of legislation marks the beginning of a second phase. An organized effort is financed; work by professional and public associations coordinated; and relationships maintained with the executive and legislative branches of the Federal government.

Phase Three: <u>Tooling Up</u>   Estimated 5-year period

Following passage of enabling legislation, a management organization is established. Plans are developed and early contracts signed. Operations begin.

Phase Four: <u>Steady Operation</u>   Estimated 5-year period

Organized efforts will continue to be developed until the point is
reached where objective standards of equal service are being
fulfilled and the special services required by trained specialists
and organizations are in operation.

TIMETABLE

More than a decade will be required for all phases, and this assumes intelligent planning, effective organization, steady energy and only minor opposition
or obstructions in the way. Many of the important steps in Phase One are
being undertaken today. Nevertheless, before legislation can be introduced,
a carefully scheduled series of action will be required. Assuming a broad
area of agreement among interested groups and sufficient resources, a
minimum of 18 months will be needed.

Legislation may require less than a year to move through Congress when
strongly backed and faced with only token opposition. Routine technical problems may double the time, however. The authorization of expenditures is
contained in the enabling legislation, however funds are not made available.
The appropriation of funds is a separate action which will take from six
months to a year and a half.

In Phase Three a year will be required to tool up and engage personnel,
then attention will be focused on extension of the legislation and on producing
sufficient evidence of benefits to successfully make a case for extending the
enabling act. The management system will be established and there will
have to be clear evidence that library networking has begun, if only on a
limited basis.

In Phase Four and the five-year period that follows, we have a right to
expect the development of a "steady state" of operations that can substantially
meet many of the objectives articulated by the National Commission. If the
decision to proceed were made in 1978, it would set in motion a program
that would reach to 1992.

JOINT ACTION

Congress has been compared to a steam engine; the water and fuel required
to make it operate comes from the outside. A legislative campaign organized
by those outside Congress desiring change is essential.

There are many organized groups with an interest in new legislation. An area of agreement among them is essential from the standpoint of planning a successful legislative campaign. Priorities should be jointly arrived at and a high degree of coordination achieved. The variety of organized forces outside Congress, public and private, profit and non-profit, each have their behavior limited in some ways by the rules of society while enjoying freedom of action in other ways. When there is joint action, the special strengths of each organization can be applied to advance the legislative action.

It is worthwhile to look down the road that must be travelled once legislation is prepared and introduced. The leadership in Congress allows the bill to proceed. Committee hearings are held in both houses, involving the favorable testimony of the many groups affected. Affirmative votes are required by the committees and by the two houses of Congress. The legislation is signed by the President and becomes the law. This only opens the curtain and allows the play to begin. It is now necessary to implement the program. The funds authorized by the enabling legislation must now be appropriated. A continuing campaign is necessary to obtain annual appropriations and assure effective use of the authority and funds which Congress allows. Organized efforts which produced the statute should continue until the program is well on the road.

A review of the conditions that are regarded as desirable for passage of a bill will add to an appreciation of the large task ahead. The goals inside government are (1) substantial support in Congress, (2) champions in the House and Senate, (3) the understanding and cooperation of the Executive Office, (4) positive legislative services from involved agencies of government, or at a minimum, concurrence when requested for opinion.

Outside government there should be sufficient backing to support favorable responses within government. (5) The groups directly affected, such as libraries, the States, and the client institutions should be unanimous in their support. (6) Little expressed opposition should come from private industry and tangible support from some quarters is desirable. (7) Community leaders who can express the national interest should be in the forefront. (8) A discernible public need should be shown and supported by users of libraries and information services. While these conditions will never be fully achieved, they represent the challenge that faces the legislative strategist.

One organization alone will not have the resources to wage a legislative campaign in support of library development. A broad consensus is required. This will not be easy when the various groups, sometimes with competition or opposing interests in library legislation, are considered. (1) Within the Federal government, there are the operating libraries and information centers. Each of these established programs have staffs and special concerns.

(2) Professional groups, such as the American Library Association, are directly affected as are umbrella organizations, such as the National Education Association.

(3) Client associations will examine the program from the viewpoint of the institutions they represent, such as the Land Grant Colleges, Universities, and Community Colleges. Each will look for some benefit built into the new program. (4) State library agencies, county and city libraries and their boards, have direct relationships to members of Congress. (5) Individual libraries, and the institutions they serve, carry prestige, in many instances, that produces national publicity and projects an image of excellence. (6) Private, profit-making corporations, suppliers of services, have established lines of communication to Congress and quickly recognize any interest they may have in the outcome of public questions. (7) Although cautious about support of what might be labelled political activity, the non-profit foundations can provide resources for basic planning. (8) In the course of the campaign, it will be important to obtain the assistance of major economic groups— industry, labor, and agriculture as well as general constituent groups— women, consumers, social and ethnic associations. Their support will be of value although their active involvement in library legislation may be minor. Campaign muscle will have to come from those individuals and groups that are closest to the library and information field.

Generalship which marshals all available resources and brings them to bear at the appropriate moments is essential. Division in the ranks is a call to Congress to decide among the contestants. A confusion of voices in the hearings, appeals for amendments or differences even on small points, will produce the reasonable response, "Go home; work it out and come back another time." Considering the wide variety of interests in libraries and information services, it will be a major task to obtain a high degree of unanimity and to infuse a coalition with fervor needed for the intensive activity of a legislative campaign. The differences among organizations can produce strengths. Their resources will vary and a legislature campaign requires many kinds. They cannot be measured entirely in tangibles—dollars, membership lists, and publication outlets; the intangibles, personal influence and a knack for politics, can be extremely important as well.

CONCLUSION

The time has come in the view of the writer for some form of Federal action, whether this proposal or another. The technology is ready and organized for networking. Not more than five years ago this was probably untrue.

For several years Federal administrators have told libraries that it was time for a change. Some years have passed since the National Commission was asked to come in with something new. Legislation will not be drafted at the White House Conference. Nor can the White House Conference carry on an organized campaign in support of new legislation. Are citizens meeting for the first time expected to complete a complex task that thus far has been beyond the capacity or will of industry and the profession?

Urgently needed, in my opinion, is an informal dialogue among key representatives of the varied interests in the field in an attempt to establish a working foundation on which a legislative program and an organized support effort can be built.

Chapter 26

THE GOVERNANCE OF LIBRARY NETWORKS: ALTERNATIVES FOR THE FUTURE—RESPONSE

William J. Welsh

The Deputy Librarian of Congress
Washington, D. C.

Eighty-nine years ago today, Montana was admitted to the Union as our forty-first state. The question facing us today concerns how we can get Montana, Mississippi, Missouri, and Massachusetts, and every other state in this country into our proposed new union, a union of libraries and information services coming together to provide information to every citizen in the country who needs it. (I use information services in the broadest sense.)

Librarians, information scientists, and information users have been debating for years the pros and cons of networking—now we seem to have emerged on the side of _pro,_ and if so, the time has come to decide how the network will be structured, who will manage it, and how the policy issues will be decided. John Bystrom has presented some tangible and practical ideas on how a nationwide network structure might be governed (Chapter 25), and it will be through just such discussions and arguments as those we have heard in the past two days that the reality of the network will be formulated, chipped and chiseled out of ideas previously cast in concrete. As we all know, such conferences could go on forever. We must begin acting on our premises, but it is imperative to realize that any plan set forth for a network governance structure will raise objections, and there are reasons for most of us to object to any structure headed by some sort of ultimate library authority. These objections should be heard. Before examining the substance of the governance structure, then, let us consider who will be affected by the idea of a national network headed by a national board.

In a discussion of the national library board concept embodied in the Council of Library Resources' Technical Development Plan on October 26, 1978, at the annual meeting of the Association of Research Libraries, I identified twenty-one possible objectors to this concept. There are: NCLIS, LC, ARL, ALA, COSLA, IIA, OE, CCC, AAP, AAUP, NLM, CRL, NEH, NEA, ASIS, SLA, GPO, NTIS, USBE, NSF, and MF. I could add to that list, but I am confident that the audience here today could identify a host of additional objectors and reasons why each might be opposed to the creation of a national network headed by a higher authority of some sort.

I could advance a number of reasons why LC would object to the concept. Al Trezza could offer reasons why NCLIS would object. The National Library of Medicine may object because that library already has its own well-structured, self-sufficient, and efficient network which serves its clientele well. How would state library interests be represented? Several states, such as Washington, have model networks of their own—others are members of regional consortia, well served by their bibliographic systems such as AMIGOS, SOLINET, etc. The states may benefit from getting federal funds, but may lose their voice in the process. And public and school libraries—why should they enter into such a structure, possibly predominated by large federal and research libraries which presumably know little of the problems such libraries have? Information brokers, developers of bibliographic systems which are doing quite well financially, may see a threat to their market if such a national network develops—why should they participate? How would the interests of OCLC be protected? What about the publishing community and university presidents?

All of these objections must be considered; each of us has a vested interest in seeing a network established with a governance to protect our concerns. But let us also look at the problems we have encountered, and will continue to encounter, because of the very lack of a national locus, a forum—problems which might have been avoided if such a structure existed. We might be further advanced by now were there a place where policies could be discussed on a national level, input made, consensus reached before individual actions were taken, with oft distressing results.

The decision to revise and adopt AACR II caused an enormous amount of consternation in the field. What will happen when the question of need for AACR III is raised? Will we be forced to repeat the same painful process because there is no national forum in which to discuss the proposed revisions? What about the problems we face in implementing the new copyright law? How will copyright clearance be affected? What about the problems of machine-user interface? How will rates and fees be set?

Shouldn't we accept the fact that we have challenges which are not being addressed in any coherent, systematic fashion? Can we set aside our parochial concerns, create a forum for most of those possible major objectors I mentioned earlier, and present to Congress a plan that will be funded because we have collectively demonstrated the need? I believe that we can and that we will. But now for the difficult question: Can we do so without recognizing and accepting that at least in some instances and for some programs there needs to be a body that can serve to oversee programs, add a focus to the network? We seem to agree that there are serious hazards in centralized authority, but what are the alternatives? Can we continue to tolerate the present unstructured approach? And if we cannot, then we must ask ourselves: Who is to provide this focus? Some of you may say ALA should play this role, and in many cases it has done so; apparently it didn't, however, in the case of AACR II. Others, including John Bystrom, say the National Commission on Libraries and Information Science should play this role. But NCLIS cannot provide this forum either, at least not under its present mandate; it could, however, be changed to do so. At present it is a board, but it has no operational responsibilities—the Commission itself stated in its 1975 report that:

> The National Commission is a policy-making and planning body. It is not empowered by law to operate programs. What is needed, as a matter of first priority, is a locus of federal responsibility, some agency in the federal establishment, where policies with respect to libraries and information service activities can be transplanted into action.... The important thing is that the new national program will require new administrative and operational functions and that at present there seems to be no natural home to accommodate them.

The report goes on to say that the body need not be federal, that it could be a quasi-governmental agency. Here, then, we have NCLIS telling us it does not have the authority to be the locus—what then can serve this purpose, can provide a national focus, can aid in solving our problems before we go too far? There is no perfect solution, ladies and gentlemen, which will provide the necessary focus and totally account for our concerns. But there are proposed structures which might meet many of our objectives and answer some of our objections. The point is to turn away from negativism and work towards something which we can shape into a positive force.

We have heard John Bystrom's proposal for a network governance structure. Another option exists, and that is the proposal prepared by the Council on Library Resources and published as part of the document "Towards a National Periodicals Center—A Technical Development Plan." This proposal details requirements for a national periodicals center, but also considers the need for a governance structure, and sets forth a two-tiered approach with a national board overseeing separate governance boards for specific, carefully selected programs, such as the periodicals center, a preservation program, etc. The choice of a governance structure is up to you—let me just review a few points in John Bystrom's proposal, as well as

some of the points of the CLR structure, to determine whether either of these
meets some of our objectives. These are the options confronting us, and the
decision is yours.

If we agree that we do need a locus for determining policy and carrying
out planning which is divorced from the operational management of a national
library service, one option, as John Bystrom recommends, is that this body
be the National Commission with a new look; he wants to see the Commission
strengthened, but with the board structured as a public rather than professional body. This is necessary, he suggests, to allay the suspicions of the
public, who sees it, as it is currently composed, as a body which only takes
into account its own interests. I too believe we need a national library board
of some sort, but believe for it to be strong and effective, it should be composed of knowledgeable persons who know the fields of library and information
science and the needs of the publics they serve, for they are the very people
who are capable of determining policies and providing practical guidance.
One of our present problems, as I said, is a lack of focus, with our leaders
unable to get together on a concrete program, so that it is obvious to most
that we are a splintered group with little backing from our constituents. The
top layer of the governance structure, therefore, must be composed of leaders
with strong voices who are truly capable of setting policy and providing a
focus.

Disinterested citizens may well be uninterested. This is our idea, we
must determine what is necessary, and we must not let the management be
taken from our hands. This board might be quasi-public, like the boards for
the National Endowments for the Arts and Humanities and the National Acad-
emy of Sciences; it should be neither solely federal nor solely private. John
Bystrom tacks onto this board an Advisory Council, A Center for Policy
Studies, and so forth. It seems to me his proposal has too many components
devoted to planning, and I believe one board must take responsibility for the
development of programs and policy planning. But I do agree with John
Bystrom on one count—the advisory board might be built from the Commission, with changes in their mandate to allow not only for oversight but also
for program responsibility. If the Commission could serve as the core group,
with representatives of ALA, ARL, LC, CLR, etc. and the private sector
folded in, a strong committee of leaders could be built to fulfill the purposes
I mentioned earlier, rather than a splintered configuration of citizens who
may have little knowledge of the needs of libraries. Such a board is proposed
in the CLR plan; it includes NCLIS, but is not based entirely upon it, as John
Bystrom proposes.

A second feature of John Bystrom's structure is a public corporation to
oversee the nationwide library information service; this corporation will
contract with agencies for necessary services, provide oversight, but will
not actually run the service, if I understand him correctly. This would be

a grave mistake in working towards our goal. By trying to mandate a nationwide library service, we may lose many of the programs which are already
functional on a local or multistate level. We must let the nationwide service
evolve from existing programs and services; voluntary participation is preferable. The CLR proposal, on the other hand, suggests an evolving network
which would offer options which local and regional groups could choose to
participate in, assuming benefits would accrue to them by so doing. Some
of you will say we have gotten nowhere so far by waiting for voluntary cooperation, but I point to the regional and multistate bibliographic systems already in existence; obviously their members are deriving certain benefits,
or these programs would not be as successful as they are. In the CLR plan,
the network grows naturally; states and regions will join if it helps them;
if it doesn't, there is no reason for them to do so.

The idea itself of a public corporation has merit. As John Bystrom says,
it is "designed to combine the flexibility of private corporation enterprise
with the ability to use the resources of the government." What I object to is
his conception of the corporation as an additional layer in the governance
structure. He proposes that there be a board to fulfill the need for the national locus, a board which is divorced from implementation; several sub-
groups to advise and carry out planning, R&D; then the corporation, with
its own board of directors, then the regional agencies (possibly interstate
compact agencies), and then, and only then, do we get to the regional or local
level and the systems that exist today. Coming from a large bureaucracy, I
know what happens when too many levels of responsibility exist—each level
waits for the next to act—I don't want to see a mammoth superstructure
develop if it can be avoided.

Compare to this the CLR proposal—two levels only: a national steering
group, followed by one operational level, a level which is broken down into
program elements, each with its own governing body. There will be a periodicals system component, a communications system component, a bibliographic
systems component, and a preservation systems component. The periodicals
system, quite manageably sized, will be the lead-off program. This will
allow all of us to see what the demands are, the constraints, and the benefits.
If the periodicals system is successful, others will evolve as they are needed;
this incremental approach, with only two levels of responsibility, will help to
avoid the growth of another rigid bureaucracy, and not incidentally, will require a lower level of funding than John Bystrom's scheme.

In considering the governance structure as it affects the local level, CLR's
plan allows for the evolution of components from existent systems, and again,
a possible unnecessary level—the regional agency—suggested by John
Bystrom is avoided. The CLR-envisioned network, for example, will actively
encourage the development of interlibrary loan networks through fiscal incentives, such as an incremental pricing policy and use deposit accounts. All

libraries will eventually have access, but financially, they may be better off to form a regional consortium, thus regionals will develop in response to need—a compact agency foisted upon a state with an already functioning network may be unwanted and unnecessary. Thus, as other systems develop to serve needs, the network will evolve, but without an intricate and costly structure thrust upon us from above. As the CLR report states, "It is inconceivable that there will be or should be a formal hierarchical and prescriptive centralized agency charged with operating a national library system. Instead, that system is likely to be a composite of many activities carried on in many places. It is essential, however, that all parts operate against a common backdrop of basic services that are stable in quality and assured of continuity."

I mentioned funding. From where I sit, funding is going to be limited in the coming years, and if money is limited, priorities must be set. Our systems will grow, but we must first show that a few programs, programs providing a necessary product, can be well-managed. I think John Bystrom's suggested budget is unrealistically high. In these times, the less our initial request to Congress, the more palatable it will seem. In this case, less would seem to be more.

Public relations efforts, a technical development plan, plans for legislation—all are necessary as John Bystrom suggests, but before we approach this more detailed level, we need a strong and consolidated effort to agree on certain priorities, starting with the NPC, and prove not only our need for that system, but also our collective strength. This requires a reexamination of allegiances, an end to pettiness, and a compromise of egos. As professionals, each of us has a responsibility to put aside our prejudices and to prove ourselves capable of providing a national library service. We must remember that this system is not for ourselves, but for the benefit of library users. The users have too long been thrust out of mind when the subject of networking is discussed, and the longer we talk, the less we serve our clients. Let us remember what we exist for, and put our minds and efforts to the proper objective, the provision of information to all who need it.

Chapter 27

THE INTRUSION OF REALITY

Anthony W. Miele

Director
Alabama Public Library Service
Montgomery, Alabama

As I see my role on this program, it is to respond to Dr. John Bystrom's
paper (Chapter 25) from the point of view of a State Librarian. I have a very
talented staff and I try to take advantage of their many talents. Therefore,
I asked them to also read the paper. With the benefit of their thoughts and
ideas, I was better able to approach my task of responding to the new federal
legislation, as proposed by Dr. Bystrom.

Inherent in Dr. Bystrom's paper are the following assumptions:

First, it is possible to separate the development of library
services from the political process.

Second, it is desirable to achieve such a separation.

It is my belief that such a separation is both unattainable and undesirable.
Further, to attempt such a separation is to ignore every lesson learned about
the political process.

The labor leader Sidney Hillman once defined politics in the following
way:

"Politics is the science of how, who gets what, when and why."

This is a broad definition and I find it to be particularly useful. It is a definition which includes everything from the exercise of citizens' voting rights to
the maneuvers of power blocks attempting to control the policies of private
organizations or public agencies.

Before proceeding, I wish to state that I am in favor of most of the goals
proposed by Dr. Bystrom. What concerns me is the likelihood that the

methods outlined to achieve those goals will cause their attainment to go un-
realized. For example, the strengthening of the National Commission on
Libraries and Information Science is an objective which must be achieved.
However, attempting to reconstitute the National Commission as a "public"
body is not going to enhance the National Commission's reputation as an informed, disinterested agent, representative of the citizenry as a whole.

My feeling is that the way to strengthen the National Commission is not to
form a new library bureaucracy. Rather, the present law should be amended
to give NCLIS both policy making authority and operating authority. To me,
this is much more feasible than to establish an additional body such as a
public corporation. The more bodies involved, the more roadblocks. The
simpler an administrative structure is, the more efficient it operates. Further, there is no guarantee that a public corporation will be responsive to
the wishes of the Commission, Congress, or, for that matter, anyone else.

It will take the cooperation of everyone to make a nationwide network of
library and information services possible. Cooperation is, or should be, the
name of the game. It is the duty of the library community to display this cooperation and assist the National Commission in realizing the goal of developing a network of library and information services. As an aside, I hope the
National Library Service Network will not be called the U.S. Library and
Information Service because the acronym for such an agency would be USLIS
or "useless."

We have in the United States a discipline called public administration
which is devoted to exploring how government actually works. In examining
the relationship between public agencies and their interest groups, the scholars have, time after time, documented the control over agency policies
wielded by the interest groups. Furthermore, the Congress itself is well
aware of such influence. A discussion of interest groups must be grounded
in reality. In regard to this aspect of the paper, I would recommend reading
such basic texts in public administration as Robert C. Fried's Performance
in American Bureaucracy or Carl Lutrin and Allen K. Settle's American
Public Administration: Concepts & Cases.

Speaking to the effort of Dr. Bystrom to eliminate all interested parties,
I would like to know, in a society that runs on information, how we are going
to exclude "those interests in the private sector which might be affected by
decisions of the board"?

In reviewing Dr. Bystrom's other recommendations for the National Commission, I have the following reactions:

Support for the Creation of an Advisory Council to the Commission. I do
like the idea of an Advisory Council. This works well in many situations.

Being a state librarian, I of course would be concerned that state libraries be represented. The make-up of this Advisory Council must be representative of the library and information community as well as the user community.

The Advisory Council should definitely have a clearly defined and substantive role in formulating policy. The lay board of the National Commission could then act on their recommendations and translate our libraryese into terms that could be more easily understood by the non-library related.

Establishment of a Center for Policy Studies Under NCLIS. This is a fine concept, long overdue. We are in the era of "cost-benefit" and lack the funds to independently experiment on ways of upgrading library services.

Reassignment of Responsibility for the Federal Library Committee. The Library of Congress should be officially declared The National Library. We all know the Library of Congress has been acting in this capacity for many years, but it must be established so by law. Before going further, let me state that I fully realize the political struggle this will cause. I support the idea of placing the federal libraries under the umbrella of the National Commission in order to guarantee making the collections of these libraries available through the national network.

Legislative Authorization for a Study of Federal Government Requirements for Information Services and Networks. Excellent idea and also long overdue.

Congressional Directives to Federal Agencies to Support and Participate in Particular Phases of National Program Development. This is a logical step when national program development gets underway.

Separation of NCLIS from Administrative Ties with USOE. This step is also logical, overdue and necessary for NCLIS to step out on its own. The USOE umbrella is chock full of holes when it comes to libraries.

Develop Relationships with Field at Policy Level. This particular item deserves further elaboration. I suspect that we are using the word "policy" too loosely. Administrative agencies, such as NCLIS or the Alabama Public Library Service, do help make policy. However, we are responsible to legislatures and presidents and governors who are elected to a policy-making role.

In discussing the proposed public corporation, I would like to lay the groundwork by returning again to Hillman's definition of politics as the "science of how, who gets what, when and why."

Without, at this time, comparing a public corporation to NCLIS or the Library of Congress, let's look at the virtues, or lack of virtues, of the

proposed corporation. First, can a public corporation be non-political?
The Corporation for Public Broadcasting was repeatedly cited as a role
model. I am firmly convinced that no one can truly believe that the Corporation for Public Broadcasting and its Board of Directors are removed from
the political world. If you will permit a few citations from The New York
Times:

> Friday, August 11, 1972
>   Headline: "Macy Resigns as Public TV Head"
> "John W. Macy, Jr., the embattled president of the Corporation
> for Public Broadcasting, resigned his $65,000-a-year job yes-
> terday. He had been at loggerheads with the White House and
> some elements of Congress over the political and financial di-
> rections public broadcasting has taken."
>
> Wednesday, May 9, 1973
>   Headline: "Public Broadcasting Due to Name Killian Chairman"
> "Dr. James Killian, Jr., was expected to be elected chairman of
> the board of the Corporation for Public Broadcasting today in what
> informed sources said would be an attempt to give the impression
> that the board is 'independent' of White House control."
>
> Friday, November 4, 1977
>   Headline: "Carter's TV Nominee is Assailed"
> "President Carter's nomination of a former White Citizens Coun-
> cil member from Mississippi to the board of a major public
> broadcasting agency, the Corporation for Public Broadcasting,
> has led public interest and civil right groups here to try and block
> his confirmation."

In Martin Mayer's book, About Television, published by Harper & Row in
1972, he says the law establishing the Corporation for Public Broadcasting
actually forbids it to operate a network. This is a trap we would not want
the National Commission to fall into.

One more item about public corporations. Those who accepted the idea
of a public corporation for the U.S. Postal Service are now strongly ques-
tioning their original position. Granted, a public corporation for knowledge
may not yet be as large as the postal service, but potentially it could even
be larger.

Another quote, also from the New York Times of November 4, 1977:

> "The Corporation for Public Broadcasting is often characterized
> as a 'heatshield' between Congress and the public broadcasting
> stations that receive Federal support."

This public corporation concept for library development will not work. In the final analysis, it is an attempt to remove library development from public accountability. This is a risky strategy to advance when public accountability is becoming, along with cost-effectiveness, the standard by which spenders of the public treasure are judged!

To analyze the proposed corporation, we must first face the problem of whether the board will consist of 12 or 13 members. Whatever the number, the members of the initial Board are scheduled to be appointed by the President. Afterward, to fill vacancies, we have the following situation. The President will still appoint, but:

- one-third of the Board is to be nominated by NCLIS;

- one-third is to be nominated by regional Federal-interstate compact agencies (more on these later);

- one-third is to be nominated by the Board itself.

The Board is going to consist of nominees who are themselves nominated by appointed bodies. Even if the "rule of three" of presenting three nominees for every vacancy is followed, a large number of political interests and library interests are also going to have, at best, only indirect input. In such a situation, I fear they will also lose their interest. Worse, they will maneuver to have the rules changed.

I would feel much better if the members of such a public corporation were nominated by such elected officers as the Speaker of the House, the President Pro-Tem, and the majority and minority leaders. This would serve several purposes:

1. Involvement of elected officials

2. Resulting in involvement of powerful interests

3. Which would further result in commitment of the elected officials and powerful interests to the work of the corporation in furthering library development.

The proposed encouragement of national networks, using many millions of Federal dollars, is a different matter altogether. Obviously, funding is a critical factor in this whole network. The questions that come to mind are:

How will the funds be distributed?

Will they go to libraries directly?

Will they go through state libraries?

Will they go directly to regions and then filter down to the state
library agencies ?

What happens to the categorical grants we now have ? Will they
continue or will they be stopped in order to get initial funds
from Congress to support a National Commission network ?

Bystrom mentions matching funds stating that they would not be required
in the proposed federal funding pattern. I am not sure I can accept that.
The matching funds are what has made it possible for me to increase our
state funding in Alabama. Requiring matching funds for LSCA monies has
proven to be an effective means of developing local commitment. Commitment, or at least concern, invariably follows to allocation of funds. Maybe
some states don't need this technique—but in Alabama we have needed it
and we still need it. I would like to think that before the idea of matching
funds is discarded, it be given very serious consideration. Rather than help,
it may hurt the chances of some of the smaller states participating in the
network.

A word on the limiting of the annual appropriations of the Library of Congress because of the ceilings Congress places on its own operating budget.
We must plan for a time when we are going to all have to live with limitations
and justify our expenses. If it wished, Congress could just as easily limit
the funds going to a public corporation. We can't escape tight funds by trying
to hide in a "non-political" role.

Here we are talking about a creature of Congress allocating Federal dollars which would potentially benefit powerful interests "back home." The
whole concern might look better to Congressmen if we could clear up another
problem—that of regional level library services.

Let's talk about regions a little bit. I am concerned about the relationship
of the state library agency to the regional level of the national library and
information service proposal. Will the state library agency be the contracting party ? Who will divide the libraries into regional areas—the National
Commission ? Will the states set their own boundaries and can they determine in which region they will be located ?

Who will select the regional board members—the governors of each state
and each region ? Who will coordinate the joint action for legislation ? The
concern about which region a state is going to be in is a vital one. I certainly
wouldn't want to be in a region where the library has no say on what goes on
in that region. In addition, what happens to the regions already in existence ?
Will they be disbanded, merged, or what ? One thing is certain, with all
these types of cooperative networks springing up throughout the country,
there definitely needs to be some kind of coordination if information services

are not to become repetitive and competitive and then become more costly
on the user and the taxpayer.

Dr. Bystrom talks about an act that would determine the procedure for
setting up Federal interstate compact agencies. He anticipates that most if
not all existing regions would become compact agencies. My question is
how does this relate to state library agencies that have already set up interstate compact agencies for library services? What happens to these compacts that already exist between states? Are they wiped out? Are new ones
established on a regional basis or do they continue to exist along with the
new regional interstate compacts?

I would like to refer to the proposed legislation. Title I and II of the proposed legislation should be combined into just one Title and reworded so
that the proposed items relate to the National Commission instead of a public
corporation. Title III should be all right except that I would like to be certain that states would have some say where they fit in—state libraries in
particular. Title IV—Library Coordination—is fine—that can stay the way
it is. Funding could be the same as stipulated in the proposal except that it
would all go to the National Commission instead of as outlined in the paper.

As to the outline of action, Bystrom says legislation must be obtained to
carry out the program that has the support of Congress. This calls for a
strategy extending over many years and passing through several phases. I
can't agree with him more. I am going through the same thing now in Alabama
trying to get a multitype system law through. I can't emphasize strongly
enough that it takes joint cooperative action by everyone in the library organization to see that legislation that is needed will pass. I believe that the type
of plan proposed is necessary but my major objection is the proposal for a
public corporation.

OK, "how, who gets what, when and why"? In particular, how are you
going to get the states to give up the level of control they now have? State
library agencies are creatures of the governor and the legislature. We depend on them and they know it.

State legislators and governors also have, in their state library agencies,
a place to get things done. When an individual legislator or the governor or
another state agency has a request, they tend to get very fast action out of a
state library agency. Unless the regional agencies can respond in the same
manner, they are not going to get very far. To this end, the requirement
for matching funds is necessary to get state involvement. When state monies
are spent, the state legislature soon develops an interest in the product that
is purchased.

This point must be stressed: the American system is a federal system based on the federal-state-local pattern. Whatever emerges must be consistent with this pattern to have even a chance at success.

Taxes are raised on this pattern. Officials are elected on this pattern, the realities of power outside Washington exist on this pattern. To cite but one example, to establish an inter-state library compact in Alabama you have to work with the Alabama Public Library Service; the same requirement exists in the other states.

Additionally, LSCA is administered on a state level—as is ESEA. We at the state library agencies, and in other state agencies, are a part of the political process for library development. To involve the states, the state library agencies must be consulted.

Since the outline of action presented by Dr. Bystrom is clearly dependent on foundations which are open to question, I will not comment in this area except to continue the pig analogy he applied to the Congress. To me the pig is still in the poke and I am not buying.

In Bystrom's conclusion, he says the time has come for some form of federal action whether it is his proposal or not. The technology is ready and organized for networking. I agree wholeheartedly with what he says— the time has come. As our new incoming governor in Alabama has said, "It is time for a new beginning."

Before closing, I must make two additional points.

1. Dr. Bystrom is clearly to be commended for having the courage to take the first step and put together some concepts for public criticism. His paper should be received—and applauded—on this basis. Personally, I will reserve full criticism for draft #2 and how it addresses the questions raised at this meeting.

2. I, too, do not have the answers. Perhaps, at most, I have been forced to accommodate more to the political realities which surround the working life of the head of a state library agency.

Whatever plan is presented to Congress, it must be a plan which functions, and functions well, in the same political reality. To do so it must include, not exclude; it must involve, not alienate. Above all, it must not overlook what is in the pursuit of what we wish it to be. And there is no doubt that this is just the beginning of a long period of discussion on a very complex subject.

A final word. I would like to read a couple of paragraphs or so from a statement that was made by a concerned citizen of Alabama at one of our five district meetings held prior to our Governors Conference, which will be held on January 7-9, 1979. Oh yes, contrary to what some of our library media says, the Alabama White House Conference has not been torpedoed— it is well and raring to go.

> "I am on the side of the people who say that we have to plan ahead, cozying up to our county commission, to our state legislators and to our members of Congress if we are to get the job done.
>
> Anybody who says that there is no federal interest in libraries does not know what he is talking about. Anybody who says that there is no state interest in libraries does not know much about what he is talking about either.
>
> It has been my experience for a long time that in a public relations program, worked out not so much by the people who work in that particular field but by the general public, properly and patiently presented, will help in bringing about an improvement that is unbelievable compared to what we had when we started."

That, ladies and gentlemen, is part of a statement made by former Congressman Carl Elliott, who along with Senator Lister Hill, both gentlemen being from Alabama, were the fathers of the Library Services and Construction Act back in the 1950's.

Chapter 28

THE GOVERNANCE OF LIBRARY NETWORKS: REACTIONS

Dick W. Hays

Associate Commissioner/Director
Office of Libraries and Learning Resources
U. S. Office of Education
Washington, D. C.

My invitation asked me to react to the governance of library networks. John Bystrom's paper provides the immediate focus for this attention. Indeed, Professor Bystrom has provided many thoughts which deserve consideration. He has provided some "fresh thinking" in a number of areas.

I should quickly note that the use of the term governance usually causes concern about who is going to control what. When governance is applied to the flow of information, anxiety tends to increase. However, there is also concern about the compatability of information networks and resource sharing arrangements. These arrangements are rapidly proliferating at the local, state and national levels. As we think about how to design and operate networks to share bibliographic data, library materials, and human expertise, we need to keep in mind such factors as:

1. Management and organization

2. Standardization

3. Criteria for network membership

4. Choice among complex technological options, e.g., tele-communication devices, computer configurations, micrographics, etc.

5. Interrelations among networks

6. Performance measures

7. Financing

8. Network design and governance

These networking issues do not exist in a vacuum. They need to be examined as a total picture—of how all levels of government work together to serve better the individual library user.

Library services, as with most public services, have traditionally been the responsibility of local government. In brief, the Federal role has been to stimulate, prod, encourage, and promote and, hopefully, provide leadership. It is here that many questions are being asked about the fiscal level of that leadership at the Federal level. We know, for example, that the governance issues are affected by the present levels of support presently existing for public and school libraries: 88% from local sources; 7% from state sources; and 5% from Federal sources. These levels might be used as indicators as to where the decision-making process for resource sharing must begin.

When we consider the total effort in creating, storing, and communicating information in its great variety of forms, it becomes obvious that libraries and their information activities are a vast and encompassing concern of our society. For example, we are told that the total investment in information-related activities in the United States represented nearly 50% of the gross national product. While this measure is based on a very broad interpretation of what constitutes an information-related activity, it helps to drive home the point that ours is an information-based economy in which 90,000 libraries presently play a part.

Justification for a Federal role for libraries has rested not on operational support, but on meeting our goal of equal access and equality of service. It suggests that library resources are inequitably distributed across the nation. There also must be an incentive to make unique and major resource collections available nationwide. The support of such resource sharing efforts has been accepted as a Federal responsibility.

The base for the Federal support role for libraries, however, is clearly one which evolves in cooperation with state and local governments and treats information as a national resource. If we fail to link these resources together nationally so that all citizens can use them, we will be neglecting a very significant contribution that we can make to the quality of our life and the productivity of our citizens. Such cooperation is most appropriately fostered across institutional and jurisdictional boundaries in legislation which adopts as its prime philosophical goal the equal opportunity of access to the nation's library and information services. The structure and governance of these efforts are of key concern to us.

We are attempting for the first time in our organizational memory to promote a unified and coherent library strategy covering all the library programs

for which we have management responsibilities—elementary and secondary
school libraries (ESEA IV-B), public libraries (LSCA), and college and university libraries. It is planned that in this way priorities may be more
clearly defined in our congressional presentation.

An ideal but less realistic posture for us might be to support a new consolidated library authority to coalesce our policies. This would entail combining the key elements of Federal support for academic libraries, school
libraries and instructional resources, public libraries, research libraries,
interlibrary cooperative networks, library career training, and R&D. The
Office of Education might consider how it would address the larger issue of
consolidation at the White House Conference where these goals should pertain
—equal access, equality of service, experimentation for purposes of improved library service, and using Federal funds as a catalyst to promote
library cooperation.

A recent OE study noted the significant impact that HEA Title II-B and
LSCA III had in promoting innovative approaches to networking. A few of
the projects such as OCLC have had national impact on library and information service delivery. The study goes on to note that many products resulting
from HEA Title II-B and LSCA III have had potential for widespread application and utility in all types of libraries and information services. It estimates
that "almost 80 percent of the projects met or exceeded. . .expectations for
attaining objectives."

We feel that basic resource sharing continues to prosper through catalytic
Federal support. State, local, institutional and private funding is not designed to foster interjurisdictional cooperation. At the same time other
factors are at play:

- The increased cost of acquiring library materials and organiz-
  ing them for use;

- The growth of knowledge, with the consequent demands for a
  wide range of specialized materials;

- The varying levels of resources and funding abilities in each
  state;

- The cost of storing infrequently used materials that accumu-
  late when a library tries to be self-sufficient; and

- The requirement to serve constituencies that are not now
  being served.

These problems are not new, but they have become more serious over the
years and, as recent studies have indicated, have reached critical dimensions.

Encouraged by continued funding of programs such as Title III, Interlibrary Cooperation, and the Library Services and Construction Act, resource
sharing has been encouraged under entities called "library systems, "
"library networks" or "library consortia. " Some consist merely of informal,
mutual agreements to share materials. A large number are bound by formal
contracts and use conventional communication means, such as telephone and
teletype, computers and other telecommunication devices. Others have
worked out mutual collection development plans. The governance structures
have been just as varied.

We know, however, that there is great concern about the need for a
"national network" and for compatability among the various state and regional networks. It seems clear that networks and other cooperative activities develop at the local, state, and regional levels to meet specific needs at
those levels. It is doubtful that a "national network" can be designed to meet
state and local requirements for all kinds of information transmission. The
national network must be designed to bridge the state and regional networks.
It must allow for diversity among political entities as well as among subject
specializations such as medicine. This is the challenge now facing us.

Chapter 29

THE GOVERNANCE OF LIBRARY NETWORKS: REACTIONS

Lawrence F. Buckland

President
Inforonics, Inc.
Littleton, Massachusetts

The topic title of the day is the same as yesterday's except the "b" subfield
is changed. The "b" subfield, as you should all know if you work with MARC,
has to do with a sub-title which today is "Alternatives for the Future." I
like "b" subfields and assumed that when I was invited to speak, it would
be on technical matters. You cannot imagine the panic which set in when I
found myself required to comment on the present paper which is definitely
non-technical.

The position paper by Dr. Bystrom (Chapter 25) proposes that a public
corporation be set up suitably controlled by various boards, commissions,
etc., to determine policy, secure financing, allocate funding, and observe
progress of the National Library Network. Although I have no specific experience in the governance of anything, my technical experiences in running a
private sector business producing R&D and production services for libraries,
plus my observations of the difficulties of existing public corporations, lead
me to a position of strong skepticism. In spite of the realization that libraries need help, to have such a grand plan without knowing details of what needs
to be done, will bring down upon us objections of people inside and outside of
the network whose support we need. My feelings are so strong, that I'm
easily led to the smart alecky remark that we already have a perfect model
for a public corporation information network in the form of the U.S. Postal
Service.

When I read Dr. Bystrom's paper, I was sympathetic with his intent to
help libraries, but I was not comfortable with the approach. To pinpoint my
objections was indeed a difficult task, for the paper's objectives and approach

were quite general. I have no great experiences in such national planning matters, and I actually failed in documenting a detailed analysis and criticism of specific points. Because the paper was difficult to analyze in detail, and because it proposed such a centralized sweeping plan, my overall feeling about it was one of discomfort. As I racked my brain trying to describe my feelings in some detail, I came upon a view of the situation which startled me. Maybe you, too, will find it startling, and worse yet, some of you may be so offended with the idea as to get mad.

My discomfort over the approach of Dr. Bystrom's paper is based on my hypothesis that libraries for years have been monopolies, because users don't have alternative sources of information. Further, I feel that technology at last is the answer to breaking these monopolies and I, for one, do not want any public corporation or governance regulations to alter or stifle what I think will be a natural demolition process.

I have said that libraries are monopolies. Further, my perspective is that improvements have been slow in coming because of the lack of competition inherent in any monopolistic situation. Services do not have to be changed or improved because users of a particular library do not have access to ready alternatives. Improvements seem to come as much from peer pressure as from the economically sound pressure of "if I don't change, I'll lose the user to the library next door. "

I hasten to add that I do not believe that this monopolistic situation was contrived by librarians as were business monopolies prior to antitrust, but rather by the isolating effect of the technology of the time. Users had to go to the information, requiring considerable effort and delay. To get better service from an alternative, they had to go farther, which actually precluded this possibility. The companion problem of delays in document delivery also was not alleviated by a user's attempting to use alternative sources.

These delays irritate a library user, who is usually in an iterative information search-answer cycle, for they have negative effects on the reward process involved in learning.

In this monopolistic environment caused by inadequate technology, the quality of the service provided to the user is almost totally dependent on the librarians. We know from experience that some fight the monopoly and are very helpful in trying new ideas whenever they can and providing the best possible service within the system. Others we know follow the notion contained in the British Museum's title of "Keeper of the Printed Books" and are not always helpful because they are discouraged, misinterpret their role or cannot see how they could do better.

When I read and hear all of the complex social theory expounded at this conference which affects individual behavior, and, therefore, network governance, I wonder if librarians who didn't start these monopolies may, in acting naturally, want to continue them.

The new technology, I believe, will solve enough problems so as to break up any so-called monopolies. The impact of the use of low cost communications and terminals will be to solve the delay and data delivery aspects of the access problem. The implications of this future solution boggles the mind, but the important point to make is that this new technology offers a new capability, namely that the user now will have a choice: to which library or data base will he log-in.

Those organizations not chosen will be in serious trouble for they will not be used. The traditional performance measurement of use is circulation, and new but analogous measures will continue to measure the value of services and will be used to determine financial support.

Another improved service, which will be brought about by using the new computer and storage technology, will be the publication and storage of a range of forms of information—not just the printed book. Again the user will have a choice and his decisions will affect what services are used. These services will allow the user a choice of data displayed ranging from answers to questions of fact, through awareness services, to reviews and programmed instruction, to original articles and books.

The implications of this dimension of choice on the part of the user are also mind boggling. The prospect has implications for the public and private publishers of information who, in response to demand, will in turn require authors and editors to augment traditional text treatises with alternate forms. These alternate forms are appearing already and will continue to grow in number.

Another aspect of the rapid availability of information in different forms pertinent to library networks is the prospect that some of these information services may be provided by organizations outside of the library. The simpler types of fact retrieval may be operated by administrative or management groups. As more and more complex topics are successfully taught using programmed instruction, some present uses of the library in teaching will move away. There are examples of both of these occurrences already appearing in industrial management training. Librarians ought to examine their future role in these areas to see to what extent their reference functions will be abandoned by users and their bread and butter support of teaching will disappear.

The third effect of this innovation is the lowering of costs so that many more library functions can be performed locally. This sets up a possibility for networks which allow lots of opportunity at the local level again: the new features are the options for local user choice.

There are undoubtedly other applications of the new technology to the future of libraries; however, the two mentioned, namely ease of access and availability of alternative information forms, will suffice for the present. The point to be repeated is that these innovations will offer the user a choice and this choice will cause the existing monopolies to fail. This phenomenon will be a natural one and will progress as long as no external force tampers with the process. My concern with the Bystrom proposal in its present form is that it could possibly alter this course of events.

Because the development of these new innovations and the effect of completed developments are so complex, they will not occur in one development cycle but will follow a process which Mathews has described and called successive approximations. My concern with governance through an organization such as Bystrom proposes is that this natural development of the network will be altered by promoting or discouraging specific functions according to forces not directly related to experience in measuring the choices of the users. It is a question of governance that creates services that users "should have" rather than governance which creates services they want. It may be a dream, but I would prefer that the network development be ungoverned, because it seems to me the best way is to let new developments break up old monopolies.

I realize that this wish for no governance is an extreme stand, and I take it here 1) because I believe in it as basic guidance and 2) because most of what has been written about governance is pretty vague and I don't want to support something which is undefined or has no limits.

It is an extreme position, however, and I will back off from it by listing some exceptions which are useful functions which ought to be attended to by some sort of "governance." The first of these functions is the development and adoption of standards. Standards are absolutely necessary and will continue to be so if we are to be able to have universal access and processing of library information resources of the future. These standards have to do with character value assignments, data message structures and communication processing functions. The collective skill which has already been mustered in developing standards has put us in the position that the cost benefits derived from further development and use of standards far outweigh any risk that an early standard will block a future opportunity for development of a new network service.

Also, the standards which are being developed are open ended with respect to the processing of content, so they are unbiased with respect to disputes such as those concerning catalog practices.

My observations of the large number of libraries which can process MARC II records vs. the small number of libraries which can process all of the different abstracting and indexing service tapes reinforces my view of the need for standards.

The capability of the computer in coping with significant measures of non-standard practice is causing an insidious disease which will be debilitating and should be watched closely. The switch of the position OCLC transaction code and OCLC's use of a non-printing code for transactions when all other MARC codes are ASCII are two little problems which we can deal with but shouldn't have to. The reason we can deal with them is that we can use computers to convert data bases from one system to another. I am not familiar with whether or not BALLOTS and WLN have a transaction code, and if they do, whether it's similar to OCLC's.

The second function in which I accept governance is in the area of funding. Clearly the use of public funding for library services has been shown in the past to be worthwhile. It should be continued and expanded as resources permit, and I am in sympathy with Dr. Bystrom's effort to increase such funding.

The allocation of this funding poses very difficult problems. The current method of federal allocations of funds to states and towns, though somewhat haphazard, seems fair. It does not handle centralized funding of development, however, and it seems that some governance of cooperative funding in this area is necessary. One would hope, however, that the results of centralized funding would be more productive than some of the large centralized funded projects to date. If governance can do this, I wish you luck in your efforts.

Chapter 30

THE GOVERNANCE OF LIBRARY NETWORKS: REACTION

William DeJohn

Director
Pacific Northwest Bibliographic Center
University of Washington
Seattle, Washington

It is difficult to feel comfortable in reacting to a paper on future federal legislation on governance and structure of a nationwide network of library and
information services when there appears to be no commonly accepted definition of a nationwide network and no concensus on what it would do or how it
would do it.

Dr. Bystrom's paper raises many questions:

1. There is no stated definition of a nationwide network in the
   paper, or in what specific agreed upon direction it should
   go—I remind you of what Susan Crooks said (Chapter 19),
   "an organization must know where it wants to go before
   structuring governance."

2. My overall impression of the proposal is that of a superstructure imposed from the top, not built from the bottom
   or grassroots.

3. What is the relationship between the proposed strengthening
   of NCLIS, the establishment of a public corporation and
   regional activities compared with the present informal coordinating library groups that meet together such as the
   Network Advisory Committee (NAC), Council on Library
   Resources (CLR), Association of Research Libraries (ARL),
   NCLIS, LC, Regional Network Directors and others?

4. Bystrom's proposed public corporation will not..."compete
   with existing federal functions such as categorical programs."

Does this mean that the proposed funding of $200 million
for the first five years would be in addition to the approximately $300 million appropriations approved by the Senate
and House Conference Committee for fiscal year 1979?

On the National Commission (NCLIS), I would like to know if in suggesting
a change for the Commission, from a professional to a public body, is there
evidence that such a change would be beneficial and not be unduly affected by
political appointees? We have enough problems with library politics without
mixing in party politics.

Is there a real need for NCLIS to take under its wing the Federal Library
Committee? Carry out a study of Federal Government requirements for
information services and networks? Why should there be a moratorium on
further implementation of Federal Government networking?

On Dr. Bystrom's public corporation proposal, Henriette Avram made
some pertinent comments (Chapter 21) and several others have, I hope, put
this idea to rest.

On regional or multi-state library organizations, I wonder how familiar
Dr. Bystrom is with regional multi-state organizational development and
functions in the last few years? His statement that "a strong regional level
can serve as buffer against arbitrary Federal dictation," frightens me with
its implication going back to the proposed public corporation and a strengthened National Commission.

I could go on, but let me only mention my surprise at the statement under
proposed Title III to "authorize establishment of Regional Library and Information Authorities, with NCLIS authorized to set up specifications including
the division of the nation into regional areas. When states had organized to
meet these conditions, they would request approval as a Regional Authority."
Does this mean that if the states don't organize, they cannot be designated a
Regional Authority and cannot take part in the nationwide library network?
Believe me, the states are not interested in having regional compacts imposed from Washington, D.C. States are capable of cooperation together
when the need is there, as has been demonstrated.

State libraries and regional networks need to define and agree on their
relationships and roles in a national network. From a political viewpoint, I
believe that regional networks need state library agencies for political and
funding reasons. On the other hand, state library agencies need regional
networks for technical expertise and networking capabilities. Very few state
library agencies have technically competent automation staff, but regional
networks do and a partnership will be necessary.

The paper achieves a purpose in that it raises many provocative questions for discussion, but I, for one, see no practical solutions yet. I agree with Henriette Avram in pursuing the idea of an independent study, possibly utilizing the methodology followed by the A. D. Little study of OCLC, in deter-, mining a structure for a nationwide library network service.

As I looked over the agenda for this conference, I noticed one missing element: user expectations and service to users. I would like to raise the question: Is the library user going to gain anything from the White House Conference and from the structure and governance of library networks in light of developing technology?

Concerning the White House Conference, I believe users may gain if 1) the delegates are educated as to what libraries and information and library networks are all about; 2) there is follow-through by all state library agencies so that we can capitalize on specific needs of the delegates so that they can become a positive force in the community, it might be possible. However, if the White House delegates spend time talking about computer library networks, rather than user concerns, then I think we'll have failed to move from the technological to the human aspect of networking.

One thing the White House Conference delegates will discover is the splintering of special interest groups among the library and information community.

A few days before this conference I met with a group of public and school librarians to talk about cooperation and how I saw them fitting into the nationwide network. These library staff members send a message: "Don't forget us," they said. What they meant was to remember that they deal directly with the users and they want to know more about how they relate to the nationwide network.

A month ago I made a speech to a group of local businessmen in which I encouraged them to demand library service from their libraries. A man came up to me afterwards and told me that his librarian had never offered to obtain a magazine article for him that he was looking for recently. He finally drove 70 miles to his state university where he found it. I'll always remember his words: "I needed that article. It was important to me because my client wanted it and I wanted to keep my client." My question is: Why didn't that librarian offer to obtain the article? How could this patron have reached the National Periodicals Center through his library?

We all have our own horror stories upon trying to use a library. Why do they occur? Is it the library staff or the user? Is it the "unpredictability"

of our users, as Shirley Echelman mentioned (Chapter 32)? Or the inability
of library staffs to negotiate and listen to their users about what they want?

There are some other things I want to mention: 1) I don't think the user
is understood by network people. They are unpredictable; they frequently
are not sure what they want. Who is going to help them gain access to information? Who is responsible for the interface between the user and the library
staff member? And the resources? 2) I don't think the library staff member
is understood by network people. In the Joe Becker type of network (Chapter
7), librarians frequently refer title and subject requests to other levels in a
network. Who's responsible for the interface between library staff members
at different levels in a network?

Reference and information functions of libraries are not being emphasized
nor are they being developed, which may be why some users are setting up
their own information networks outside libraries. To me, this is the crucial
level of service and use of networking.

People make networks work. People at all levels. We are not involving
people at local levels so that they feel a part of what is being developed and
can convey that feeling to their users and potential users.

I would feel more comfortable if as much time, effort and money were
being spent on the human factors in networking as on the technological factors.
I believe that since our funds are being channeled mostly into the technological
aspects of networks at the national and regional level, then that is setting our
priorities. So, even though we might give lip service to our concerns for the
user and the human factor, I think that our spending priorities in the near
future will continue going into the technical aspects unless we make sure that
one of the major issues at the White House Conference is the human factor in
networking and, furthermore, that all of us begin tomorrow to examine the
human factors in our programs. You and I have the ability to become change
agents and insure that the human factor is considered and acted upon. If we
don't, no one else is going to do it.

The Committee under CLR, NCLIS and LC to link bibliographic utilities
has $6 million available. Six million dollars. Bill Welsh and Henriette
Avram are concerned with the user aspects, but they have other battles to
fight—we have to lobby for our users—no one else will.

To summarize:

1. Bystrom's idea on governance is premature at best and has
   several flaws.

2. If we can bring the human element/aspect into our discussions on networking instead of our emphasis on the computer, then we have a chance.

3. The interface between users and librarians and between librarians and other librarians is an important facet of guaranteeing equal access to information and to a nationwide network.

I would modify Henriette's call for a conference on education of people about networks and suggest that Galvin and Kent, for their next conference, also have Sara Fine develop a workshop on the human behavior aspects of networking.

Chapter 31

GOVERNANCE, FUTURE ALTERNATIVES: DISCUSSION

The discussion which follows has been transcribed from tape recordings,
summarized and edited. Comments and questions have been attributed to
speakers when their identity was provided. The editors of these proceedings
take responsibility for any errors in fact or interpretation resulting from
this process, since it was not feasible to provide proofs to discussants for
checking.

Maurice Freedman, School of Library Service, Columbia University

My remarks are directed to my former colleague Mr. Welsh. I appreciate your several references to me in your listing of agencies which might
find reason to offer opposition to a national library agency. I am glad to
know that the concerns that have been represented by so many people, and
that you have chosen to identify with my name, have achieved the level of
recognition that needs to be considered, at least in a public speech. Let me
share several of these concerns with you.

You did LC and CLR (the Council on Library Resources) a great disserv-
ice by saying that they have put the users out of mind. The National Program
for Acquisitions and Cataloging (NPAC), the various efforts toward Universal
Bibliographic Control, CONSER, and many other programs, have been directed toward satisfying the needs of the nation's research libraries and their
users. In the case of NPAC, they have been extraordinarily well served.

What the concern is, however, is that there is little tangible evidence
that public library bibliographic access and interests have been a concern of
the Council on Library Resources or the Library of Congress (in this case
the proponent of this National Library Agency, and in your person, LC the
endorser). In 1904 shortly before the publication of the first ALA cataloging
rules, but after the 1901 inauguration of the LC card service, Charles Cutter,
one of America's two greatest cataloging theorists (the other being the

Russian-born Seymour Lubetsky), warned that the interests of the public libraries and, yes, the children will be safeguarded by the rules-making bodies, and the research library constituency cannot be assured.

In recent times there have been many opportunities by LC to have included people who have had as their concern the bibliographic control and access of materials for public and school libraries, but who, as well, have been critical of the provision of this service by our de facto national cataloging center, LC. For example, a bibliographic advisory committee was previously appointed by LC. The person who suggested the committee also suggested a slate of names which included Paul Fasana, Seymour Lubetsky, Joseph Rosenthal, and Sanford Berman. Of these names, Joseph Rosenthal was the only one selected (and he of course has publicly endorsed AACR 2). Instead of Sanford Berman, Francis Hinton of the Free Library of Philadelphia (and the assistant head of the Catalog Code Revision Committee) was appointed. Sanford Berman, an independent thinker, as were all of the people recommended, has eloquently advocated bibliographic service for the public and school library users.

In a paper you gave to the ARL and which I cited in my article "Processing for the People," you stated that LC's first responsibility was to the nation's research libraries. I have seen nothing subsequent to that 1974 or 1975 statement that indicates either a change of position or even an enhanced concern for the non-research libraries. Finally, CLR—and I am reminded of that lovely homily I heard for the first time yesterday, "The Golden Rule: the agency with the gold, rules"—has been in the vanguard of promoting the bibliographic interests of the nation's research libraries. I literally cannot list the host of successful ventures that CLR has funded which have attempted to help the nation's research libraries and/or LC.

One may wonder as did the gentleman next to me at yesterday's meeting: "What do all of these bibliographic concerns have to do with governance and a national library agency?" The agency proposing the national library agency, CLR, and the agency endorsing it, LC—although showing a sensitivity to criticism—have shown little response to the substance of the proposals of the criticisms. I ask you, what is there in CLR's proposal and your institution's posture that should lead me to believe that the baby issuing forth from the CLR/LC union would not be its parent's child—that is any different at least in terms of past services than it has been.

Let me say I have no opposition in principle to a National Library Agency, but its auspices give me great concern. I would welcome your telling me why the future will not be like the past and welcome also for one or more of my many colleagues who have been so devotedly concerned with public and school library bibliographic access an invitation to at least participate in LC's selected committees. Dr. Hayes' point yesterday, that we should include all viewpoints and resolve them, is especially well taken. Finally, if you prefer to deal with organizations rather than individuals, I would suggest representation from, or selection by, the Public Library Association's Public Library Catalog Needs Committee and that they be added to the list of those who are usually invited to and participate in planning national bibliographic services.

"Processing for the People" was intended not as a denial of the needs of the research libraries but as a positive statement and a plea for the kinds of bibliographic services public and school library users need and deserve, which Charles Cutter originally identified in 1904.

William Welsh

Guilty on all accounts, Mitch, and that's why I was trying to say last evening and again today—we need a forum so that we can bring together all vested interests and to avoid the painful process of AACR 2. I think that this is a very serious deficiency, and I look forward to something constructive to follow from this session so that there is a beginning of a forum, so that your views can be adequately represented.

Maurice Freedman

Can I suggest as a practical suggestion that existing groups have additions made to them, particularly that bibliographic advisory committee. That's not a forum.

Gaya Agrawal - Robert Morris College

We want Federal government support because we are afraid there is not enough of a market from end users to survive in the free enterprise market. We want a monopolistic situation free from antitrust law and the Federal Trade Commission, because we want everyone's dollars to serve a small percent of end users (some user studies show only 20-30% of the academic or public community are using the library). Because we don't want to conduct valid and reliable consumer research on end users, most of the surveys are conducted by librarians who are middlemen in marketing terms. And not the end users. We are also afraid that the product will fail on the drawing board, similar to several other consumer products, and because we are not sure if we can use innovative approaches in marketing and sales promotion of the product.

John Linford - NELINET

Susan Crooks, in her comments, said that "what's best for OCLC may not be best for the National Network," as one of the considerations they used

for the ADL study. I'd like to offer two corollaries to that, one of which is
"what's best for OCLC may not be best for OCLC's own constituents, " and
which leads into the next one, "what's best for the National Network may not
be best for the libraries in the nation. " Now this is not a reason to abort
the National Network, but it is however a principle that must be kept in mind
as the National Network is implemented. Too often we've seen national level
organizations, both governmental and nongovernmental, acquire a life of
their own, becoming nonresponsive, which in itself is a benign characteristic
if we aren't paying for it, but sometimes counterproductive or destructive.
A model similar to the program proposed for the National Periodicals Center
is a comfortable thing for me. Federal and philanthropic funding, plus low
overhead, central development and direction, combined with wide participative input and laissez faire operational participation, is a very comfortable
thing and I would support such an approach. It allows development efforts at
the top which can be built up from the bottom based on exercise of judgment
at both ends.

Barriers to networks seem to be a function of standard behavior patterns
on the part of librarians. When NELINET first got started in 1964, we were
probably the only network (we may not have been, but it appears that we
were the only network at that time) to be dealing with computerization in
libraries. Once we found out that NELINET did not fall flat on its face,
other networks decided to climb in on the thing, and it was obvious that the
concept would work. CSLI is another example where entepreneurs in the
library field spottily got CSLI going; they picked up on and bought the CSLI
package. As other librarians found out that it worked and didn't fall flat on
its face, they also bought in. Now this is evident by the clustering that you
have seen in a map of CSLI's present customers. It's a very clearly clustered concept.

Libraries in a given area watch what's in their area. The National Network has a similar problem with this behavior pattern. We only have one
chance (I don't know how many national networks we'll have a chance to put
together). If the first one doesn't work, we're just out of luck. As Henriette
Avram says, this is a fear syndrome, but I think that we'll just have to deal
with that one.

I want to emphasize that I have strong support for the activity that Henriette Avram and the Library of Congress have been engaging in. There may
need to be a forum of some kind, but it does not need to be a public corporation. The models that we've got for public corporations really wind up being
COMSAT, which sells a very popular product at a profit, or the Corporation
for Public Broadcasting which sells a similarly popular product only because
it can subsidize the cost and sell it for a low enough price for people who
can afford it or want to afford it. Amtrack sells an overhead-ridden semi-
popular product at a loss, and the Post Office sells a popular and potentially

profitable product at a deliberate loss with subsidizing by the first-class postage payers. So I don't know which of those models we fit into, but I suspect that none of them really fit what we have to need as a public library corporation.

Ruth Risebrow - University of Arizona

I'm reminded of the Gilbert and Sullivan song, "I am the very model of a model major general." What we have here, what we're talking about, is a major general model, and as that first great model in the library field, the Dewey Decimal System, was very important to the future of the profession, this is probably the most important thing in the future of the profession at the moment. As an engineer first and a librarian second, I am aware that a model must be specific before it is generalized. It is generally designed, operated, and then modified before it is generalized and accepted. However, I think much of the unease of some of us here is the fact that once the government, whether it's federal, state, or local, blesses a model we are going to be stuck with it—that it is not particularly easy to modify once it has been approved by the government. However, it is very important when designing a model to know all the factors involved, and I think William Welsh's idea of a forum of the strongest representation we can have from all interested parties, whether they are private or public bodies, is very important. And I think we have had here some very good, if not always official, representation of the various bodies concerned. I for one would like to thank the people at Pitt, Shirely Echelman and all the other speakers on the panel, and particularly this panel this morning, for having presented themselves as targets for arrows.

Marge Lippendott - College Center North, Community College of Allegheny County

What we're talking about at this conference is revolution. Revolution is what this country was founded on. There are three positive aspects of revolution: (1) the role of maintenance, and not in a negative sense but in the maintenance of what is good; (2) the role of transition, to help people see what's better; and (3) the role of visionary. And we need all three roles, and at different times we can play all three roles.

William Welsh

I have asked Robert Wedgeworth if we can schedule a two-hour program at the ALA Midwinter meeting where the National Periodicals Center plan can be presented so there can be an opportunity for input, and I realize there has not been.

I don't regard this as a revolution; I think this is an evolution. I think revolution implies blood, the burning of existing structures. I hope the message that we get here today is we're simply going to build on the strength that we have. We are a very powerful group in this room, representing very powerful institutions. I think it just needs a little sharpening of focus—a transfusion, not a loss of blood.

Gerald Sophar - U.S. Department of Agricultural

There has been some unhappiness regarding the structure and the thrust of the White House Conference. The American Society for Information Science was unhappy too. We were unhappy that a large lay delegation would appear in the White House Conference and probably be an uninformed group. So we did something about it; we put together a publication called "Eighteen Issues for the White House Conference on Library and Information Science Services." We had 25,000 copies printed (through the courtesy of Wiley and Company). We have addressed such issues as information, literacy, cost of information, information as a national resource. Unfortunately we only got this done in October, but we are sending this out to all of the remaining state conferences and to lay delegates. So here's one professional society that tried to act instead of just being unhappy.

I hear a lot of concern about the user. For some reason librarians believe that they are close to the user. I don't think they're as close to the user as they think they are because most of them do not understand marketing and the market. With this feeling in mind and because of my background, I persuaded our director to ask for funds for a market study of "who are our customers?" and "what do they need?" The market study is going to concentrate on the people of the U.S., the end user, and I would suggest that other library organizations think in these terms.

My final remarks refer to the question of a National Information Policy. Being in Washington I'm just as disturbed as others are when you don't know whether one should go the route of fee or no fee for service; there is no national policy. But I'd also like to point out that in the general structure of our society it's usually the weaker groups in our society that ask for national policy—the consumers, the librarians. With strong groups in our society (e.g., the medical fraternity), just mentioning national policy will bring loud protests; they don't want to be touched. So when you think of national policy, ask yourself the question—are you asking for visibility or are you asking for national policy?

Part Six

CONCLUSIONS

Chapter 32

LIBRARY NETWORKS: POSSIBILITIES AND PROBABILITIES

Shirley Echelman

Assistant Vice President and Chief Librarian
Chemical Bank
New York, New York

I would like to begin by thanking Tom Galvin for inviting me to speak to this
very illustrious group of information managers, librarians, information
users, policy makers, communicators and other influential folk. When Tom
called last March to ask whether I would take on this assignment, I was
puzzled by his request. I pointed out to him that I was neither expert nor
even initiate in the subject of networking. He replied that he hoped that I
might be able to "put the content of the daytime sessions into a broader perspective...and address larger issues such as ultimate service and information delivery objectives of networks." Well, the challenge of such splendid
functions as "putting into broader perspective" and "addressing larger issues"
overcame my sense of caution and I accepted; which may prove the contention
of some computer scientists that rational decisions are best made with the
aid of computer analysis of the factors involved, and not by the human brain
working on its own.

In any case, being mindful of my non-expert status and of the fact that we
have just finished two full days of discussion, as well as drinks and dinner,
and have the better part of one more day's work ahead of us, I do not propose
to attempt a very serious expostulation of issues tonight. What I would like
to do is to take a more or less lighthearted look at some of the issues that
have been raised at this conference from the point of view of four different
characters whose lives may be affected by network development, and to pose
some questions that they might ask if they were with us tonight—and indeed,
some of them may be with us tonight. Before I do that though, I have a serious concern that I would like to share with you, and which is not part of my
prepared text.

Some remarks made during the past two days, some discussions I've had
with attendees at this conference, and some recent reports that have come
to my attention worry me greatly, and I should like to put some bits of information before you tonight and share some of my worries.

The first relates to the exchange between Al Trezza and me about Joseph
Becker's remarks of yesterday. I will not review that now because you all
heard them, but I will say that my worries are not allayed. The second—
the Network Advisory Committee report on the development of the bibliographic component of a national library network; the third—a recent report
to the Association of Research Libraries member libraries on legislation
for a national library agency.

These matters were discussed by the SLA Board of Directors at its meeting last Saturday, and it has asked me to convey to you its deep concern
about the apparently unrepresentative planning, development and current
interim management leading to the creation of a national information service
network. SLA's Board urges the fullest participation by and consultation
with representatives of the library and information community in all stages
of planning and implementation for this network and its components.

A national information service network will be a source of great power in
our information-oriented society. The implications of structure design and
governance need to be widely discussed and understood before specific commitments are made. I am not at all sure that these implications have been
addressed. Now, back to the prepared text and the points of view of four
different characters whose lives may be affected by network development.

The first character is the library user. I will not say the ordinary library
user because, as those of us who work in libraries know, there is no such
person as an ordinary library user. Library users are extraordinary in our
society, in that they are active initiators of searches for information, instead
of being passive recipients of information packaged and transmitted to them
in various modes.

They are also, as any reference librarian can tell you, somewhat unpredictable. It is these two characteristics that are central to the organizational
issues that we are facing at this conference. To state the matter a little more
succinctly—library users ask questions, and—you never know for certain
what question they are going to ask next! The need for resource sharing,
bibliographic access to collections other than one's own, and rapid communications capabilities arises from these basic characteristics.

Librarians have long exerted themselves to attract information seekers
and to be prepared for the unpredictabilities of the search. Indeed, being
prepared for the search is the grand game in many ways.

Library users (or readers, as they used to be called in the days when reading was a publicly-laudable activity) may ask three questions of libraries. These are:

1. Where do I find information on "x"?

2. May I have the documents containing information on "x"?

3. What information on other topics is there in this place in which I might be interested if I only knew about it?

The ability to answer questions 1 and 2 is vastly enhanced by well-designed and adequately-funded library networks. Indeed, it may be that most of us have gathered here in Pittsburgh to improve our capacity to answer these two questions. Question 3, in my opinion, is the most crucial question that a reader can ask in a library; the question which has the greatest life-enhancing potential, both from an individual and a societal point of view. Yet it cannot be answered by a librarian, or by the most sophisticated network yet imaginable. It can only be answered by serendipity; by an act of communion between a single reader and a collection, a communion which is mundanely called "browsing." There are compelling organizational and economic reasons why information policies must encompass and promote the concept of library networks, but one side-effect of network building is to decrease the reader's ability to browse creatively in a single place; to satisfy "idle" intellectual curiosity. This is a loss for which we, as a society, may make considerable payment at some future time.

Let me illustrate serendipity with a short tale I heard recently from a librarian in a great state university. It seems that a new graduate student appeared at his elbow one afternoon and stated that he was starting on a research project having to do with the relationship between rainfall and the per hectare yield of various grains. He was specifically interested on this particular afternoon in investigating rainfall records and yields of ground-holum on the plains of Abbenay. The librarian was puzzled by the question—he had worked with agricultural researchers and students for many years, but he had never heard of ground-holum. Abbenay didn't ring any bells either. After due consultation with standard agricultural science reference works failed to produce the answer, he advised the student to query AGRICOLA and offered to arrange an appointment with the literature searcher. The student agreed to a time for the interview, thanked the librarian, and wandered off.

The student was a curious young man by nature, but proud. He didn't recognize ARGICOLA but it seemed somehow familiar. He wandered idly over to the catalog—where he had not been able to find Abbenay or ground-holum—and looked up Agricola. He discovered that there was a book on the subject in the collection. He found it in the stacks and borrowed it (in English translation, of course). Tacitus' biography of the Roman Governor of

Britain interested him mightily, although it had nothing to say about ground-holum; and he began to read widely in his spare time on the early history of the British Isles. He eventually gave up agricultural research for Anglo-Saxon history and became a famous scholar in the field. I don't know whether he ever learned of the transmogrification of Agricola from diplomat to data base.

From the viewpoint of the library user, the important functions of networks are most likely to be improved information retrieval capabilities, improved document delivery facilities, and expansion of referral services. The cost is measured in decreased creative browsability.

The second character through whom we may consider networking is the library manager. Like the wise son in the Passover service, our library manager knows most of the questions to be asked, and she knows many of the answers. Many of her concerns are addressed in the Montgomery paper (Chapter 18), and I would like to comment briefly on this paper from the library manager's viewpoint. First, I agree wholeheartedly with Montgomery's premises that behind each barrier to networking is an unmet expectation, and that expectations play a major role in governance. This is true in all governance structures, I think, be they in the profit or non-profit sectors, academic or government, past or present. What Montgomery is saying is that people involved in a governing activity will try to formulate and direct that activity so that it does what they want it to do; and when more than one person is involved, political action of one kind or another is the inevitable result.

I have spent a great deal of time during the last two years traveling around the United States and Canada and talking with librarians. While much of this talk was about issues of exclusive or specific interest to the organization for which I was traveling, a great deal of it was about current issues of interest to the profession as a whole. One of the issues frequently discussed was net-working. The people with whom I talked about networking were mostly members of Special Libraries Association, but they were from all types of libraries, with the possible exception of school libraries. Many were managers of libraries or of departments of libraries. My lasting impression of these discussions is that, while librarians are enthusiastic about the possibilities for improved service through networking arrangements, they have two major concerns.

One concern is that network membership shrinks the decision-making options for managers of individual libraries and departments. This may be partially a psychological reaction, but there seems to be at least some reality in it. Management is essentially a decision-making and coordinative function —anything that limits individual decision-making opportunities can realistically be perceived as a diminution of the management function.

Another and, I think, a deeper concern is that the best library service is that which allows for the most contact between librarian and library clientele. The questions that library managers are asking are—does network participation increase or decrease the distance between us (the library staff) and our clients? Does it tend to set us further apart from the public we are supposed to be serving? If it does, what will be the consequences in terms of short and long-range local public support for libraries, and in terms of our own satisfaction in our work?

It is true, as Montgomery's paper points out, that self-interest, timidity, fear, and jealousy are factors which raise barriers to progress toward co-operation among libraries. However, if anyone thinks that these factors are unique to libraries, he or she simply has never worked in any other kind of institution. All institutions in society are victimized by these flaws in the personalities of their personnel. The barriers thus raised may be more intractable than those raised by legal or economic factors, but they are a fact of life in all but the most Utopian societies.

My third character is the lay delegate to the White House Conference. I say that he is my third character, but although I have pondered him long and hard and have made mighty attempts to project myself into his persona, he remains elusive and ghostly.

This lack of definition arises, in large part, from the fact that no positive qualifications were required of these delegates—in fact it was apparent at several of the state conferences that the main qualification for lay delegates was that they have as little experience with the organization and function of libraries as is possible for a human being in a literate society. Therefore, the best I have been able to do is to formulate some basic questions that I would hope an intelligent non-librarian delegate might pose when confronted by a proposal for a national network such as that outlined in the Bystrom paper (Chapter 25). These questions might be:

1. What is a national network? This question needs no comment, other than to state that a good pamphlet on networks should be available to WHCLIS delegates, and I assume that NCLIS is assuming responsibility for provision of such a pamphlet.

2. Is there any institution in our society with which a library network could be compared and with which the lay delegate is sufficiently familiar for the comparison to be meaningful? I can think of three possibilities for analogy, but none of them are very satisfactory.

    The first is the Postal Service, which is a distributed network for delivery of documents. In every reasonable

society, it is an integral part of the national information
system. In the U.S. it is both computerized and labor
intensive; it is increasingly expensive and apparently
increasingly inefficient. It is also less reliable, albeit
sometimes quicker, than its 19th century predecessor,
the Pony Express.

The second is the Federal Reserve system. It is a semi-
voluntary hierarchical network, with a federal regulatory
structure. Its purpose is to increase the stability of
commerce in the U.S. by insuring a reliable banking system. It is somewhat successful, although not entirely so,
since it seems to be losing members because of the high
cost of membership vis-a-vis demonstrable benefits. In
any case, it is not a really satisfactory analogy because
of the arcaneness of what it is supposed to do. Library
networks certainly do not wish to be perceived of as
arcane.

The third possible analogy is the food distribution system
which could be characterized as an informal network.
Membership is voluntary, Federal government regulation
is moderate, it is a nationwide system for the processing
and distribution of vital goods. On closer examination,
however, certain negative characteristics appear which
mitigate against analogy. The system is increasingly
mechanized, increasingly centered on packaging and marketing rather than on product integrity and equitable distribution, and increasingly expensive. In addition, the
primary producers (read: authors) and the final consumers (read: library users) seem to be losing out to
the middlemen. Although one may recognize many simi-
larities here to library networks, the analogy could be
detrimental to the development of understanding or
sympathy.

Despite my lack of success in finding an analogous system, I think it is important to continue the search so that
lay delegates can see the picture of network possibilities
in terms that they already understand. Perhaps NCLIS
should concentrate some effort in this area. In any case,
I return to the questions that a lay delegate might ask.

3. Why do we need a national network? Will better library
    service be a certain result? I think the answer to this is
    a qualified "yes," but we librarians are going to be hard-
    pressed to prove it to the public at large.

4. Is it worth the money it is likely to cost? This question
will also be asked by my fourth character, into whom the
lay delegate melds at this point.

That fourth character is one who is beginning to emerge as the central
character in any discussion of such issues as those we are addressing—the
citizen-taxpayer. His questions might be seen more in the nature of challenges to the development of networks than as disinterested questions by
some. And yet, he is all of us here, all of us who work in libraries, and
most of us who use them. His basic question is: Will the cost of networks
be greater than the cost of current library service, and if so, will the benefits be so evident as to outweigh the additional cost?

The issues raised by this question are major elements in the debate over
information policy, and indeed they relate to other national debates over
economic and social policy. Some of these may be:

If the nation adopts a national network concept, how will this affect the
job market for librarians? Is the adoption of the concept likely to exacerbate
our increasingly intractable national unemployment problem? If the answer
is that more jobs will be created, or at least that none will be lost, are other
demonstrable savings going to be effected? If they are largely effected in the
area of resource sharing, how will this impact on the publishing industry and
specifically on employment in that industry? There is considerable evidence
that library resource sharing does not have crucial impact on publishing at
large, but what about scholarly and reference-work publishing?

Another set of questions deals with document delivery issues. Is document
delivery really better (i.e., surer and/or quicker) under network arrangements than it was prior to the birth of the network? What will be the impact
of publication-on-demand and delivery via facsimile or home television to the
ultimate user on the need for sophisticated library-centered document delivery systems? What about the impact of full-text retrieval from computer
data bases?

The last set of questions has to do with who will be in charge and who will
participate. I hope taxpayers will ask these questions. There are a whole
group of them and they relate to such societal issues as participation by the
private sector of the economy in systems supported by public money, part of
which represents tax contributions of the private sector itself; the role of
the expert in the governance of societal systems; the thrust of our society
toward homogeneous middle-class goals and the effect of this thrust on our
long-cherished commitment to individual freedom; the inherent power of any
network to control and censor what goes into it as well as what comes out;
the anonymity of management in any large institution and the protection from

reasonable public oversight that this anonymity many confer; and the issue of equality vs. egalitarianism, that is, participation by all vs. governance by all.

It appears that I have been more serious than I meant to be. I would like to close by sharing three aphorisms with you, and by hoping that you will remember them from time to time when you think about libraries, about information networks, and about information policy. They are intended as road signs indicating caution and not as stop signs.

1. Diversity is as important as efficiency.

2. Serendipity can be as interesting as sex, and its effect may be more lasting.

3. Curiosity, not computers, led to the discovery that $E = Mc^2$.

DISCUSSION

Allen Kent

Although I agree with just about everything you say, there was an element in your talk that sounded to me as if you suggested there is something sinister about government. I used to feel that way a number of years ago. I used to feel that government was non-responsive, irresponsible, wasteful and lazy. And then I began to roam the halls of Washington. I began to sense in every agency that there was at least one person in middle management who was responsive, who was trying hard, who was working hard, and was trying to do something useful. It restored some faith in government, and I began to sense that these were people not too much unlike me. They had some elements of leadership, some elements of clay feet. In many cases, events began to overtake plans and programs and they felt they had to do something. And they had to make some moves, despite the risks.

The second thing that occurred to me was the comments made by some after President Carter met with Menachem Begin and Anwar Sadat—the sinister element of meeting in Camp David—obviously an Israeli encampment or settlement.

The third point that was raised in my mind when you talked about serendipity was a wonder how much serendipity the Chemical Bank uses in dealing with Eurodollars and dealing with profits in the banking industry.

Shirley Echelman

I don't know that your comments need any answer. If there weren't a certain element of serendipity in dealing with Eurodollars, we'd be a little better off in terms of the dollar in the international money market. I don't mean to suggest that I think that people in government are any more sinister than any of the rest of us. I am only worried about the maintenance of a participatory democracy, and I recognize Jefferson's words about vigilance and I want them to be applied to the development of library networks as well as to any other developments.

Henriette Avram

I wanted to comment on Shirley Echelman's presentation. The Network Advisory Committee minutes that she was reading from need, I think, some further explanation, rather than being taken out of context. First, I would like to say that the Network Advisory Committee membership, and I give this to you from memory—and it's not complete—is made of people from the University of Chicago, BALLOTS, OCLC, Washington Library Network, SOLINET, NELINET, CLASS, MIDLNET, NLM, NAL, the Council of Computerized Library Networks, AMIGOS, FEDLINK, the American Library Association, the Special Libraries Association, the Association of Research Libraries, the Chief Officers of State Library Associations, Information Industry Association, the American Society for Information Science, and the American Association of Publishers. There may be others I can't remember at this time.

The other thing I would like to note is that the announcement that Shirley Echelman made has been publicly made by me at least four times in the past few months—in fact, it was made by me about three o'clock this afternoon. I described this project to this group. In addition, it has been announced twice at ALA—this past June meeting I gave a presentation and it was announced, and Jim Haas of the Council of Library Resources announced it at ALA when the members of the Network Advisory Committee gave their presentation to the community describing the events and the proceedings and what was going on in the Network Advisory Committee.

The National Information Network (or Service) that Shirley said we are developing is really nothing new. It is not really the national information service, it's what I call the library bibliographic component; it's what Jim Haas calls the "comprehensive computerized library database"—and what it is really is the linking together of the present utilities. It is linking together Washington Library Network, the OCLC, and BALLOTS, and perhaps, depending upon some of our own internal problems, the Library of Congress.

At least the Library of Congress will continue its MARC projects and its giving of bibliographic services to the community.

Now, the people that are working on this—the committees with CLR— it's just really new and all the pieces aren't in order yet, but the one committee that will be going forward on this is Fred Kilgour, myself, Rod Swartz, Ed Shaw, Carol Ishimoto, and Herman Fussler—this is a sort of a program committee. So this has not really been a secret, and given the terms that you read from the minutes, it sounds like that. SLA has been invited to participate in this, and in fact, one of my staff members attended and gave a presentation for the network committee of the Special Libraries Association describing all of these activities. We are trying to open this up just as broadly and completely as we possibly can in terms of our abilities to communicate.

Beth Hamilton - Illinois Regional Library Council

It is difficult not to trust Henriette Avram to the fullest possible extent, but I think that the point that Shirley Echelman is trying to make—and she can correct me if I'm wrong—is that although this is communicated to the library community, it is communicated as a fait accompli and we have not been given a chance to vote on the components of the Network Advisory Committee, nor have we had representatives come back to their constituencies and explain to us the rationale for these decisions. Is that right?

Shirley Echelman

Well, that's partially the case, but I'm also concerned with the list of organizations that Henriette Avram has read to you and of which I was aware, of course. Given the Advisory Committee made up of all of those groups of people or representatives of all those groups, it had decided, or at least the steering committee of that Committee had decided, that they themselves wanted to constitute themselves as the governing board. They then discovered that action had been taken by three organizations which prevented them from doing so. I'm concerned about that kind of apparent pre-emption.

Maurice J. Freedman - Columbia University

As Henriette Avram has heard me talk too many times for her satisfaction about subject headings in LC, I have heard her network speech innumerable times. And I will have to say, having been at many of those sessions you talked about, including this afternoon, I heard no reference at all to legislation being introduced in Congress in May. And I had, up until this point, a great deal of faith and credibility in Al Trezza's saying there is no plan, nothing is in place, there is no structure, and the White House Conference is wide open. And it just seems to me the establishment of a national utility seems like an inappropriate action prior to the White House Conference. It would seem that the White House Conference should first assert that we need such a facility. I never heard any reference to legislation.

<u>William Welsh</u>

What we have just observed is the typical problem of communication, especially amongst librarians. Shirley Echelman was giving three, or at least two, separate reports. The legislation has nothing whatsoever to do with Henriette Avram and the networking group. The legislation stemmed from a draft proposal that the Center for Research Libraries put forward. The Center for Research Libraries, for reasons which should be obvious to each of you, has a vested interest in the future of the National Periodicals Center. They would like to be a part of that activity, so they drafted that legislation. Subsequent to that, there was a meeting called by the Center for Research Libraries in conjunction with the Association of University Presidents. Jim Haas was invited and asked if the Library of Congress was going to be represented—he hearned that LC was not—so he put my name forward. When Gordon Williams called me to ask if I would attend, I said "Yes, is NCLIS going to be represented?" And the answer was "No." So I was able to get NCLIS represented. When I walked in that room—and this was less than a month ago, I believe—I discovered that ALA was not present, and I was deeply concerned.

But this is the problem we are dealing with and if I say much more, I'll be telling you what I am going to say tomorrow about the whole problem of the National Library Board. But there are a number of movements afoot and the reference to the May 1 date (I don't know quite how that May 1 date came about—it's actually May 15, as I understand it) and the magic of that date is, that is the date by which Congress must introduce authorizing legislation if it hopes to get approval for appropriation language in the subsequent fiscal year; but there is this movement to try to get the National Periodicals Center into being.

What I want to tell you tomorrow is that we have a problem, and it is represented in this room. We lack a forum. One of the things I'll be saying tomorrow is that during the most recent meeting of ALA in Chicago, Dick De Gennaro and a number of others spoke about the necessity for postponing the adoption of AACR2. My response, as the representative of the Library of Congress, was that I was not prepared to respond to any single individual, that what we lack in this country to a degree that is absolutely shocking is a forum, there is no gathering together of everybody who has a vested interest so that all of the people who have something to say can be heard, and then we can move in a collective manner. I am deeply distressed with the situation.

There is one more element that perhaps you don't know: there was a press release on October 16 which proposes that there be a research library network. This is a joining together of the BALLOTS system with the RLG group and, as expected, there was some reference to an expectation that it would be expanded. This is another major development proceeding from an obvious logical grouping together of libraries; in consequence the effect of this upon OCLC is hard to determine, but I am simply bringing that to your attention so you are aware that there is another complication.

But the message I want to leave with you is that in this country we lack a forum to discuss national concerns and move in a collective manner to a solution that meets all of our needs. It is virtually impossible to get everyone's interest represented, but we've got to do a better job than we are doing now. We've got to get the publishing community involved, the private sector, SLA, ALA, and a whole list of organizations that have a vital interest in what we are doing. And tomorrow, when I list just some of the objectors to a national plan—the last set of initials I was going to list was MF—and that was going to be Mitch Freedman.

Shirley Echelman

I did not come here as a representative of the Special Libraries Association, I came here as a working librarian in a small library in the private sector of the economy. And one of my concerns is that some of the developments that are going on seem to me—and I may very well be wrong—but they seem to me to assume that if the needs of the major research libraries in this country can be met, then somehow all of the rest of us working in the thousands of small special libraries, medical libraries, public libraries, school libraries, and other kinds of libraries, will somehow fall into the system. And I am not sure that that's going to happen without some design and planning.

Joseph Anderson - State Librarian, Nevada

My concern is very similar to the one that Shirley Echelman just mentioned. I am here representing a small state, far from the seats of decision making and power in Washington. I also represent a small state library. But as in the administration I have served in for the past eight years, and one I anticipate serving after tonight, I am here representing my state and I am here with a charge to bring back a report as to the nature of the unfolding concept of network. We realize very clearly how dependent we are on other resources in the nation. From my perspective, hearing the process of the conference to this moment, we have laid out to the taxpaying public of the state of Nevada that here is now an opportunity to prepare for a first step at the national level to develop the information resource and access to it. We've sold access to resources to our senior, advanced and aged political decision makers.

We've even sold it to the new ones coming aboard in state government and in county and municipal government. And the appearances of what goes on now or say from this moment forward, will be severely damaged by activities of perceived special interest groups—and libraries are a special interest group—with the impropriety of having activities, agencies, organizations who are not responsive to the tax system of the state or of the nation.

We are not elected people, we are professional people in a field; if we go back home and explain to a state legislature what is happening at the national level in a professional forum in terms that they can't handle, this will be counterproductive to say the least. So I would urge that the powers that be do not take publicly perceived action, which may lead those of us in the hinterland to suspect that the decisions are already made and that we and our citizens are merely rubberstamping things that already have taken place.

Chapter 33

A SUMMARY OF ISSUES FOR CONSIDERATION AT THE
WHITE HOUSE CONFERENCE
ON LIBRARY AND INFORMATION SERVICES

Thomas J. Galvin

Dean
Graduate School of Library and Information Sciences
University of Pittsburgh
Pittsburgh, Pennsylvania

INTRODUCTION

Creation of an effective national library and information network to serve all
Americans is a cornerstone of the proposed national program for library and
information services described by the National Commission on Libraries and
Information Science in 1975. The Commission writes:

> America has an abundance of recorded information, not a short-
> age. However, this precious resource is concentrated in rela-
> tively few locations, often virtually inaccessible to millions of
> people, and is lying largely untapped. Thus, the challenge is to
> find the means for making these resources available to more
> people through an effective identification, location and distribu-
> tion system. (Toward a National Program for Library and
> Information Services: Goals for Action, p. 5)

The key to effective sharing of recorded information is the development
of a nationwide network of libraries and information centers, comprising, in
the words of the National Commission, "an integrated system encompassing
state networks, multi-state networks, and specialized networks in the public
and private sectors." (Goals for Action, p. 49)

Because of the centrality of the library network concept to the national
program for library and information services, it is clear that issues relating
to the governance, design, structure and funding of networks should command

329

an important place on the 1979 White House Conference agenda. In order to further the identification and definition of these issues, as well as to provide an opportunity for librarians and other information professionals to participate directly in formulating this portion of the White House Conference agenda, the National Commission joined with the Graduate School of Library and Information Sciences of the University of Pittsburgh to co-sponsor the 1978 Pittsburgh Conference on the theme, "The Structure and Governance of Library Networks" as an official Pre-White House Conference.

On November 6-8, 1978, nearly five hundred librarians, information specialists, representatives of the information industry, and other interested individuals met in Pittsburgh for three days to explore issues relating to library networks. The Conference was open to all who wished to attend. This paper, intended as a resource document for the White House Conference, constitutes a summary of the major topics discussed at the 1978 Pittsburgh Conference. It is based on position papers prepared in advance and distributed to participants prior to registration for the Conference, papers presented at the Conference itself, comments made during six scheduled discussion sessions by members of the audience, and data gathered through a questionnaire distributed to all Conference participants. *

THE CHARACTER OF LIBRARY NETWORKS

The National Commission defines a library network as:

> Two or more libraries and/or other organizations engaged in a
> common pattern of information exchange, through communica-
> tions, for some functional purpose. A network usually consists
> of a formal arrangement whereby materials, information and
> services provided by a variety of types of libraries and/or other
> organizations are made available to all potential users. (Li-
> braries may be in different jurisdictions but agree to serve one
> another on the same basis as each serves its own constituents.

---

* The opinions of Conference participants reported in this paper are largely
derived from a "Summary of Preconference Questionnaire Responses:
1978 Pittsburgh Conference on the Structure and Governance of Library
Networks" prepared by M. Evalyn Clough, Assistant to the Dean and
Lecturer, Graduate School of Library and Information Sciences, University of Pittsburgh, and James M. Matarazzo, Assistant Dean for Student
Affairs and Associate Professor, School of Library Science, Simmons
College, to whom grateful acknowledgment is made by the author of this
paper.

Computers and telecommunications may be among the tools used
for facilitating communication among them.) (Goals for Action,
pp. 82-83)

In its simplest meaning, a library network is a mechanism created to facilitate the sharing of resources among libraries for the mutual benefit of their
clienteles.

American libraries have a long tradition of sharing bibliographic data and
of sharing books, journals and other media through interlibrary lending.
More recently, libraries have joined together to share storage facilities,
specialized staff or services, to purchase materials, supplies and equipment
jointly, and to realize the benefits of cooperation in many other functional
and service areas. The exponential growth in the number of items published
each year, the rising cost of books, periodicals and other library materials,
the increasing demands placed upon libraries by their clienteles, and the
development of supportive computer and telecommunications technologies
have all served to stimulate library network development. Several hundred
such networks are now in existence in the United States. Some are international in scope, some national, some regional; many are statewide or
purely local. Some are limited to a single type of library (public, academic,
school or special), some to a single subject field (e.g., medicine); others
encompass all subjects and more than one type of library. Some involve
significant participation by the private, for-profit sector. Some library networks perform only one function (e.g., the cataloging of books), others provide a number of services to member libraries. Some networks are governed
by formal consortium or interlibrary cooperation agreements, others by
contracts, still others by the full or partial merger of formerly autonomous
libraries into organized library systems. A significant number have no legal
or contractual basis for existence beyond informal institutional agreements.
Characteristically, network membership is entirely voluntary, with participating libraries free to withdraw at any time. Network operations may be
financed entirely by institutional membership fees or assessments, by fees
for services, and/or from a combination of sources, including state and/or
federal grants and gifts from foundations. Funding is, at present, typically
on a year-by-year basis. No comprehensive coherent national plan or set
of guidelines has yet been developed or implemented to bring about integration or rationalization of the variety of networking activities and structures
that characterize the contemporary library scene.

MAJOR ISSUES—FINANCING THE NATIONAL NETWORK

The authors of position papers, panelists, speakers and participants at the
1978 Pittsburgh Conference identified funding as their highest priority concern in the future development of a nationwide library network. No accepted

general plan currently exists to provide the new funds needed to establish
and maintain either the national network or the subsidiary regional, state or
local networks that it would ultimately comprise.

At the national level, a number of complex fiscal issues emerged that
demand consideration and resolution. One is the question of optimal balance
between publicly-supported or publicly-subsidized information agencies,
such as libraries, on the one hand, and the emerging private, for-profit
sector, popularly known as the "information industry," on the other. As the
National Commission has observed, it seems "crucial that information activities in the public and private sectors operate in harmony with one another
and in consonance with the national interest." (Goals for Action, p. 26)
Any increase in public support for enhanced library service through network
development may be viewed by some as an inappropriate incursion by government into the arena of the private sector. Conversely, if effective access to
information is both the right of every American and a vital element in the
survival of a free, democratic society, then it is clearly the responsibility
of government to assure through the use of public funds that every citizen
has adequate library service.

Historically, the burden of public support of library services has fallen
most heavily at the local level. State, federal and foundation funds constitute,
at present, only a small portion of total library support. The result is
marked inequality of access to information within most states and among the
states. The goal of equality of access to library and information services
for all Americans appears to require that the states and the federal government assume a greater share of library costs. In particular, a new balance
among federal, state and local funding seems essential to meet the initial
costs of establishing and operating library networks. The responsibility of
the states and the federal government for equalizing access to information
needs to be made explicit by statute and through appropriations. The costs
of creating and maintaining the national network cannot be met from currently
available local sources of support. Increased federal funding is consistent
with the view expressed by the National Commission "that the total library
and information resource in the United States is a national resource which
should be developed, strengthened, organized and made available to the maximum degree possible in the public interest." (Goals for Action, p. x)

Priority concerns include substantially increased federal funds to establish new operational networking programs at the national level, to expand
and enlarge the national bibliographic record, to support expanded national
programs of the Library of Congress and other federal libraries, and to
provide financial incentives to encourage regional, state and local network
development. To achieve true equality of access, state and federal funds
are needed to reimburse larger and more specialized libraries which will
inevitably lend more materials to other libraries than they will borrow from
them.

Both existing and proposed networks currently face major financial problems. Chief among these are the need for assured, long-term, multi-year funding and for more effective methods of allocating costs among network members in a manner commensurate with the benefits of participation. Uncertainty remains as to the method by which federal and state funds can most effectively be channeled to the local level, as well as with respect to the ultimate role that state library agencies can or should play in the planning, development and operation of networking programs. What priority can or should be given to funding network development in a time when local libraries are severely pressed to finance existing services to their clienteles? And by whom should these priority questions be decided?

MAJOR ISSUES—THE STRUCTURE OF THE NATIONAL NETWORK AND ACCESS TO ITS SERVICES

A central concern of participants in the Pittsburgh Conference was the recognition that some existing library networks are exclusionist and elitist in their membership. Because the bulk of print resources are concentrated in a relatively few large libraries, these libraries, understandably, are exerting a major influence on the design of emerging national networking structures. Smaller academic, public, school and special libraries are apprehensive that their clienteles, who collectively constitute the majority of library users, may be granted only limited access to network resources, or, especially in the case of children, excluded from participation and access entirely. Particular concern was expressed for the clienteles of the nation's 74,000 elementary and secondary school libraries, since the national record of school library participation in network planning and network services has not, to date, been impressive.

It is, however, a generally accepted planning principle that the success of a library network depends upon its ability to offer comparable benefits to all its members. So long as it appears that smaller academic, public and school library collections contain few items of interest to large research libraries or their clienteles, there is little prospect of parity. Federal and/or state subsidy to large net lenders in exchange for guaranteed access for all potential network participants may be necessary and appropriate to resolve this problem.

The sciences of network planning, design and evaluation are only in the early stages of development. Much network planning is based on unverified assumptions about use patterns. Trial-and-error methods currently predominate in the absence of rigorous empirical approaches to the formulation of network performance objectives and evaluative criteria. Computer simulation appears to offer a promising alternative to present methods for estimating cost-effectiveness, cost-benefit, and for addressing such complex technical design questions as multiple-function versus single-function or single-subject networks.

MAJOR ISSUES—NETWORK GOVERNANCE

"Governance, in the context of library networks" write K. Leon Montgomery and Ed Dowlin in their position paper for the Pittsburgh Conference, "is the sum of the relationships between participants (and their institutions) and the network organization(s).... Governance permits those using and running networks to express their interests and concerns... to establish goals and objectives as well as the policies by which these... are to be achieved." It was the sense of the Pittsburgh Conference that questions of network governance at national, regional, state and local levels are among the most difficult and complex issues that librarians will need to address in the near term. Conversely, failure to resolve these questions is likely to prove the major obstacle to the optimal development of library networks to benefit library users.

At all levels, a major issue is the autonomy of individual libraries. Network participation inevitably carries with it some obligation to subordinate local interests for the collective benefit of network partners. The prerogatives of exclusive local ownership and control of library materials must be modified when these resources are, in some sense, "pooled" with the holdings of other libraries in a networking mode. Buying decisions, for example, can no longer be made unilaterally at the local level. Moreover, if participants are to achieve the level of confidence in the continued ability of networks to assure access to needed items that is essential to long-term financial support of networks by their members, individual libraries must make long-term acquisitions commitments. It is questionable whether participation in the network can continue in the traditional voluntary form for member libraries, given the high level of mutual dependency associated with the networking mode of operation. A major concern is the prospect that the freedom of individual libraries to establish local service priorities may be compromised by the overriding necessity to meet obligations imposed as a consequence of network membership. A second major concern, that network participation may carry with it undesirable or unsupportable requirements for modifying local bibliographic practices, may prove somewhat less troublesome than had been expected, in light of emerging technological developments.

Most participants in the 1978 Pittsburgh Conference appear to be seeking to create library networking environments that will enable individual libraries to maximize the gains and minimize the risks attendant on whatever losses of institutional autonomy may accompany network membership. Governance structures that assure full participation and democratic decision-making are viewed as essential to this goal. The view was strongly expressed that network governance should be characterized by the maximum possible decentralization of decision-making authority. It is recognized that national and state-level leadership are essential, but not at the price of national or state control.

Governance questions are heavily influenced by network technology. The problem is perhaps analogous to citizen control of the military in a democratic society. How can those librarians and lay authorities (e.g., library boards, school superintendents, college administrators) who lack technological expertise participate effectively in the formulation of network policies that are dependent on understanding the capabilities and limitations of the technology that supports and determines the very character of network operations?

Of specific concern to delegates to the White House Conference will be those issues that relate to governance at the federal level. Given limited resources, the entire proposed national program cannot be brought into existence at one time. National priorities for the orderly stages of network development must be established. Participants in the Pittsburgh Conference generally acknowledged the need for a locus of federal responsibility for network policy planning, research and development. Other functions might include managing a coordinated, integrated national network structure, obtaining and distributing federal network development funds, coordinating existing federal library programs, and, possibly, regulating library networks as a public utility.

Several specific models for a federal library authority were identified and considered at the Pittsburgh Conference. One approach would involve an expanded role for some existing federal agency such as the Library of Congress, the National Library of Medicine, National Agricultural Library, Office of Libraries and Learning Resources in the U.S. Office of Education, or the National Commission on Libraries and Information Science. Alternatively, it was recognized that a new federal agency may need to be created. Two models, a public corporation comparable to the Corporation for Public Broadcasting or the Communication Satellite Corporation (proposed by John Bystrom in a position paper commissioned by NCLIS), and a National Library Board (suggested in the National Periodicals Center Technical Development Plan released by the Council on Library Resources just prior to the Pittsburgh Conference) were examined in some detail.

Several other major issues of national legislative concern that merit the attention of White House Conference delegates emerged in relation to network development. One is the need to make explicit, by statute, the federal responsibility for assuring equality of access to library and information services for all of the nation's citizens. Adequate library and information service for all citizens will require a sharing of the costs of those services among federal, state and local governments. Federal regulation of non-voice tele-communications in the public interest is considered vital to library network development, as is ultimate resolution of the copyright question in a manner that balances proprietary interests against the public interest in effective access to recorded knowledge. Congressional action may also be required to provide an adequate statutory base for interstate library networks. Irrespective of any possible assumption of operational responsibilities by the National Commission on Libraries and Information Science, attention must be given to the question of the future of that agency as a policy planning, research and coordinating mechanism at the national level.

Fundamental governance issues also exist at the state level. Goals for Action proposes a central role for the individual states, and for state library agencies, in the development and implementation of the national program. Yet some state library agencies lack the statutory authority required to assume leadership in multi-type library network development, while most are neither supported nor staffed at a level appropriate to the expanded responsibilities envisioned for them. Concern was expressed at the Pittsburgh Conference that state boundaries not serve to restrict network development along natural geographic or special interest lines, and that state agencies not become the sole channel through which local and regional networks can access federal funds.

MAJOR ISSUES—EDUCATION, RESEARCH AND DEVELOPMENT

Participants in the Pittsburgh Conference identified a variety of urgent needs in the areas of education and training in relation to library network development. The capability of librarians to understand and utilize network technology, as well as to manage that technology for the optimal benefit of their clienteles, must be enhanced through improved and expanded educational and in-service training programs. A special concern was expressed for the education and training of network executives.

A high priority was assigned to an expanded national research, development and demonstration program in relation to library networks. Among target areas identified were research to enhance understanding of patterns of use of print and non-print materials, to improve network design and evaluation capabilities, and to deepen current understanding of the complex operational interrelationships among network functions. Additional priorities in research and development included standardization of bibliographic data formats, retrospective conversion of bibliographic records to machine-readable form, improved document delivery capability, and experimentation with new information storage and telecommunications technologies such as videodisk, home computer, cable television and communications satellite.

CONCLUDING COMMENTS

The 1978 Pittsburgh Conference reflects the significance of library networking and library resource sharing as major developments in the improvement of library and information services to the nation, as well as their centrality to the proposed national library program. This suggests, in turn, that networks should be a major agenda item for the White House Conference on Library and Information Services, since equality of access to information for all citizens can be achieved only through the creation of effective structures for sharing recorded knowledge.

The 1978 Pittsburgh Conference identified a number of issues and concerns that are widely shared by librarians, information specialists, and others who have a professional responsibility to meet citizen information needs. The importance of a coordinated national program was recognized, as were the needs for education, research and development to enhance the ultimate quality of service to the individual library user.

The growth of library networks, and their growing importance to librarians and library users, has resulted in the emergence of a number of fundamental policy questions. Among these are, what should be the design and structure of a national library network (or networks), how shall these be managed, and how are they to be financed? The objective of the 1978 Pittsburgh Conference was to provide a national forum for the identification, elucidation and discussion of these issues as a contribution to the creation of an action agenda on library networking for delegates to the 1979 White House Conference.

Chapter 34

CLOSING SUMMARY

Alphonse F. Trezza

Executive Director
National Commission on Libraries and Information Science
Washington, D. C.

During these past three days the audience has listened to the presentation of five position papers and summaries, one dinner talk, twenty-two panel reactors, and six discussion sessions. In addition, there has been much discussion on the topic of the structure and governance of library networks, and many questions have been raised about the White House Conference on Library and Information Services and about the Commission. My task now is to try to shed some light on some of the questions that were raised, clarify some misunderstandings, and provide at least a few of the major themes that seemed to have emerged from the conference.

I have been asked what did I think of the conference. Was it helpful to the Commission? From my personal vantage point, I think its been wonderful. Wonderful because all of you had an opportunity to express yourselves on a highly controversial and basic issue—the structure and governance of a National Library and Information Services Network. The diversity of opinions here is only a microcosm of the diversity of opinions throughout the country on this very basic issue. I personally do not feel, for example, that we are nearly ready to introduce legislation for governance. There has not been enough public discussion or sufficient opportunities for people to react.

I would like, first of all, to review briefly the background and status of the White House Conference. When the resolution calling for the White House Conference was passed by Congress, one of the goals set forth in that resolution stated that "productive recommendations for expanding access to libraries and information centers will require public understanding and support, as well as that of the public and private libraries and information centers." It further stated that the National Commission, a permanent, independent,

executive agency, was to plan and conduct the conference, and that they were
to work with the states and provide them with technical and financial assistance to enable them to organize and conduct conferences and other meetings
in order to prepare for the conference. It went on the say that the Commission had to insure participation from a broad spectrum of Americans.

During the hearings for the White House Conference bill, it was clear that
each state, if the state desired it, was to have a conference. In addition,
conferences for the territories, the District of Columbia, and for American
Indians living on or near reservations were planned. As of late October,
1978, twenty-four state and territorial conferences and the Indian conference
have been held. Between November, 1978, and the end of April, 1979, which
is the deadline, there will be thirty-three more state and territorial conferences. One state so far has decided not to have a conference. All the others
will be represented at the National Conference October 28 to November 1, 1980.

In trying to determine the agenda for the National Conference, the Commission had to face the problem of providing for grassroots input. Thus, the
emphasis on the state conferences. What are the issues that must be discussed to satisfy the needs of the users ? President Carter, in August of
1976, stated that "if we are to succeed in developing libraries to their full
service potential, we must have the interest and participation of large numbers of the American public. This conference should be the combination of
an extensive process of citizen involvement in library policy, making its
beginnings at the grassroots. Results from the state conferences can be
pooled at the White House Conference. We will then have a sound foundation
upon which to devise complementary local, state and Federal plans for library and information services in a decade ahead. " When I testified before
Congress not too long ago about the Commission's budget, the point was made,
for at least the third time in three years, that the Congress is expecting the
consensus developed at the White House Conference to point the way for library legislation for the 1980's. The Congress is going to look, I think, with
a little bit of reluctance to moving on legislation before the White House Conference is over.

We are committed, as you can see from my earlier statements, to working
with the states for grassroots input. It is our hope that the states would first
of all consider their own basic needs, both local and state, and see how these
impinge on national responsibilities. Their recommendations would be re-
layed to the National Commission and the White House Conference planning
staff for use in planning the National Conference agenda.

Identification of issues the states feel express national concerns would
thus provide the basic input for setting the ideas for the National Conference
agenda. The Commission, however, was anxious to obtain recommendations

from national sources as well. Our plans, therefore, included three sources for input. One was to seek geographic input. This was to be accomplished through the state conferences. The second source was to plan three to four theme conferences on major issues. So far we have planned three. The first theme conference was a small invitational conference on the basic issue of Federal funding of library and information services. The plan called for two sessions, one held in June with participants representing the library and information science community. The participants in the second session held in September included representatives of the Administration, the Congress, and organizations concerned with public policy, especially fiscal. A paper was developed by an outside contractor—it was shared first with the library group, and then with the group of public policy people. A revision of that paper, which is only a background paper and has not been endorsed by anyone, will be available shortly and will be shared with the delegates to the White House Conference, the participants to the Federal funding conference, and with anyone else in the country who so desires it. It's a carefully prepared paper, and it reviews the options of Federal funding—categorical grants, revenue sharing, block grants, etc.

The second theme conference is on another major issue—governance. About a year ago, Tom Galvin, Allen Kent, and I planned this conference. And I must say we are gratified, at least I am very gratified, with the results of it. The third theme conference, which Charles Benton, the NCLIS Chairman, mentioned to you in his opening remarks, is planned for spring 1979 and will address the issue of literacy—and not just print literacy, but media and computer literacy. With these three theme conferences, we have another opportunity to discuss, essentially with professionals, national issues of major concern.

The third source of input will come as a result of the Commission's open invitation to every professional library and information association in the country to participate. They have all been invited to send us recommendations and to suggest ideas and topics that they feel ought to be considered for the agenda for the White House Conference. I have publicly issued this invitation at local, state, and national meetings over and over again. The deadline for organizations and associations is the same as the states—the end of April 1979. You heard the comment from the ASIS representative at this meeting. They have published a group of six papers and are sharing these with the states and with the Commission. They have identified some issues they feel are important. ALA is working on issue papers. Other groups, I'm sure, will also participate.

Through the three sources I have just reviewed with you, we hope to determine the major issues for the White House Conference agenda. How do we plan to accomplish this difficult task? Are we going to follow the lead of the

White House Conference for Handicapped Individuals, who received 35,000 resolutions from the states and regions? They did reduce these to 3,500 for the national conference, but were never able to get around to voting on them and had to do so later by mail. The Commission's tentative plans are to limit the number of broad issues to a half dozen—each of these issues will be sub-divided into a number of topics, we're not sure how many, as we have to first determine the issues. What these might be is hard to say. I suspect funding and governance may be two of them and literacy a third. We're still getting input. The agenda still is not frozen. It is still in a state of flux. The tentative plans for the structure of the conference is something like this: the delegates are going to spend most of their time in work sessions—small work groups of about twenty-five people, discussing issues and coming out at the end of the conference with recommendations for action—recommendations to the Congress and to the President. First of all, the Commission is required, within 120 days, to produce the final report and submit it to the President. The President is required, within 90 days after that, to produce his report to the Congress for action. That's the schedule. We're hoping that the conference is going to produce recommendations for new legislation and for revision of existing legislation. In addition, we expect ideas which can be implemented by you and me in our various capacities throughout the country at the state, local, institution, association, or agency level. That's the plan.

Now, who are these delegates who are coming to Washington after being selected by the states? The state conferences, in accordance with the rules developed by the Commission and based on the law, require two-thirds of the participants to be lay delegates. We use the term, non-library related. These people, in other words, are users—these people are the ones we are trying to serve. They are in the majority. One-third of the delegates represent the professionals. The states, in selecting their delegates to go to Washington, are doing so on a two-thirds/one-third formula. Some states are electing their delegates; some are selecting them. Some delegates will be at-large delegates. Altogether, we will have approximately 760 official delegates and another 340 or 350 alternates—about 1,100 people who will participate in the meetings and the discussions. These delegates, then, will be coming to Washington. The states themselves have an obligation and a responsibility to orient these delegates once they've been selected and the state meetings have ended on the recommendations adopted by their conferences. The National Commission, through its White House Conference staff, is planning an intensive orientation program for the delegates starting in January 1979.

As the delegates are selected and are officially registered by the Commission, they will be given materials so that when they arrive in Washington they will have a basic level of understanding of the issues. What they will

get are briefing papers, fact sheets, etc. We are also planning an orientation
session in each state with the delegates. The idea is to make sure that when
the delegates get to Washington they will all have a common base of information and understanding. This, we feel, will help insure a productive conference. That's the present plan. This, then, is how we are working toward
developing the issues, orienting the delegates, and structuring the conference.

Let me share a few more of our plans on the structure of the conference.
We plan an opening and closing session. At the closing session we will adopt
recommendations and actions and present them to the President of the United
States. The discussion sessions will be held on Monday, Tuesday, and
Wednesday. In addition, we are planning some general sessions, but these
will be held only at meal times. There will be national speakers at these
general sessions. As you can see, we are planning a generous part of our
time for discussion. The delegates will have exactly one night off. They are
going to work four and one-half days, because the American taxpayer is
spending $3,500,000 for this conference, and we must use it responsibly.
We are trying to make certain that the use of those funds will benefit the
people of this nation—the delegates are coming to work, not to visit Washington. If they want to visit Washington, they can do so with pre- and post-
conference tours, but during the conference they are going to work. Hopefully, then, the conference will produce recommendations for action, and that
is the beginning of our job.

Implementation, as was said a little while ago, is the key. When you leave
here today, what are you going to do about all the issues we discussed on
governance? Are you going to go back to your busy jobs and forget it, and
then next year when you go to ALA or one of the other national conferences
and they talk about governance you get up and talk about it again and forget
until the next time? How are we going to make sure that we somehow move
the agenda and get movement on the ideas that we think are so basic? Governance, for example, is so important and so basic we had better start getting
some consensus between now and the end of the White House Conference so
that we can go to Congress and the Administration united in the action we
need.

You have another important decision to make. You have to decide how
you can influence the delegates in your state who have been elected to go to
Washington. If you are not a delegate yourself, remember that, like your
Congressman, your state delegates represent you. The delegates in your
state are your representatives to the National Conference. Just as you voted
yesterday for your Congressman, these delegates are yours. And you may
influence them, if you so desire, to represent your views at that conference.
It is the democratic process.

Now, let me mention one more thing on governance. There has been a lot of discussion about governance; one possibility is a public corporation as suggested in John Bystrom's paper (Chapter 25). Another form is a national library board which has been included as a suggestion in the study on the National Periodicals Center. I have heard comments during this conference that the Commission has a hidden agenda, and the Commission has made up its mind on the issue of governance. Let me assure you that this is just not so. The Commission, for example, has not taken any position on the recommendation for a national library board. You will recall the Commission had a periodicals task force which issued a report called, "Effective Access to the Periodical Literature: A National Program." This report recommended that a national periodicals system be established with three levels, and one of those levels was the National Periodicals Center. In the report, it was recommended that the Library of Congress be the administrator and the operator of the National Periodicals Center. It further recommended that the Library of Congress should undertake a technical development design. The Library of Congress asked the Council on Library Resources to undertake the design study for the implementation of the proposed National Periodicals Center. The design study has now been published and its recommendations, including the idea of a national library board, need to be discussed and analyzed so that a consensus can be built to assure successful implementation. William Welsh indicated that he is planning a public meeting at ALA for this purpose. The Commission, when it meets in March, 1979, will consider the recommendations of its Advisory Committee on a National Periodicals System and at that time will, I trust, take a position. But as of this moment, there isn't any Commission position on a governance mechanism. It could take the form of a public corporation, an existing agency, a national library board, etc.

In the Commission's national program document, the need for a Federal locus of responsibility is expressed. What the document states is that much discussion on this issue is necessary. It is a forum, such as this Pittsburgh Conference, that will help to determine what kind of governance mechanisms the library and information community will support. Then the Commission can take a stand, support the decision, and work toward making sure it becomes a reality. So, let me again assure you that the Commission's view on governance is still open. Remember, we are still open to ideas for the agenda for the National Conference as well as ideas on any other major issues. We are working toward implementation of our national program objectives, however, and we are not standing still.

The Commission works on implementation through a variety of methods —task forces, contracts on research projects, interagency agreements, etc. We are working with the Library of Congress, for example, on an authority file project. We support the Library of Congress and the activities of its

Network Advisory Committee. We supported a study in cooperation with the National Bureau of Standards on computer-to-computer protocols. Earlier I mentioned our work on the periodical access program. You heard Patricia Pond refer earlier to the school/library media center report (Chapter 23). The report will be published in December, 1978. The Commission is moving ahead on the pieces of our program document that contribute toward a broad, national library and information program to serve users.

We must always remember that we exist to serve people—not to serve ourselves. We must not get caught up in the details of technology nor in the process of what we are doing. We cannot lose sight of our reason for existence. As William DeJohn pointed out (Chapter 30): Is what we are doing really going to benefit the user, or is it simply another one of the process details that professionals spend most of their time trying to solve. Our challenge, however, is serving users.

Let me close with some comments on implementation and then I'll be glad to respond to questions. The implementation responsibility for the recommendations that result from the White House Conference belongs to all of us —the Office of Education, the American Library Association, the Library of Congress, the Federal libraries, the National Commission, other national associations, state regional groups, and finally, you and I as individuals. It will never happen, however, if we do not organize for implementation.

William Welsh has mentioned the lack of public forum, a national forum, to come to grips with certain issues. I used to like to think that the national associations provide the forum. To some extend they do and must continue in this role. But, in addition, forums such as this one are equally essential. And, perhaps, the Commission will sponsor the kind of activity that Henriette Avram mentioned last night—that is, a well-selected group of people representing various interests to look more closely in a responsible way at major issues and require them to go back and report to their organizations and get a definite commitment on some of these issues. Our task forces, incidentally, are put together on a representative basis, such as the one we put together to study the need for a national periodicals system. We now have an Advisory Committee to the Commission to recommend implementation of a National Periodicals System. In forming the Advisory Committee, we asked the major library and information science associations, as well as the private sector, the information industry, publishers, etc., to recommend individuals to serve on our Advisory Committee, thus assuring us of a broad spectrum of representation.

Finally, I think I can characterize what we've been doing these last two and a half days as creative discontent. Incidentally, a number of speakers have been relating stories their father told them, so let me tell one too.

When I was growing up, one of the things my father warned me was that in controversial and difficult matters to "keep one thing in mind. Crawling out on a limb," he said, "is bad enough, but cutting the limb off behind you is inexcusable." I'm hoping that neither the Commission, nor its staff, will ever crawl out on a limb, let alone cut it off behind them.

We need your support, we need your input, we need your help. This is a public appeal to you to keep us informed so that we can reflect your ideas and your needs. Remember, the Commission exists to try to improve library and information services and to advise the President and the Congress. Our job, then, is to find out what you and your users want.

INDEX